Advance Praise for the *Off the Street* series

If I was to describe the characteristics of the cop I'd want protecting my town, they'd have to be an almost superhuman blend of cunning and driven---cunning enough to think like a crook, to consistently out-fox the criminals they're tasked with catching; and driven, as in driven like a freight train, with an unrivaled passion, to get the bad guys.

Detective Baughman harnesses his fantastic passion, putting a unique voice to paper. He gives us a glimpse into his dark world — a rarely seen criminal world filled with horrible people and yet, somehow, we walk away with a brighter outlook on life, knowing there are cops like Baughman out there protecting us and our loved ones. For that, the world is a better place.
 ~ **Andy Cashman** - Network Television Producer

Here is a powerful view from the inside, as only a detective who fights vice can know it. *Off the Street* is another nightmare for your bedside, one you won't be able to set aside or get out of your mind.
 ~ **J. Ross Baughman**, Pulitzer-Prize winning journalist and author

Detective Baughman has created an eye opening "MUST read" about the seedy underworld of the prostitution subculture. His story line is filled with images that compel you to see how violence and manipulation are the crafty tools that pimps use against vulnerable young women! If you believe that prostitution is a victimless crime, you will think again!
 ~ **Lieutenant Karen D. Hughes LVMPD** - Vice Section

Real peopleA story of Detective Baughman m God.
 ~ **Bill Hart** ff Sergeant (Retired)

Excellent. A must purchase start reading you will not be able stop. To keep it short and simple.........it will keep you intrigued all the way to the end.
 ~ **Regina Porter** - Special Victims Unit, Victim Advocate

Baughman serves up an action-packed ride into the dark underbelly of the sex industry. *Off the Street* is an inspired page turner about one undercover detective's fight against the pimps and bad guys--who are prostituting women and girls into human trafficking.

~ **Aaron Cohen,** author of *Slave Hunter*

OFF THE STREET:
Redemption

by

~~Chris Baughman~~

Behler
PUBLICATIONS
California
USA

Behler Publications
California

OFF THE STREET: Redemption
A Behler Publications Book

Library of Congress CIP data is available.

FIRST PRINTING

ISBN 13: 978-1-933016-64-1
e-book ISBN 978-1-933016-65-8

Published by Behler Publications, LLC
Lake Forest, California
www.behlerpublications.com

Manufactured in the United States of America

Table of Contents

Preface, *i*

1. The Gateway, *1*
2. Purgatory, *6*
3. A Meeting of Minds, *14*
4. The King and I, *19*
5. Homecoming, *31*
6. A Butterfly in the Spider's Web, *41*
7. Locusts, *49*
8. The Hero Judas, *57*
9. Purpose, *66*
10. A Las Madres Tormento, *72*
11. The Path, *83*
12. Broken Souls, *90*
13. Hoop Dreams, *94*
14. The Trishula, *100*
15. The Wolf Hunt, *106*
16. Hell Freezes Over, *111*
17. The Needle, *119*
18. Worlds Collide, *128*
19. Untold Truths, *133*
20. Game of Wits, *143*
21. Raiders, *154*
22. The Front, *163*
23. Namaste, *172*
24. The Serpent, *180*
25. The Keep, *188*
26. The Last Bastion, *197*
27. Angels, *201*
28. The Event, *208*
29. The Void, *218*
30. The Rift, *225*
31. The Pain, *231*
32. The Collectors, *237*

Acknowledgments, *247*

The Promise

To my dearest daughters, Christian and Tiara, as a father, I wrestle with the same thoughts; have I given you the best of me? Have I told you how much I love you? Have I held you in my arms tightly and whispered in your ears

"…there is nothing more precious to me than the both of you."

You were selfless enough to share your father with the world. My promise to you is that I will continue to fight the bad men, but, if a time should ever come when either of you call out for your daddy, I would stop the world to be there for you.

I love you both.

Preface

At the outskirts of the city, I lean with my back against the driver-side door of the crimson Ford Mustang GT I call The Beast. Beside me on the hood, steam escapes from the cover of a small — or is it tall? — cup of hot Starbucks coffee.

In this serenity, I can remove myself, if only for an instant, from the chaos and lose myself in the night sky. Tonight the view is unobstructed. Not even the bright lights of my city can compete.

Glimmering against the opaque blanket of night is the star Vega, radiating gently in the heavens. From where I stand, it appears calm and beautiful, even though its brightness fluctuates and is, at its core, at war with itself.

My city, Las Vegas, is the glowing star of the nation and is also, at its core, at war with itself. She has been shamelessly stripped of her dignity and left bare, branded with the tag line, "What Happens in Vegas, Stays in Vegas."

For the time being, I can only watch in disgust as those entrusted to shape her image fail to protect her purity.

They promise visitors that anything goes here, as though we don't care what's done in our home, that there's no pain, no penalty, no guilt in the morning. They do this with no thought as to what else they invite into our community to feed upon the good people who live here.

I know the Las Vegas Strip too well, where traveling billboards of women dressed in near-nothing crawl along the corridor. 1-800-Girls2u.

Gaggles of people milling on corners sport T-shirts that advertise "Hot Girls in minutes." Smut peddlers congest the sidewalks, the veins that support my city, by cramming card stock photographs into visitors' hands. Their messages show women spread-open, with absurd little markers super-imposed to afford them the barest of modesty. Those possessed by greed, grab stacks of magazines cramming them into newspaper stands, "Women for sale!"

While I respect and value the freedoms given us by the Constitution, and champion freedom of speech, I demand to know where is the freedom, the justice, in beating a woman throughout the day and bartering her out at night? These dark souls have caused my city to slip into the abyss.

The people who keep Vegas living and thriving wish to see Vegas' beauty free from the haze and gloom of the pamphlets, billboards, and magazines that litter our streets.

Yet my city grows weaker through the crippling blows by litigators, who represent the very thing I fight to abolish. Instead, human traffickers flock here, funneling in women and children, making them into slaves in our city.

I shake myself out of my reverie and dive back into the underworld, amongst the privileged dregs to find what is lost.

1
The Gateway

The coffeehouse is nearly empty as I sip my tea and wait for Detective Catherine Hui to show up. My phone conversation with her earlier in the day was brief. "Hey, Cathy, what does your schedule look like this evening? I'd like to talk a bit about the young woman you arrested the other night. Eliza was it?"

I had offered to meet at her office, but she demurred. "No, I don't want people asking questions. There's a small coffeehouse just south of our building. But just so you know going in, I arrested and charged her with solicitation."

Even though P.I.T., or The Pandering Investigation Team is regarded as one of the top in the nation, our ability to destroy criminals who force women into prostitution is based largely on the leads we pursue—our breadcrumbs, so to speak. Even though Cathy arrested Eliza, she has developed a bond with her, and because of that time and care, a gateway into Eliza's world has materialized. This is the first step in saving a life.

Apathy is the attitude carried by many in our position. Across the nation, "prostitutes" aren't seen as women, or even as people. They become more akin to heads of cattle.

They are considered by many as acceptable losses, casualties of their own chosen career path. I blink and can picture a sea of faces, and my mind is flooded by the pain of a thousand empty eyes. No matter how expendable Eliza may have looked to others, Cathy has made her the exception, and believes I can offer some light. People like Detective Hui are a rarity in the Age of Me, Myself, and I, and I can't help but mentally salute the young detective.

I haven't waited long before the shop's front door pulls open, and in walks Detective Hui. She's dressed casually and totes a black oversized purse. After grabbing an iced something-or-other from the counter, she looks to the corner of the room and spots me. With a smile and wave she makes her way over.

After our usual hellos, "how you doing," and general joking around," Cathy turns all business as she digs into her purse and pulls out two sheets of paper.

My eyes drop to the memo.

From: Catherine Hui
Sent: September 14th, 5:56am
To: Chris Baughman
Cc: Lt. Karen Hughes

Tonight we arrested Eliza Serra, I.D.# 5343333. I placed a seventy-two-hour hold so that you could have the opportunity for an interview. She requested a hold anyway so that her pimp couldn't bail her out before she had a chance to speak with you. He got Eliza a year ago, but now she wants to turn him in. She has managed to stay hidden from him for about a week. She has been staying at her mother's house. Eliza stated that the pimp— or P.I.—continually calls her, and has sent people to follow her mother around, probably hoping to catch her and bring her back.

The P.I. goes by Macc, and has ten girls who work for him. For the most part he keeps them separated. She also said he recently put $25,000 cash down on a car. There was also some mention of a hidden place where he keeps his money. I know this will sound crazy and I'm not sure how accurate this is, but she said he bragged about a vault, and the only way to open it was with his eyes.

She refused to write a statement or give a taped interview, but would consider it if and when you showed up. Eliza is very scared of this man. She has been severely beaten, the abuse has been constant. The last time she tried to leave, he beat her and chopped off all her hair as she lay on the ground.

I fear if she is released before you are able to talk to her she may end up going back to him. If you have any questions please feel free to call me.

Thank you,

Detective Hui

Shaking my head, I release the memo. The sheet floats downward and gently lands on the table.

I take a sip from my tea. "So, Cathy, what do your instincts tell you about Eliza?"

"The same thing I thought that night; this girl needs help, Chris. I'm not in a position to help her, not like you are."

"And you're sure about her?"

Leaning in slightly, she places her elbows on the table and interlocks her fingers. "Chris, I know what I'm talking about here. She is in danger. I don't know how, but I just got the feeling she wouldn't be able to take much more."

I heed her words, for I am kin to that dread. "There anything else I should know?"

"Yeah, there's a bit more," she says, pulling out a sheet of paper. "He's around thirty-four years of age, maybe five-feet-ten, one-sixty, with black hair and brown eyes. I guess that $25,000 he put down was for a new Mercedes-Benz. It's supposed to be jet black. Eliza said he has guns, several of them, and has threatened her with them."

Cathy flips to the next sheet of paper. "I listed the women for you by order of importance. First off is a Hispanic they call Mya. She is twenty-nine years of age and has been there for about ten years. Secondly, there's a white girl, around thirty, who goes by the name Katie. She has also been with him for about ten years. Bianca is a black female, twenty-seven years old. Eliza said she has been around for seven years. Ally is another white girl. She is believed to be around twenty-six. He has also had her for seven years. Gina, another one, is twenty-six years old and been in the picture for the last six years. Faven, nineteen, mixed Asian and white. He brought her in just under one year ago. Yolanda is a white female, maybe nineteen years old. She's new also. He has been pimping her for about one year. Joy a black girl, twenty-two years old. She has been mixed up in this for the last four years. Eliza heard his newest turnout is a nineteen-year-old. She hasn't met her, but he snagged her two months ago. Like I said earlier, they are supposedly spread all across the city."

"Damn..." With a sigh I massage my temples. "That's ten different women if we include Eliza."

The young detective leans back in the seat and rubs her neck. "I know this'll be difficult. I'll help however I can."

"Did she know or give any clues about his personal history, hobbies, or achievements?"

Cathy bites the bottom of her lip, searching her memory. "She mentioned something about him being a local basketball star. Or maybe he was good at basketball...something along those lines. You know, Chris, sometimes...sometimes," Cathy pauses.

"What up, Cat?"

She slowly lowers her gaze. "I just wonder how bad it actually gets."

"How bad can it get? Not enough of us ask that question. It would terrify people to even consider it. Truth is, all our children are prey. Here's a riddle for you. Which of these men commit the worst crimes: a rapist, a kidnapper, a murderer, a slaver, a thief, or an abuser?"

"I don't know. I guess if I had to choose..."

"Wrong," I interject quickly. "You don't have to choose because we can't separate one part from the whole."

"I don't understand."

"You asked how bad could it get, and you need to consider the violent nature of a murderer, the depravity of a rapist, the cunning of a thief, the hatred of a slaver, the indifference of a kidnapper. Imagine the worst that someone possessing *one* of those characteristics could do. Now imagine *all* of those qualities stagnating in one person. Consider how dangerous they'd be. You do that, and you'll begin to understand exactly what pimps are. They are the embodiment of the worst that mankind has to offer. How's that for bad?"

"God!"

"No, Godless," I say, scooting back my chair. "You've done an amazing job laying out the battle. I doubt anyone else could've done better."

She manages a smile as we walk to the door and I hold open the front door. "Thanks. That means a lot coming from you."

I say through a grin, "You're the one who found her, not me. Have a good evening, and be careful tonight."

I don't take my eyes away until her red taillights fade—two fireflies in a sea of darkness.

The pimp is an inexplicable aberration, and I wonder how they can walk, speak, or even exist without hearts. They feel no guilt, remorse, or shame. My time in PIT has shown me what I fear most in man. If this epidemic continues to spread, what will the world will be like?

Once I have talked with Eliza, there will be no way to stop what's coming.

Macc, I'm coming for you.

2
Purgatory

County. This building never changes. It's still cold and still pale. Waiting for the garage door to the parking area to lift, my thoughts run to Eliza. I jot down her jail identification number inside in a small notebook and place it in my back pocket.

It wouldn't surprise me if she got herself arrested on purpose. If so, Eliza's play here is smart. County is the perfect refuge, where Macc can't touch her.

I make my way into the building and move past the plastic bench chairs and medical station, past the clerical staff, who work behind steel doors and thick Plexiglas, and into the Search room. A few corrections officers slip on rubber gloves and call the names of newly registered guests, a carnival of criminals, all circus freaks.

They look at me as I study them. Those who've already been searched stagger into line. One of the corrections officers operates a camera. Its bright flash sears the retinas of inmate number-so-and-so while painting the pale walls behind him in light. Partially blinded, rubbing his closed eyes with his index finger and thumb, he steps away to the next ride.

"Next!" yells the camera man. I only hear the voice of the ringmaster coupled with carnival music. "Come one! Come all! Step right up! Get your free cavity searches and complimentary mug shots here!"

I round the corner and see a couple of booking sergeants inside their office. One plugs away at a computer terminal hunt-and-peck style. The other takes a moment, stretching and yawning in his reclining office chair. After a second or two, he knocks back a little of whatever is in his coffee cup. "Excuse me, I'm Detective Baughman with Vice. I'd like to speak with an inmate." I reach for my notebook in my back pocket. "Here is her I.D. number."

"All-righty. What have we here? Eliza Serra. That sound right?"

"That's right."

"You just made it. She's already upstairs, and is scheduled to be released within the next few hours. Looks like your girl's been here over two days."

Two days. Here is a good hint about the underlying tragedy. It tells the true tale of prostitution in my city, and an insight to the simple minds that created the laws to stop the problem.

Every woman arrested in my city for solicitation automatically receives a seventy-two-hour hold. I understand the intention of the hold and why it's implemented. No one could stomach the old rhythm, where a woman was arrested, booked, bailed out, and put back out on the street the very same night. Instead, the prevailing wisdom was that she might benefit from three days of reflection, a chance to sober to her situation.

If we're lucky she might even have a change of heart. I know, however, that this band-aid cannot stop the hemorrhaging wounds which afflict Vegas because these women are handed all the risk and take all the punishment. Meanwhile, slavers continue to benefit and continue collecting their blood money.

It seems broken that society should take this attitude.

I pull back the door to an interview and peek inside. To my left is some kind of restraint chair, dark molded plastic with thick straps dangling from it. Four wheels are bolted to the bottom. If there are wheelchairs in Hell, they can't look much different.

Nice ambience. I doubt this room's going to help make her feel comfortable, so I guess I'm on my own.

I drag the small metal table out of the way and push it against the wall, and arrange two chairs face-to-face in the middle of the room. I don't want anything to come between us; not fear, distrust, or even that metal table.

A few more minutes pass, and the door opens under the screeching protest of hinges ground down to metal on metal. One foot in a standard-issued orange rubber slipper lingers at the threshold, and is tentatively followed by the rest of a young woman draped in County's dark-blue inmate scrubs.

She moves slowly, her head hanging, weighed down by misery and hardship. I look at her and feel I can almost see through her. She's hollow. As the door swings closed, I search for the soul of this young woman. I know, even from my studies and experience, that there are places where no person was ever meant to travel.

Five hundred years ago, my ancestors were taken, and even to this day—so many generations later—many still struggle to recover from that journey. It is one thing to be brutalized into compliance because even the smallest shreds of dignity and pride can still survive under such circumstances. It's entirely another thing to surrender. A soul that has truly given up is nearly impossible to resurrect. It's a place where hope is laid to rest, a void, where emotions like love and hate don't exist. It's my job to wade in this desolate land, through the damaged pool of lives left in ruin, seeking anyone who holds an outstretched arm. I only pray that we aren't too late for Eliza.

She moves deeper into the room, eyes fixed on the ground. The sound of her soft slippers skips off the walls. She is closed off; her arms are crossed, her hands grip her thin triceps, leaving indentations from the pressure with each anxious shift. Nerves. Bad ones. Her gaze pans left, then right, searching the cement floor for the legs of a chair. At this point she couldn't care less about her surroundings, or the people in them, be they friend or foe. Her indifference tells me we may already be too late.

Timidly, she places herself on one of the two chairs. I move around her to the other, giving as wide a berth as the modest room allows. Going into this, I know two things; she wants help, and yet she's terrified of what I may ask in order to free her.

I lift the chair and move it back slightly, putting roughly three feet between us. For the first few minutes neither of us speaks. Sometimes, by doing or saying the least, the most is accomplished. The sound of inmates cursing and corrections officers barking seeps in through the crevices.

I don't rush her. It's a kind of dance to find trust, and I let Eliza take the lead.

I notice her short brown hair, neatly trimmed but still uneven. I have seen this before. This whole scene is a direct passage ripped from their annals of abuse. Chastened. I recall Cathy's words, "The last time she tried to leave he beat her and chopped off all her hair." As if beatings and threats weren't enough, he humiliated her, stripping her of her glory and beauty as well.

"Are you him?" she asks softly.

Am I him? A simple yes or no answer might end this conversation more quickly than I'd like. "Who were you hoping would be here?"

"The one they all talk about. The one who scares them. I'm sorry, but I won't talk to anyone else."

"Why?"

"People say he's the only one who cares about us, about the girls."

"Do you remember Detective Hui?"

"Yes."

"Well, I can tell you she cares for you a great deal. In fact, I'm here because of her. Please don't make the mistake of thinking that 'this man' is the only one who cares."

As we move further into our conversation, she relaxes. Her arms and hands drop from their crossed position onto her lap. Her breathing becomes more rhythmic, steadier.

Scooting my seat a tad closer, I make myself available, both physically and emotionally. "It doesn't matter who or what you were yesterday, Eliza. If you choose, this moment can be the place you start to take your life back. If we're going to move forward, you'll need to lift your head because you've got nothing to be ashamed of."

This is a curious moment. Can Eliza truly hear my words and feel my sincerity? Can she sense my concern, or does she feel I'm like every man she has met while in Macc's clutches?

Her head slowly rises until our eyes are locked. Amazingly, hers still carry a look of innocence in spite of the dark eyeliner and mascara caked on her false eyelashes. After two days in jail, whatever lipstick and makeup foundation she may have been wearing has faded.

Closing her eyes, she inhales deeply. Even though we are locked behind bars, thick walls of cement, and submerged in the pungent aromas of a jail, Eliza fills her lungs with a fresh new air. Her spirit seems to float from her body, as if she's awakening from a coma. She opens her eyes and leans forward. "So what happens now? What am I supposed to do?"

I'll require some time to strategize on Macc's downfall, which can't happen without her involvement. There's also the not so small matter of figuring out how to best keep her safe. I don't want to overwhelm her during our first meeting so I keep it simple. "Nothing. You aren't supposed to do anything just yet." I can see confusion spreading across her face. "Eliza, I don't know where you'll end up when this is all over, but wherever that is, I'll be there right alongside you. You don't need to decide anything at the moment. I'm going to leave a phone number for you. I'll have it put into your property. That way we won't need to worry about anyone finding it on you. Think long and hard about what you want and where you want your life to take you. I'll only ask you to consider one thing. Will you be able to promise that you'll trust me and remain with me until we finish this? I've got your back in ways that you couldn't understand. When and if I need you, I've got to know that you'll watch out for mine."

"What if I can't do what you need me to?" Eliza asks, biting her lip. "How do you even know you can trust me? I don't even trust myself sometimes."

"Eliza, I may not need to involve you at all. As for whether or not I trust you, you sought me out. I trust you."

"I...I don't know."

I need to ease her apprehension. "We're in territory you don't know, and I'm attempting to create a relationship."

"A relationship?" She cracks a smile. "I have to warn you that most of mine don't make it, and lately, none of them have lasted more than a few hours."

"Wait, did you just make a joke?" It warms my heart that she can find some levity among the tragedy that has defined her for too long. "You'll be out of here shortly, so have you made arrangements to go somewhere safe?"

She nods. "My sister will be here for me when I get released. Macc doesn't know where she lives."

She has a sister. Good. This means she will have someone to lean on if she chooses not to use me as her crutch. "If there are any problems, I want you contact me. If your sister can't be here, have the jail staff call me before you walk out those doors. By now, I'm sure Macc knows you're in here. Remember, my number will be in with your property, okay?"

"Okay," she says. She allows a glowing smile to spread across her face.

"Let's get you out of here," I say, standing. "I'm sure the processors want to get started on your releasing paperwork."

"Wait!" she whispers as we walk out the door, "I don't even know what to call you."

"Chris, and I'm very pleased to finally meet you. Oh, and, Eliza, no matter what you decide what you want to do, either way, please call me."

As I open the door, she walks past me and can only shake her head as she smiles—seemingly shell-shocked at how a glimmer of hope could come from so much sadness. I smile on the inside as well. Together, we coast through a sea of criminals, past photo booths, and corrections officers grinding feverishly to complete more bookings. Soon we find ourselves back outside the sergeant's office. Despite all the congestion, traffic and chaos around him, he sits tranquilly at his desk. Man and coffee mug, in perfect harmony. I almost hate to pull him from his peace. "Excuse me, Sarge?"

"Hey there, Detective. You all finished?"

"I am. Thank you for the help," I say, handing him Eliza's inmate card.

"All right, let's see here," he says to himself lifting himself out of his chair. The sergeant hands the card to a corrections officer. "Here's Inmate 2593333. Can you get her back to her housing unit?" He looks at me with a smile. "Okay, Detective, that's it. Come back anytime."

He thinks of her as Inmate Number 2593333. To me she is no longer seven numbers in the system. She has a name, a soul, and a chance. Welcome to your resurrection, Eliza.

As I travel back across the city, I glance at the many billboards lining the freeways. Regular night clubs promote themselves using half-naked women. Outright strip clubs and internet based porn sites now advertise along our thoroughfares.

The sickness is spreading. At times like this I can't help but wonder what travelers must think while passing through our city. Or maybe they don't. Perhaps they feel that the Devil's work has already been done here. Our elected officials have let things go from bad to worse so quickly, and the many good people who live and contribute here have begun to believe there is no hope left, no virtue, and nary a soul left to fight for it.

With all the ways we've presented our city, it really is no wonder that men with the most evil of intentions have migrated here. They dig in like ticks and suck the life out of the families here.

I have seen them all my life, those who look to take advantage of the naïve. Of course, to be taken advantage of, one must embrace the deceiver on some level.

To some extent, Eliza believed in Macc, but thankfully she managed to hang on to some shred of her soul. That is a small miracle in its own right. One of the key elements of control in this world is to systematically breakdown the will, the heart and soul of a woman. Declare love, but shower them with hate. Show them kindness, and then feed them violence. Introduce them to an avenue of escape, but not before riddling it with booby-traps.

What is the pain threshold of the human spirit? How much can be endured before life becomes more of a curse than a gift? Eliza Serra may very well have reached her breaking point, and I can only hope that she allows me to shoulder some of that weight.

3
A Meeting of Minds

There are rules of engagement. Traffickers have theirs, and I have mine. Pimp law versus my hybrid mindset of Criminal Law infused with Street Rules.

The hands on the old diner clock read 11:15 p.m. I peer out the window at the glowing moon before directing my attention back to my partners, Al Beas and Trey Gethofer. Although barely occupied, the diner still has life. The scent of fried eggs, bacon, and coffee fills the room. Aromatherapy. The few customers scattered about seem to all be polishing off the last bites of their meals. It's quiet here, except for the faint pinging of metal on porcelain and glass. Short-order cooks straighten up their work stations while waiting for the next order.

"So what's the deal, Chris?" Al asks dropping a straw into his Sprite.

"Cathy Hui found a girl who's a definite victim. She may even come forward as a witness. Of course, we have a bit of a problem, since we've got no idea who's been trafficking her. She only knows him by Macc, so for all intents and purposes, this guys a damn ghost. Still, the fact remains she needs our help and protection. Her name is Eliza Serra. She is around eighteen years old and somehow managed to get into a world that she wants to escape. "

Trey leans back, raises his arms and stretches. "So let me get this straight. You don't even know if this chick is on board to testify, yet she needs our protection?"

"I spoke with her over at the jail, and have a good feeling about her."

Al interjects, "All right, so let's just say she's with us on this thing; you said this *puto*'s a ghost and we don't know shit about him."

I hedge. "That is not entirely true. We know he got his hands on Eliza about a year ago; she's tried to leave him in the past, but he disciplined her through beatings. Also, he recently chopped off her hair. According to Eliza, he goes by Macc. He's around my age, maybe a little older, and he recently bought a Mercedes-Benz from a dealership somewhere. To purchase this car he took $25,000.00 from some type of high tech vault. He has about ten different women, mixed races and all ages, and some have been with him for at least ten years. Our victim tells us that each of them has a nickname. They don't speak to each other using their real names. According to our victim, he uses violence and fear to control them."

"Damn, that isn't much to go on," Trey injects, sounding slightly annoyed, "but I guess, at least it's something."

He's right, we don't have much, but I think it's one of those rare cases where we can make some assumptions. "Well, let's look at what we have."

Trey inhales. "First off, he's smart. He's been running women for ten years, and we don't know who the hell he is. That's pretty impressive."

Al weighs in. "He gave 'em all fake names. That means we're going to have one hell of a time tracking them. Shit, this dude's got ten girls, and he hasn't popped up once. Last douche bag we put away only had three, and he was all over the damn city. This guy is low key, which means we probably won't catch him slipping on the strip."

"You said he was about thirty-four, so if he's been at it for ten years, he started around twenty-four," Trey says. He points his pinky straight upwards and affects a dismal British accent "I deduce, my good sirs, that this knave has spent some time either in the 'militree' or at 'uni-vuhh-city!'"

Al rolls his eyes. "Nice going, Sherlock."

"That was Shakespeare, dumbass."

"Hey, how about this?" Al offers, ignoring Trey, "He just bought a new Benz, right? If he wants to act like a successful businessman, he's probably going to go to one of the few places in this city for the best in vehicle servicing. Am I right?"

"It's possible," I say. "So let's sum up what we have so far. We figure this man is intelligent, both street smart and quite possibly an intellectual. We think he may have spent some time abroad through either the military or college. He has been operating in this city for ten years, which is shameful, but also a credit to him. As Al pointed out, he's not impulsive. I think it's safe to say he's probably doing quite well in the money department. Ten women, even if they only make a thousand a day, that's ten thousand for him. So he has to have a safe place to keep that money, right?"

"Damn, 10k a week?" Trey is amazed to contemplate the numbers, and just shakes his head. "Good luck explaining that. Unless…" Trey has picked up the scent.

"Unless what?"

"Unless the son-of-a-bitch owns a business, too."

I feel some pieces of a complicated puzzle being moved into place. "I can't think of a better way to move and hide money. He has a box at some Fort-Knox-type vault, which means he's too savvy to just throw everything into a bank. We have ourselves a ghost." I look across the table at two of the best cops I've ever worked with. "I have a couple ideas that I hope will shed more light on this Macc dude. Obviously, we're going to learn quite a bit from Eliza. So, gentlemen, who's ready to do some damage?"

Trey nods his head, suggesting that he is prepared to walk the dark road once more.

"So, that's it. Macc's the next motherfucker on the hit list." Al says before taking another sip from his Sprite.

Trey shakes his head and grows introspective. "Doesn't it seem like as soon as we get one, another fucker pops up who is always more messed-up than the last guy?"

Al agrees. "I feel the same way, and it makes me sick. It's getting worse every day. I can't turn my head without seeing more of these pieces of shit."

They're right. It's only getting worse. Not a day passes when I don't receive a call from some mother or father in small-town Middle America asking for my help. God only knows how they find me, or who directs them. The questions are always the same: "Are you the man that finds girls and can send them home?"

Each request is the same, and every one of them stings. What am I to say? I'm a detective and maybe their last chance to find a lost loved one. I know how it feels to die a million times over because I have heard all of the prayers and the cries of a thousand parents who only want to hold their children once more.

I have felt many dark things in my life. I've wrestled with loss; lived stricken with illness, and even been broken. However, I have felt nothing as morbid, as lonesome, as when I first felt the breaking of a mother's heart. This kind of pain is not natural. It is hellish. When a mother's heart is shattered and left in ruin, something truly beautiful in this world dies. And this brings me back to our current case.

"I imagine Eliza will call early tomorrow," I say, looking at Al and Trey, "I'd like someone to roll with me to meet her if that's the case."

Al and Trey simultaneously scramble for their cell phones and start blabbering loudly, acting as if they're having full on conversations. Of course neither of them bothered to dial a number or even hit the send button. No one likes waking up at the crack of dawn, especially after burning the midnight oil the previous night. "Great," I say, quickly making my choice. "Al, thanks for stepping up."

Trey acts as if he just won the lottery. "Sorry, Al, but it's about time you carried your own weight."

The conversation ends, and we dig into our pockets to pay our bill. "Al, I'm going to be in a little later than normal. Do me a favor and try to stay free in the latter hours of the evening."

"What's up?"

"I have a couple ideas about how to get more information about Macc. I need to go somewhere, but I can't take either of you."

"What?" Trey fires back before I can even finish. "Somewhere you can't take us? What the hell are you talking about? I'm sorry, but one of us is going with you tomorrow."

"Trey's right, it's not a good idea to be rolling around solo."

"Guys, I appreciate it, but this time you're both just going to have to trust me. If either of you came, it'd only do more harm than good."

Frustration punctuates Trey's words. "At least tell us where you're going."

I know Trey and Al. If I tell them where I'm headed they'd follow, and they'd stick out like salt in a pepper jar. "Guys, I'm going back home. Think of tomorrow as kind of a family reunion for me, and this is one party neither of you will want to crash."

"Home, huh?" says Al. "You sure you want to make that trip alone?"

I only nod. Al understands my dilemma. I could never take them with me. There are places in this city that aren't open to the public, especially if they carry badges. Membership can't be bought; they must be earned through fist fights, broken bones, and the shedding of one's own blood.

"Be careful, man. When was the last time you went back?"

I tighten my lips and shake my head as we step into the parking lot.

Three car doors slam, three engines turn and just like that, we go our separate ways. I take the side-streets home. It's calming. I move through Vegas slowly, in and out of her hidden places, the small pockets unseen by most. "From whence you came, you must return," a small voice tells me. So I use this time to acclimate myself, to my city, her vibe, her heartbeat. Tomorrow, the prodigal son returns home.

4
The King and I

Today, I'm weary. I couldn't sleep last night. I was haunted over and over by the same childhood torments, both dark fantasies and sick memories of diving into the bathtub as the sound of exploding gunfire pinged off the walls and echoed through the neighborhood. I heard the sound of my mother's voice. "Chris, if you hear guns, run fast, and get home." I remember the parents, cousins, and friends of families holding carwashes and barbecues just so kids I grew up with could have decent funerals.

We bounced around so much then, from one gang-torn neighborhood to the next, never staying long enough in any one place for me to get too comfortable. Every time I made new friends, it would be time to move again, and this cycle would repeat itself throughout my entire childhood. When I was a child, this felt like a curse.

Nowadays, I see it from another angle. What had been a curse is now a blessing because I can return to any neighborhood in this city. Every project and gang turf holds a friendly face, and this has proven to be an invaluable resource.

It is strange the way memories can come back to life when all the stars align.

Al had asked how long it had been since I'd been back. Now I can tell him I was there just last night, through my nightmares. My dreams reminded me how life there had been good and terrible at the same time.

The year was 1987, and the place was Gerson Park. Some called it by its first name, almost casually, while others simply called it "The Park" with ominous tones. For the mothers who tried their very best to raise children here, it had a yet another name.

Hell.

Gerson Park was one gigantic square, easily eight blocks in all. It was comprised of unit after unit of two-story, condo-like tenements. Back then, this gigantic project was home to of one of the most vicious gangs Las Vegas had ever seen. It was also my home. I lived just across the street, at 1917 Balzar, or 40 Block, proud home of The 40 Boys gang.

There wasn't much to do in hundred-degree weather, and what little there was seemed to transform everything outside of my home into a massive, war-torn battle ground. I sought an oasis. I'd heard about a community center with air conditioning, ping pong, pool tables, even books and magazines. There was one problem; any oasis worth getting to was always surrounded by danger that's equally remarkable. This center was hidden somewhere in the depths of The Park's decrepit buildings and hopeless landscapes.

In looking for the community center, I must have looked like fresh new meat for the GPK—the Gerson Park Kingsmen—another local gang. The word on the street was out; the younger the gangster, the better. The earlier they could be taught the trade, the more successful, violent, and dedicated they would be.

Gangsters knew how to play the system. They hand some new kid a fistful of crack cocaine and sit back and watch him sell it. No muss, no fuss. Once his fists are empty, he turns in all the money and they slide him fifty bucks. Although fifty dollars means nothing to the pushers and masterminds, it's a small fortune to many of the families here. Imagine the sensation of power a child would have. He gets a bona fide gangster watching over him that's matched to a pocket-full of cash.

The best part, if the kid gets caught, he's only tried as a juvenile. Maybe he goes to a youth camp. Maybe he gets probation. Either way, he earns his stripes for the gang, and the adults move on to the next kid. Some great cycle this is. Everyone wins and everyone loses.

I can well remember the heat of that summer. Even at dusk, the streets still burned long after the sun had gone down, turning the rubber soles of my shoes to gum. It was a dangerous time all over Vegas, but even more so in this labyrinth of side streets, alleys, and tenements. But somewhere nearby was a place of refuge, and I was determined to find it.

Crossing the street, I looked up and saw a pair of green and white tennis shoes dangling from the phone lines, slowly twisting from a faint summer breeze. They'd taken a beating from the sun, but they looked brand new. I glanced down at my own beaten and broken down shoes and found it hard to fathom someone buying new shoes just to hang from a phone line.

With every step, I moved deeper into the abyss. It struck me that almost everything here was dying. Even at my feet, the patches of dead grass seemed only a spark away from transforming into fields of flame.

At thirteen, I was a prime candidate for gang recruitment. I could almost hear the cheesy pitchman selling this dream like a placebo.

"Welcome to fabulous Gerson Park, home to the Kingsmen! You are about to enter a land where reality is only limited by your nightmares. We have it all, from flaming police sub-stations, to lurid acts of violence. No matter what you seek, we guarantee you will be sure to leave here more appreciative of where you came from. Health risks include unexpected pregnancy, sexually transmitted diseases, gang violence, police brutality, crack cocaine and PCP addiction, random mauling, bullet holes in your body, causing minor blood loss, and in some extreme but not so rare cases, robbery, mayhem, and murder."

I carried only one thought as I ventured into Kingsmen territory, *I only have to make it to the recreation center.*

After five minutes of walking, I was deep into "The Park." I should have been at the recreation center by now. Where was I? I took a wrong turn, and it was getting darker. I turned in circles, looking for any recognizable landmark, but found myself surrounded by graffiti, roll calls, and gang charters listing people I'd heard of only through whispers— Poncho, Monster, Shooter, and Mad Cap. The green spray paint trailed from the names like blood from a wound.

Panic consumed me. I was lost in Hell. Maybe I'd recognize something if I went a little further. As I continued moving through the darkness, between boarded up units and trash-filled alleys, I was drawn towards the sound of music floating through the air. Like an ancient captain lured in by the song of a siren, I followed it, hoping someone could point me the way out of here. I emerged near a small parking lot filled with cars painted in different shades of green. Beautifully painted '64 Impalas, Caprice Classics, even the occasional Cadillac Deville wore patterns of swoops, swirls, cubes, and checkers.

Tearing my eyes off the cars, I lifted my head to find I was smack-dab in the middle of the very thing I'd been trying to avoid. I could do no more than twist my body, sneaking peeks at close to thirty men and teenagers all around me. Each had on more green than the last guy. I stood there beside those immaculate cars trying to remain invisible, but my clothes gave me away. I was in the wrong color, without even one stitch of green to show.

Beneath the blue moonlight, the whole crew danced and chanted the lyrics to NWA's "Dopeman," while tossing up gang signs to the heavens. Thankfully, no one seemed to notice me as I worked my way through the crowd.

One man stood out and caught my eye. Like a king, he sat on the hood of his Impala, as if it were a throne. It had dazzling chrome trim that picked up twenty different hues of green, all swirling along its length. It sparkled like a star.

Compared to his court followers, the King was much more serious, more imposing. His arms and hands were massive and his skin was the color of night. He reminded me of the Incredible Hulk, only instead of *being* green, he wore it.

I made my way past two kids my age who were leaning against a tree. *Keep moving, Chris. You're almost out of here.* All I needed to do was get across the street, and I'd be home free.

I'd made it to the other side. I'd made it, and without drawing any attention to myself! I could have jumped for joy. Instead, I made a big mistake. I saw a huge Super Big Gulp cup a few steps away, sitting upside-down at the street curb next to a gutter drain. What is it about an upside down cup that screams out "CRUSH ME"? I should have counted my blessings and kept on moving, but I was elated at having escaped danger, and couldn't help myself. I took one, then two, and three giant steps and jumped into the air and came down on it full force.

Cr-rrumple, POP!

What was that pop? I looked down and saw the smashed cup and small shreds of saran wrap. I had no idea why the cup made such a peculiar sound, but I kicked the remains into the gutter.

Just that fast, my cloak of invisibility disappeared. "Hey, motherfucker! What the fuck is you doing!" The two kids from under the tree sprinted to the scene of the crime, screaming at me.

"What?" I shrugged my shoulders, and took a step back from them.

"You just crushed our shit, nigga!" They sounded like drill sergeants, screaming so the whole world could hear.

I turned my head looked across the street. The music had been turned down. No more Eazy E. The entire gangster party was on hold. They were more interested in the cup killer than they were in NWA, or their 40 ounces. It was obvious they wanted to see how these two handled me. The two kids, one with a flat top and the other slathered with Ash Curl, surrounded me, then looked across the street at the thugs, and waited to see what they'd dictate for their next move.

Their voices floated across the street. "Fuck that nigga up!"

"Whoop his ass!" The two gangsters-in-training were happy to oblige.

"We gon' fuck you up. That's on Gerson, nigga!" Flat Top said, while raising his clinched fists. Ashy Curl stood next to the curb and took up his best boxer's stance.

As the peanut gallery across the street cheered on the baby gangsters, I panned the streets. I didn't even know where my house was! Could this have happened in a worse place? I doubted it. I was so lost that I couldn't have made a break for it if I wanted to. With the luck I was having, I would run around a corner and right back into them.

I quickly spun around, looking for something, anything to use as a weapon. Coming up empty and nowhere to go, and nothing to do but defend myself, I balled my fists.

The fight was about to begin when a single voice barreled from across the street. "Bring his ass over here!"

The voice was so powerful, so confident, that it rattled all three of us. It was the King, and he never moved from his gleaming green throne. His court jesters and dancing thugs grew silent. I felt like a prisoner of war as his royal guard marched me across the street.

"Oh, man, he's gonna whoop your ass!" one of the kids whispered as he marched me across the street.

"It was a stupid cup!" I whispered back, frustrated.

"That wasn't no cup you stepped on, nigga!" interjected the other kid. "Man, you messed up bad!"

I was escorted through the crowd—a sea of green, shiny Jheri-Curls and 40 ounces—and was deposited directly in front of the King. My heart raced and I could barely breathe. Beads of sweat formed on my forehead and ran down the side of my face.

While my blood pressure raced, the King regarded me through the haze of his joint. "Do you know what you just did?" His voice rumbled like thunder.

"Yes, I do," I replied nervously. "I jumped on that cup and kicked it in the gutter."

Taken aback, the King looked at his two generals. "Did this little nigga just say, 'Yes, I do?' "

Soon they were all laughing at me. He composed himself and re-focused his attention on me. "It ain't the cup you stepped on; it's what was inside it that got these little motherfuckers trippin' on you." He pointed to the scene of the crime and pointed at Ashy Curl and Flat Top. "Hey, you two little niggas, go over and see what's left."

The two sifted through crushed leaves and debris that had gathered along the curb, looking like pigeons hunting for bread crumbs.

"It's all fucked up," Ashy Curl blurted out. "You ain't gonna be able to sell this shit. It ain't barely none left!"

"What's your name, Little G?" the King asked me.

"My name is Chris, sir. I'm not a G, either."

Erupting in laughter once again, he lifted the 40-ounce to his lips and tilted it backwards. Air bubbles rushed from his mouth to the bottom of the bottle. After nearly chugging the whole thing he wiped his lips with his thumb and forefinger. "Do I look like a 'Sir' to you?"

"I don't know. That's just the polite thing to call you. You're older than me."

"Hmm." The King tapped the front of his foot along the edge of his bumper. "All right, Chris. Well, what you did was step on about two-hundred-dollars worth of my product. You ain't got two hundred dollars do you?"

"No," I replied timidly. I then scraped together the last of my courage. "Can I ask a question, sir?"

"Go on."

"Why would they hide two hundred dollars worth of anything in the gutter? That doesn't seem too smart."

He looked around at his loyal subjects with a smirk. "I like the way this little motherfucker thinks." He leaned forward once again and extended his left hand, offering me the remnants of his frosty brew. "It's hot out here and you're sweating like a motherfucker. Kill it!"

"Umm…no, thank you. I'm thirteen years old."

"No thank you?!" He laughs again. "So, Chris, you don't drink, either? Well, you're right about one thing. You sure as hell ain't no G, but I saw you. You was about scrap against two niggas, so you ain't no bitch, either." He appeared to contemplate the situation. "So you ain't no G, and you don't want to be one. We all have to be something, little nigga. You ever think about who's going to have your back when the shit hits the fan, or how you're going to make money? What about girls, little homie? You like girls, right? 'Cause they love the Gs!"

As I stood at center-circle trying to decide how to answer him, I made my decision. Both options sucked, but I would rather fight them all than dishonor all the things my father had taught me. The way I saw it, I was going to get beaten up either way. If I became a member, I'd get jumped, kicked, punched, and stomped on. The alternative was that I say no, and still get my butt kicked by the whole group. But at least I could still look my dad in the eye when I got home. Well, once the swelling went down, that is.

"You a strange little nigga, man. You like rap music? You like this NWA, don't you?

"Not really."

"Not really?!' If I wasn't looking right at you I would swear you was some kinda white boy. Well, we need to handle this situation. I can't sell smashed up crack to my customers, and it looks like you ain't with putting in work to pay me back. You did have a good point, though. That was a dumb-ass place for those little motherfuckers to hide it. How about this? I'll find some shit for you to do every weekend. Some days you might wash my ride, other days you might be a lookout for us if the cops fall through."

What's the difference? In my mind, if I was a lookout I might as well have become a dealer, and if I was a dealer that meant I'd turned my back on everything I loved. I took another look around at his dark knights as they continued to tower over me. I couldn't breathe; they sucked all the oxygen out of this place and replaced it with smoke.

"Sir, I'll wash your car. I'll wash every car out here every weekend for as long as you tell me to. But I..." I felt terrified. As I tried to speak, nothing but a cracked whisper came out. "...I can't help you sell that stuff."

The King leaned back and pulled another drag from his weed. He lifted his face towards the stars and, like a geyser, released another plume into the atmosphere. "Listen, you ain't got a lot of options, nigga. You're going to work, and you're going to do what I tell you to. I understand you don't want to do this shit, but being a man means paying what you owe. And, little man, you owe.

"I'll admit, there is something about you I like." He got down off his throne and reached into his car and pulled out a tape. "I'm going to give you this tape. I picked this shit up when I got this NWA. Tell me what you think about it. The music ain't for me, but hell, you might love this shit. Now this is all personal. That shit you crushed and what you're going to do to work it off, well now, that's business, and you best have your ass back here in one week."

Like Moses, the sea of gangsters parted with the simple wave of the King's hand. I ran through the gauntlet, not looking back, and continued running as fast as my feet could carry me. I finally stopped at an intersection and tried to catch my breath. Just above me swung those green tennis shoes. I could almost hear them taunting me. "We own you, and we'll see you again, one week from now! Hope you enjoyed your visit, Chris."

I resumed running, my thoughts scattering about my brain. Do I tell my mom and dad? No, they had enough to deal with without me making more worries. I rushed down the dimly lit street, sprinting past one streetlight after another until I was finally in my yard and close to the front door. I quickly dug into my pocket and pulled out my house key. I checked over my shoulder. No one had followed me. I unlocked the door and made it safely inside before throwing the dead bolt. If I'd been born a cat, I only had eight lives left.

I peeled myself off of the front door, and looked down at the tape in my hand. Sweat had smeared the ink on the tape. I tugged at the bottom of my t-shirt to find a semi dry spot, and wiped the tape dry. No wonder the King didn't like it; it wasn't even a full tape, only a single song on each side – by KRS-One.

Before long, I found myself spending hours in my bedroom, huddled over my broken boom-box with a pair of needle-nose pliers, trying to manage the volume. I listened to those two songs over and over, soaking in his poetic words. It made me question everything the gangsters across the street tried to tell me. As the hours turned into days, I'd rap along to the songs. *"Poetry is the language of imagination. Poetry is a form of positive creation!"*

This man was intelligent. He wasn't talking about selling drugs or shooting up people. How could the King not love this tape? This is what should have been blaring from his Impala.

My week was up, and I was tormented by the fact that I had to go back to him. On the other hand, I couldn't wait to tell him he was all wrong, that he didn't have to be a gangster, or sell drugs. If he just gave this tape another listen, he might understand. The King could be a poet like KRS-One.

I grabbed that tape, and held it tightly like the treasure it had become, and made the journey back into the Valley of the Damned. I had no choice; I had to go back. This city's small, and this community was even smaller. If I ran, sooner or later, they'd find me.

As I ventured into the pit of darkness, I could sense something wasn't right. It was far too quiet and somber. There were no crowds or music blaring from cars. I rounded the corner to find the guys usually clad head-to-toe in green were now wearing crisp white t-shirts. Inching closer, I noticed the Cadillac sitting in the King's parking spot, and one of the King's henchmen sitting on top.

None of this made sense. Did they overthrow him? I made my way up the small mound where Flat Top stood alone. He saw me and sprinted down the hill to meet me. "What is you doing here?"

"I have to return this tape."

"Return the tape?" he whispered with urgency. "Nigga, he dead!"

"What? How?"

Flat Top looked over both shoulders to make sure we were still alone. "Look, man, he got kill't. Someone shot him and his car up. He gone, man. Just keep that fucking tape. I guess you don't owe him that two hundred dollars, neither."

"What are you guys gonna do now that your leader's dead?"

"Come here," he whispered, waving for me to follow him. We moved, hunched over like scouts, to the other side of the mound. "Look over there. See the dude in the middle? The one on the Caddy? He the new leader now. I heard em' talkin'. They gonna shoot somebody up tonight."

"Shoot somebody up? They're going to kill someone? What about you?"

"What the fuck you mean 'What about me?' I'm a gangsta! Shit, maybe one day I'll run this neighborhood. Man, you weird!" He took a quick, nervous look around. "You need to get the fuck outta here 'fore somebody see you. Don't be jumping on no more Big Gulp cups, either."

I looked back as I made my way from the mound; there was Flat Top, a figure in the shadows, standing under the darkness of the canopy. From here, he was only a silhouette, digging into his pants pocket to serve another crack-head, another lost soul. Actually, if I count Flat Top, there were two lost souls.

Some things were beyond my comprehension. Even now, as a grown man, no matter how hard I try to make sense of all the circumstances surrounding this experience in my life…I can't. So again, I'm left with no hard answers, save for one. I have no doubt that if the King had lived, my life would have taken a terrible turn.

I often hear whispers about the misguided children, our ill-fated inner city youth, all destined to become casualties from their decisions to chase easy money and street dreams. This ignorance is heartbreaking. I am a testament to two facts: Some have little to no say as to the road they will travel to meet their destinies, and if not for what I believe to have been some divine intervention, I, too, would have become nothing more than a casualty.

I look out the window at the familiar tenements as the sun says its last goodbyes to Vegas by casting gentle orange hues along the skyline. As I turn this lonely corner, things down here aren't so lovely. The trip back into my old 'hood makes me feel like a time traveler. Will things ever change?

5

Homecoming

I step out of The Beast and spot a group, all young men. Although they try not to stare, I can feel their eyes taking me in. I'm sure by now they've figured I'm not a customer. What escapes them is why I'm on *their* block—when in all actuality, I'm back on *my* block.

Not five steps away from them on the sidewalk is the cutoff switch for the main water valve to a vacant house. I give myself two-to-one odds that whatever they're peddling is hidden in there. I can't help but think it beats a Big Gulp cup. Still, it's a shame. They are soldiers in a war the devil will never let them win.

The old house I'm standing in front of shows its years, but does its best to remain well-kept, like many in this neighborhood. The man who lives here once ruled this neighborhood with an iron fist, and wore the colors of his gang like a national flag. Nowadays, this one-time King has put his colors to rest and focuses on being a father. Somehow, despite all the chaos he has lived through, the years have been kind to him, and it's not hard to believe he graduated high school only one year before me.

At nearly three hundred pounds, he's a beast of a man, yet seeing him through the living room window, I notice that he springs up easily from his living room chair when he hears the furious barking of his giant dogs, both abnormally large pit bulls. I watch him lumber to the door to investigate.

"Your dogs are crazy, Cee!" I yell. "

After he places them in the dog run I make my way up the driveway as Cee looks me over. "Damn, boy, it's been a long-ass time. Welcome back."

The sun drenched and weather beaten oak front door is older than he and I combined. But it's still sturdy. Cee leaves it open, and I move in behind him. Looking around the house, not a whole lot's changed over the years with the exception of a huge flat-screen television, where his son plays a video game.

"Hey get your head out that game and say hi," Cee calls out, never blessed with the gift of subtlety. It has been a long time, but kids don't forget. In days long past, I was a neighbor, Cee's son could be found right beside me as my honorary barbecue taste-tester.

Little Cee spins his head around to see me standing in the hallway with his father. His eyes light up. "Hi, Chris!" he shouts out. "You cooking today?"

There are few times when everything in the world is right and life is this simple. "No little man. I came by to visit your father. Maybe soon, though. Sound good to you?"

"Heck yeah," he replies with an electric grin.

"All right, son," Cee interjects, "go on and get your homework done."

"Daddy, I already did my homework, soon as I got home."

"Oh, then go do your readin' for the night."

"I already read two chapters of the book we're reading. I was assigned to read only one chapter tonight," he smiles, besting his dad, once again.

I glance over at Cee, who grimaces while rubbing his chin. "You know what, just take your butt to the back, all right?"

"Fiiiiine!" Little Cee mopes down the hallway towards the back of the house. "'Bye, Chris."

"See ya, little man."

"Come on into the kitchen, Chris. You hungry?"

"That depends, is your specialty the same as it was back in the day?"

"Well, actually I make it a little different now. Instead of frying, I do what I like to call a pan sear."

"So, pan seared bologna sandwiches?"

"It has a nice ring to it, don't it?"

"Only if it's not made with pork," I say, watching him pull mystery meat out of the fridge.

"So, you know everyone knows what you're doing now right?" Cee asks as he drops a pan on the stove.

"What *I'm* doing? You mean everyone knows I'm not working gangs anymore?"

"That's exactly what I'm sayin'. It was one thing for you to hunt down motherfuckers that shoot at parents, women, and kids in drive-by's. This hunting pimps, though, you got a lot of motherfuckers out here concerned. You ain't making no new friends. You know that, right?"

"I've heard," I say, nodding. "As for friends, the way I see it, I've already got enough."

"Brotha', you can never have enough friends. The niggas you're fucking with are connected to killers. Money buys lots of things, Chris, including loyalty."

"I understand where you're coming from, and I know you're right. But you know how I feel about this. This city and I belong to each other, and I'm not going to hide from anybody. If any of them want to see me before I see them, I'm not that hard to find."

Cee turns on the stove. Ice blue flames turn orange at the tip as they flicker beneath the pan. "Well, I hope you have people looking out for your ass. If you plan on taking on the city, you're gonna need 'em."

"I'll survive, I think."

"You know what's funny? Mutherfuckers don't even know how to describe you. I've heard so many rumors about what they say you look like, I almost started believing them. One nigga said your psoriasis was burn marks. They think you ran into a burning building to get a baby or some shit. Crazy, right?"

Cee places the meat into the pan. Its fat content's so high there's no need for oil. Almost instantly a bubble forms at the center of the meat. Grabbing a spatula, he firmly presses it back down. "Well, since you didn't come down here for one of my 'hood-famous, pan-seared bologna sandwiches, I guess I should be askin' you what's up?"

I know as well as Cee that we're about to walk a very, very fine line. Here, there are rules and serious consequences when it comes to sharing information with cops. No matter the history between the two of us, I respect this. People who speak openly about the criminal affairs of others do so at their own peril. In Cee's case, I won't ask any direct questions. That way, he doesn't have to give any direct answers.

The street rules I grew up with were simple:

Don't allow yourself to be disrespected.

Don't let anyone hurt your family.

Don't ever sell out on what you believe in.

And lastly, Do Not Snitch.

Still, to this day I hold my own rules close to my heart. Because of them, it's a very rare occasion when I reach back into my past to ask lifelong friends for help in deciphering the present. Some officers spend their entire careers trying to cultivate informants. Many go digging up old rumors, or any garbage they can find. They hang fresh charges over the heads of snitches like razor-sharp guillotines. Of course, there are those extraordinary instances when the cop/informant relationship ceases to exist, and all that's left is a friendship.

Given what I've seen, I understand why people refuse to cooperate with us. Uncompassionate police work has cost us greatly. I've always believed it's our duty to protect the people, in all aspects, and at all times, even when it makes our efforts feel herculean, because at the end of the night, those same people who went out on a limb to help us don't get to make the long drive home. They're already home.

"I'm looking for some information, Cee."

"Information, huh? About who, or is it a what?"

"That's just it. Right now, it's neither. At this point I'm not sure what I'm looking for. I have a couple things I can bounce off you, but I'm not sure about any of it." I lean against the counter. "I'm looking for someone early- to mid-thirties. He's been in the game for at least ten years, and he's controlling somewhere around ten different women."

"Fucking pimp-niggas!" mutters Cee in disgust as he places the finishing touches on his sandwich. "Is he beating 'em?"

"Really? Are there any who don't?"

Cee puts the sandwich on a plate with some chips and rubs the stubble on his thick chin. "Hmm, let me run this to little Cee, then we can finish this shit up." A few moments later he meanders back into the kitchen, "All right, what else? You know what he's pushing?"

"I've heard he's driving a Benz, a 550 AMG."

"Shiiit, a Benz? That don't help none. Names? You got *any* names?"

I know better than to expect too much. If the Benz 550 AMG is a standard edition pimp ride, then the moniker "Macc" is even worse. It's as common as any tattoo found in a Cracker Jack box. Open, apply, press for ten seconds and viola, instant pimp.

"He goes by Macc."

Cee leans against the kitchen counter, shaking his head and looking at me as if I've missed something. He takes a huge bite from his sandwich. "Macc? You said he was in his mid-thirties, right?"

"I did. Does that mean anything to you?"

"Damn," he says, sounding perplexed and looking slightly shocked. "I guess it was only a matter a time."

Based on his reaction, I'm having a few concerns of my own. "A matter of time?"

"Chris…I ain't sure how to tell you this, but a…I think you know this motherfucker."

Everything slows. I can feel my heart beating, even my breathing feels delayed. I couldn't have heard him right. Did he say? "What?"

"Yeah, nigga."

Even as a child, I chose my friends carefully, or so I thought. These men are monsters, not people. Those beliefs have served as my foundation. I pray to God he isn't a friend. "Are you sure?"

"Oh, I'm sure. Shit, you mighta broke bread with him at one point or another, for all I know." He sees that I'm dumbfounded. "Look man, you might need to dig through some old yearbooks."

I massage my eyebrows. *Please…don't let this monster be a friend from back in the day.*

"Try high school," Cee says while polishing off the last of his meal. "Chris, I know this shit bugs you. You know I'm with you, I hate these motherfuckers, too, but have you ever stopped to ask yourself what the other side sees when they look at you?"

"What do you mean?"

"Come on, man. You tryin' to tell me you ain't ever thought about it? I know this might be hard for you to see, but you ain't the 'normal' one here. Everyone knows it. No offense, man, but, yo' ass shouldn't even be here."

"I shouldn't be here? You lost me." At this point there is so much going on in my head, I can barely follow.

"I'll put it like this, you were raised in what, ten different 'hoods? Eleven? Shit, you tell me."

"Something like that. What's your point?"

"Most can't make it out of *one* without getting locked up or killed. Then there's you. Shit, I pray to God that whatever you have rubs off on my son 'cause the way I see it, you shouldn't even be alive. You ain't a gang banger, you don't sell drugs. On top of it all, you became a fucking cop. Doesn't that seem a little fairytale to you? Things just don't happen like that…not down here.

"As far as the other side of the mirror, just remember these boys, selling these girls, they feel the same damn way about you that you feel about them. You're fucking with people that no one could touch. The cold thing about it? Macc ain't the only one you know. Sure as shit, you goin' come across motherfuckers you love, niggas that loved you. The streets say you're killin' em', but you know when you're that good, it makes you something else…a target. You don't even know who your enemies are. Some of your old boys are going to smile in your face and at the same time wish you dead. I guarantee they all know who you are. They sayin, 'It takes one to catch one.' "

He knows about my taking down other pimps? My old friends wish me dead? Fairytale?

He's given me plenty to think over and set me on the path without telling me anything at all. There'll be no more questions. Our balancing act needs to come to a close because there's only so far Cee can go.

"Anything else, man?" Cee asks while rinsing his plate.

"No, I'm straight. I've got more than enough info to sort through. I'm pretty sure I owe you one."

"Well, get your ass back down here soon, and bring your grill with you. A little barbecue ought to square us right on up."

I step back into darkness and move to The Beast.

Driving out of Cee's neighborhood, I scour my memory for clues Cathy and Cee gave me. Five nine. Basketball hero. Mid-thirties. College scholarship. High school? If he attended Rancho High School with me, that would have been between '91 and '93. Of course, if he were an upper classman that would narrow the window even more. If memory serves me correctly, I know two people who match that profile, but only one fits perfectly into this puzzle. Mario Davis.

At this point all I have is speculation. I can't be sure it's Mario—at least not yet.

My cell phone rings and the numbers flicker across the screen, with no name assigned. I answer.

"Um...he...hello?"

Instantly, I recognize the voice, it's as hushed and just as timid as it was when we first met. "Eliza, hi. It's good to hear your voice. You sound good."

"Well, I've come a long way since you last saw me. I've been dealing with so many emotions lately that it's nice to be back home with family. They're helping a lot, but there are some things I just don't want them to know. Some things I can't tell them. I guess I'm afraid of how they'd look at me. I look in the mirror and don't even see me anymore. I just want to be me again, not *this*. I know I probably sound crazy right now."

She's been living her worst memories, and the nightmares attack even when she's awake. Like vultures at a carcass, they pick away at her sanity.

"You don't sound crazy, Eliza. Not even a little."

"When I think of where I've been, and what I've had to do…are you sure, Chris? I don't want to be crazy. I just want to be okay, and I'm not."

"You're waking up from a year of abuse, and you're discovering you aren't the person you were when you left. That doesn't matter, though because life is about growth, evolution, and survival. Despite everything he's done to you and everything you've seen, you're here. Be proud of that, and if you feel you aren't ready, then I'll be proud for you."

I can hear her weeping. "You can't say those things! You can't tell me I'm worth you being proud of."

"Eliza, have you ever heard of an odyssey?"

"Is that like a journey?"

"In a sense, yeah. Think along the lines of a spiritual quest. Together, we're going to find whatever it is that was taken from you. But before we can start, we need to meet, if that's all right with you."

"Yes…when?" It sounds as if her tears have run dry.

"How about tonight? Can you meet me in an hour?"

"Is it all right if my sister brings me?"

"Sure. There's a parking lot at the intersection of Pecos and Sunset, near a Mexican restaurant. Do you know the place I'm talking about?"

"My sister doesn't live far from there."

"All right then. I'll be in a red Mustang. Okay?"

"Okay, one hour…and Chris?"

"Yeah?"

"Thank you."

Her regrets have grown titan. If she's to survive stepping from the darkness into the light, she must unflinchingly stare down her guilt, the shame, and the angst that Macc saddled her with. Those emotions have become a monster. The memories of all that she was forced to do are coming back to haunt her. They're as hideous and destructive as that primordial race of giants from long ago. In the mirror she only sees Cyclops.

Eliza's certainly strong enough to make this journey, but I worry in what condition she'll arrive. The clock is ticking. My next stop is the Triangle.

The office is filled with its usual carefully constructed mayhem. Detectives move around the office shuffling through paperwork and printing ads from sites like Craiglist, backpage.com, and Eros.com. The printer spits out page after page of females for rent, women, which in almost all cases, have some tyrant behind them paying for the ads and pulling the strings.

I find Al just beyond the posse of enforcement detectives. He's leaning back in his chair, holding a large cup of coffee, and focused on his monitor. I step past and greet him with a pat on the shoulder. My desk still looks like a wasteland, littered with stacks of paperwork, binders, and pictures of prospective targets. Someday I'll find time to organize it, but not today.

"What's up?" Al slowly spins his chair to face me. "You're back from your visit. How'd it go?"

"It was helpful, but I'm not sure of anything yet." At this point, I'm not ready to tell Al that it's possible I know Macc." Maybe after tonight I'll have a little more clarity on the situation."

"Why? What's happening tonight?"

"You and I have an appointment." I fire up my computer. Normally I'd leave the navigating of law databases to Al, but under the circumstances, I opt to handle this one on my own.

"Oh," Al says, leaning forward in his chair, "she called?"

"Yeah, and 'she' is named Eliza. We're going to meet her there in about thirty minutes. Pecos and Sunset."

For the next few minutes I look inward, allowing that voice inside to walk me through the smoky maze. *Okay, if Macc is who we expect him to be, we may not find him in any law files. He may not have had any police contact. On the surface, he'll appear to be as common as anyone on the street. Is he a model citizen, or master of illusion? You know where to start; what type of identification does every good citizen carry?*

A driver's license.

From the home screen, I enter the department of motor vehicles database and type in M-A-R-I-O-D-A-V-I-S. My right hand traces along the keys, stops and hovers over the enter button. Terrible thoughts echo through my mind. *How can a man like this be the same who was beloved in his community? How could he have gone from having such promise, to such destruction? Will it be easy to ruin someone I know, someone I grew up with? Someone I idolized?*

The weight of those questions is heavy as my index finger comes crashing down on the Enter key. Mario's photo appears on my screen. There he is. Not much different from what I remember. His copper skin tone is accented by a smooth, bald head that's accented with thin eyebrows arching above warm dark eyes. A slender, nose leads to a small, well-groomed moustache. As if his smile isn't dazzling enough, he tops it all off with two diamond-studded earrings. If he's the one I'm looking for, he's a different breed. He has the look of a predator. The smile, the face, even his charisma jumps off the screen. These types of men are the most dangerous of all because merely talking to their victims is enough to hypnotize them right into their grips.

I hope I'm mistaken. *Mario, if you are Macc, I will see to it that you never smile that brightly again.*

I take the mouse, move the arrow to print, and grab the photo from the printer. "Let's roll, Al."

6

A Butterfly in the Spider's Web

With the photograph placed safely above the sun visor, Al and I drive towards our destination. I can't help but glance out the window onto the Las Vegas Strip.

Our beautiful city's lights burn brightly against a hopeless backdrop. Visitors are so mesmerized by the magnificence and the chime of dropping coins, that they overlook the lost that walk among them. Young women camouflage a fresh black eye with heavy make-up and shift against tender bruises in the middle of some swank, ultra-lounge.

We arrive and take a lap around the parking lot, which looks clear, and settle The Beast into position facing the street a few feet from the restaurant. It doesn't take long before their car arrives and pulls up nearby.

"Al, heads up. She's here."

"Cool. I'll hop in the back seat."

Al exits and I follow, standing just inside the driver's-side door.

Through the dimness, Eliza's smile shines brightly. She turns to her sister and wraps her arms around her, and places a gentle kiss on her cheek before reaching for the door.

"Hi, I made it!" She smiles as the light glistens against her short dark hair.

"So I see. You look terrific." And she did, too. Finally, I was seeing the person behind all the makeup and slinky dress, a young woman who had seen too much but was trying to wash it away, one day at a time.

"What? I look like crap. I've been crying all day, no make-up, my hair still hasn't grown in evenly. I'm wearing a pair of old shorts and a tee shirt." She looks at Al sitting in the back seat. "Who's that?"

"That's my partner, Al," I say, opening the passenger door of The Beast. "He's a good guy, but if you're uncomfortable with him being there, we'll have him wait outside. Sound fair?"

Getting in, she shoots me a smile. "Deal."

My relationship with Eliza is built on a solid foundation, but it takes Al mere seconds to annex my relationship with her into one of his own by offering a gentle smile. "I'm glad to see you like my partner." And to think I'd been worried Al would seem too imposing. "So, Eliza, have you ever given a statement before? No? Well it's no different than what we're doing right now. We're just friends talking. Nothing needs to be formal. All we're going to do is relive where you've been, what you've seen, and how you ended up here with us. How does that sound?"

"That doesn't sound too bad, well except maybe for the 'relive' part."

"Don't worry. Al and I will be right here with you every step of the way. You aren't going back in alone, okay?"

"I'll do my best," she says, pushing a smile through her terrified expression.

"Your best is all I can ask for." With that, I reach into my backpack for the recorder and place it on the armrest between us.

"Okay, here we go. Um, for me it all started with one really bad decision. It was spring break. My girlfriend came by and picked me up in what I thought was her new car. We were out having a good time, cruising, ya know, when we got pulled over by the police. It turned out the car was stolen. I ended up in jail that night, and I was an emotional wreck. I just remember sitting in the corner alone, crying. My girlfriend wasn't even in the same room. It was terrible.

"I was huddled up on a metal bench, when I was approached by a girl. She was pretty, and seemed really nice. Her name was Sadie, she was Latina, too. She calmed me down and asked what I did for work, and my age. I told her I was going into the Navy, that I'd enlisted as a cryptologic engineer. I remember her kinda laughing at me, like I was naïve or something. She told me the Navy wouldn't take a person with a felony, and that not too many people would.

Then questions started coming about what I would do now, did I have a back-up plan, did I have the money to pay for a good lawyer, and if not, how would I make that money to pay for my defense.

"I didn't have a plan. All I wanted to do was join the military. I couldn't even answer her. I didn't know what to say. I felt like my whole future was circling the drain. She could see I was paranoid, and that was when she made me a job offer. She made it seem like it was working for an escort company. After telling me about the kind of money I could make, she gave me the name and number to the owner of the company...Damon.

"Once I got out of jail, it didn't take long before things in my life started to fall apart. Because of that arrest, the Navy dropped me on the spot. So much for serving my country. I tried to get other jobs. I went around filling out applications, but they all said the same thing. 'We're sorry, there was an issue with your background check.'

"My relationship with my mom was going from bad to worse. Eventually, I got frustrated, and that turned into depression. It was bad enough that I'd embarrassed my entire family with the arrest, but now I couldn't even contribute. I couldn't get a job. I couldn't pay for a lawyer. I really felt like I was more trouble than I was worth. A few months later, I was cleaning my room, and came across that piece of paper with the number and Damon's name.

"I'd forgotten about it, but when I saw it I thought, 'Thank you, God!' I really felt like this was a blessing. I'd been struggling and was so depressed, so I figured why not? Being an escort isn't against the law, and I could help my mom with bills, and maybe get a lawyer. I mean how bad could it be, right? So, I made the call.

"A day later, Damon came to my house to pick me up. He was nice, handsome, and so kind. He just felt good to be around. So I went with him to lunch. It was beautiful, and I felt like we connected instantly, like he could actually see *me*. He started to ask me questions about my life, about my dreams. He also asked me about my family, my sisters, and my relationship with my mother. He wanted to know whether or not my parents were separated, which they are. Just a ton of questions about my personal life. Our conversation went on for hours. I told him what I loved most about myself, even every little complex I had."

In the still of that moment Eliza drops her head with a smirk, and chuckles. She seems to be laughing at her own naiveté. "You know what they say, hindsight is twenty-twenty. I realize I told that man too much, too soon, but all I wanted—all any woman wants— was for someone to listen, to hear me. I wanted to share my life, the things I'd been through, and I did. He was so into every word that I said.

"Eventually he offered me a job. He said, 'What if I could show you a way to make lots of money, without having to have intercourse with anyone?' I thought, that's great, 'cause I'm not having sex for money. Everything he said to me was perfect; every word seemed to be just what I needed to hear. I stayed with him all day. I ...I, by the end of the day I was mesmerized. I was so ready for a better life, that I left my home and family to live with him. That evening we just spent time together.

"Initially, he put me in a condo with another girl he called Joy. That night he sent me out there to work. I didn't know what I was doing or what to expect. He started pairing me up with some of his other girls." She pauses momentarily, "Do I have to tell you everything? This is all stuff I don't even want to remember, Chris."

I can only imagine how she feels. This is that proverbial look into the mirror. What's looking back at her isn't something or someone she is fully ready to see. I offer a compassionate smile. "Eliza, share what you're ready to, okay?"

Nodding, she crosses her arms and rubs the outside of her biceps. "Where was I? The girls, the girls taught me everything. What to say, how to speak, even who to look for. I can't believe I'm about to say this, but they even taught me how to 'trick fuck.' Over the next week, I tried to learn as much as I could. After two weeks, Joy vanished, and he told me we were supposed to save up for a house. It took me a few days but I'd made the money he wanted; $15,000. He moved me into a nice place in North Las Vegas and put another girl named Gina in there with me. I was supposed to be in the house all the time, he told me not to leave unless he told me to go to work. Eventually, he moved Gina out, and then it was just me and him for about five or six months. By this time I learned his 'pimp' name was Macc. So that's what I started calling him. I guess it turned out Damon was just a fake name he used."

Something has struck her, a thought, maybe an emotion, but a look of remorse spreads across her face, as tears gather in her eyes. "I brought my friend Georgia into this mess, and before long, I was the one teaching her. It was like a sickness." The tears pour down her face. "I did the same thing to my friend that was done to me. I didn't know how bad it was going to get. I didn't know it was going to be like this. Over time, I felt like I was falling deeper and deeper into this hole. It wasn't long before he started to arrange trips."

Eliza is laboring with the memories. It's rare that I interrupt this process, however tonight, I need more clarity. "Trips?"

"Yeah, um, he started becoming more demanding, not nice like he was, initially. He would make me work out of town. California, Atlanta, Hawaii. I remember my first trip. He sent me to Atlanta with Katie and Gina. When we got there, they did all the working. I didn't do anything out there. He just wanted me to see… what was expected of me, I guess. Once he felt I got it, he sent me away with one of the girls…um, Gina. He made us go to three towns. We all had a quota, and we were required to make $5,000 in each location before he would let us return home. So he set up $15,000 trips. One of those times someone slipped something into my drink."

She pauses, and for a moment I think of this man. He, like so many others traffickers, had spun a web across our nation, and moved women across it as if they were livestock gone to market. I turn my eyes back on her and watch a thin stream of tears fall down her left cheek. The emotional trigger Eliza fought so hard to hold in check was pulled. I need her to be strong. We've only scratched the surface of what I need to know. I reach across her body and pull out a small box of Kleenex from the glove compartment. "Hey, it's okay, we've got you now. You're safe."

After wiping her face she continues, "I, uh, I woke up in a hospital in some strange city, with no family. It was so cold, it just felt… cold. I've never felt so alone in my life. Gina just left me there, by myself. Macc eventually sent for me. When I got back, he didn't believe me. He made me sit in a chair, while he stood over me, screaming at me. He called me a liar, a bitch. I just remember him yelling at me 'Bitch get up, take off your fucking clothes!'

"He stuck me in a cold shower after he made me strip naked. He wanted me vulnerable. The water was so cold, and I was in there so long, it started hurting. As I stood there freezing, he gave me the option of leaving. When I took it, he started beating me, punching me in my face, my head and ribs. Another of the girls was there, and she screamed and begged him to stop, but it didn't matter. I think, at some point, the beating was less about hurting me and more about showing her what he was capable of.

"I was terrified. I just wanted to go home. He dragged me back downstairs. I, I was still naked and wet, crying, wishing someone would help me, but no one came. The other girl couldn't do anything. She was as scared as I was. He threw me onto the kitchen counter, on my stomach. He held me down with one arm, and the last thing I could see was him reaching for a butcher knife. He was zig-zagging the blade across my back. When he talked, he sounded like monster, and he kept screaming at me, 'I'll fucking kill you BITCH. You think you can just come into my FUCKING house and LIE TO ME!'

"When he finally pulled me off the island, I was messed up. I thought he was going to kill me. He just stood there laughing at me. When I looked into his hand, he didn't have a knife. It was a safety pin. I felt like I was losing my mind, like I was outside of my body. Imagine seeing yourself in a movie, but not being able to help yourself. I was still freezing, when he forced me back upstairs and threw me on the bed. He held me down by my shoulders. I was begging him to stop. I told him I wasn't lying. I tried to kick him off, to fight back. I wasn't strong enough. I was crying so badly I could barely breathe. He told me, 'BITCH, STOP MOVING, SHUT THE FUCK UP!'

"Macc kept a gun in his night stand, and pulled it out while keeping one hand around my neck to pin me down. Then everything around me went black. I was so focused on the gun that I didn't notice that he'd grabbed a pillow. He covered my face and started suffocating me with it, screaming the same thing again and again, 'Are you fucking lying? What happened out of town?' He jammed the gun into my cheek and told me if he ever caught me lying he would kill me.

"My answer never changed. I think that was when he decided I wasn't lying. Finally, he lifted the pillow from my face. He just stood over me, smiling, and saying, 'You didn't think I'd really kill you, did you?'

"Um, a while after that, I ended up leaving for maybe two weeks. I left from San Jose. I'm sorry, I can't think. I got my stories all mixed up." Eliza whispers as she wipes her tears and blows her nose looking slightly embarrassed.

The stories are always the same, but I'm nonetheless shattered. "It's okay," I say gently.

"But, um, he thought I was dead for about two weeks. I didn't want to endanger my family any more than I already had. I knew he had people watching my dad's house."

For a moment, she stops speaking. Her shoulders slump over and her head hangs. She says so much without adding another word. Her left hand moves towards her face, and she gently caresses her left eyebrow. "So, I went back to him." She says it in a manner that suggests not even she can believe it. "I'd pretty much prepared myself for the worst. Initially, he made it seem like he was glad to see me, even though he punished me for months on end."

As her tears flow, my throat tightens and jaws clench so tightly I could grind bone to dust. This is the funeral, the moment when she mourns for the girl lost to this darkness. Eliza's tears wash the stain from her soul. As she purifies her own, I fight a war within myself. Passion fueled by pure hatred burns in me, trying to seize my mind. I close my eyes.

From her cloud-soft voice comes one a heavy storm of words. "He beat me again and then gave me two options. I could either walk around bald headed, or…or he was going to bring over a group of his friends. He was going to force me to have sex with them, one after the other, or two to three at a time. He didn't care. We're nothing to him. I guess we're nothing to most people. Anyway, I guess I should just be happy I was given a choice. He completely chopped off my hair off with some clippers."

She ends her statement with an elusive almost invisible smile. For her to smile tells me that somewhere deep within her, she had hidden a fragment of light, a tiny bit of hope. Though he tried, Macc couldn't kill it in her, at least not all of it. I understand just how painful that must have been for Eliza. Sadly this part of the interview only makes the first incision. The surgery is yet to come.

7

Locusts

"Okay Eliza, I'm going to ask you a few questions. I'm looking for specifics on some of the statements you made initially. If anything specific comes to mind as we work through this, just feel free to interject, all right?

"Yes."

"You were led to believe that you would be working for an escort agency. Correct?"

"Yes, a legitimate company."

"How long had you been with him before the trip to Atlanta?"

"About a month and a half."

"Can you tell me a little bit more about your drugging?"

"Sure. I was on one of the trips. He'd sent me to San Francisco. One particular evening, I'd gone into a hotel. I think it's called The Standard."

"Do you remember waking up?"

She nods. "I remember waking up in some guy's room. The whole house was completely dark. Pitch black. When I came to, I was freaking out. The guy didn't understand why. All I knew was that I had no idea what had been done to me the night before, or even where I was. I finally managed to get out of that house. Eventually I made my way back to the hotel room where Katie was. I had to beg her to drive me back to Vegas."

As clearly as shame can be seen in her face, I hear it in her voice. "Did you ever visit a hospital at any point before you returned home?"

"Yeah, in San Jose," answers Eliza faintly, with head lowered, fidgeting with a button on her plaid shorts.

"How'd you end up there?"

"I was so sick on the ride home, and falling in and out of consciousness. I remember waking up in a hospital. From what I can recall, Katie dropped off my things and left. She told them I was a drug user. She lied about everything. I eventually got a copy of the report, which said I was an alcoholic who came from a dysfunctional family. They made it seem like I was nothing. I have a good family. One that loves me," she lowers her voice to a whisper, "even if I am messed up. I called my family, and my sister drove out to get me that night, and that was how I left."

"Is that when you came home?"

"Yes, but he was able to keep tabs on me somehow. He contacted my mother, and told her he knew I was back in Vegas, and once he found me, he would make sure I called her. At the time, she didn't know what I was doing. How do you tell your mother that? How do you say there's a man forcing you to sell yourself?"

How indeed? She says he knew she had flown in. If Macc is expert at his craft when she moved in, he is likely to have taken all of her identification; her social security card, passport, and driver's license. It's the pimp's standard protocol. If any woman looks to run from the devil, multiply her problems tenfold when it's attempted with no identity. Using her documentation, he could have easily had one of the other girls place a phone call to the airport acting as if they were her, or as a concerned friend.

"Eliza, where'd you go after you made it back to Vegas?"

"I tried to stay hidden, so I stayed at my sister's house."

"For how long?"

"Um, for like two days, after that I went to my dad's. I stayed there most of the time. I hardly even left the house. Like, we were all so paranoid and scared."

"Were you in fear of losing your life?"

"Yeah, but not only mine; my family. Imagine the thought of being responsible for someone you love being killed or hurt."

Her tears start again. She loves her family, and I can see where this is headed. The question is complex; what would a woman give to protect her family? The answer is equally thorny; her future, her body, mind, and spirit. This is far too heavy a price. What makes this even more burdensome is that Eliza could never tell her own family that she had become a slave to ensure their safety.

"So, I went back to him, Chris."

"When you went back to him, was it to the house in North Las Vegas?"

"Yeah, I went back to the house I'd paid for. The funny thing is all I went back with was a suitcase. I'd given him every cent I made, and when I tried to leave him the first time, I left everything behind. Everything I had, he bought for me with the money *I* earned for him. He gave it all to Yolanda. Part of the punishment, I guess. He had set up this whole hierarchy thing."

"You said at some point, he asked you if you wanted to leave?"

"Yeah."

"And you said…?"

"I said yes! I said it on several occasions. I remember once he told me to go. I even had a suitcase ready because I'd just come from out of town and he was like, 'I'll even take you to your mom's house.' I was like, 'Okay, let's go.' I was bringing my suitcase downstairs, and as soon as I stepped onto the tile floor to wheel my suitcase towards the door, he smacked me. He hit me so hard."

What is the tipping point? How much can she relive before her soul bursts into flame? As Eliza continues, her sadness turns into anger, and from her weakest moments, she begins to find strength. I welcome the sight of her hands balling up into fists and her teeth clenching. Even her temples flare. Whatever he did to her in that house, on that tile floor, has become the catalyst for the chain reaction that may just turn my victim into a soldier.

Her voice is different now. "When he hit me, I just fell to the ground. He kept smacking me. He got on top of me and kept moving my hands from my face with one arm while slapping me with the other. All I wanted to do was hold my head and cover my face. He blew my right eardrum out. I was crying so hard, and the ringing in my head wouldn't stop.

I continue with my questions and force myself not to give in to the horror of this young woman's story. "There another time when you walked into a closet? Can you tell me about that?"

"Um, yeah, that was the time he wouldn't believe me about being drugged. It was more of the same. We were in the bedroom. I was crying, scared, and upset when he just asked me, with this smile…this fucking smile, 'Do you want to leave?' I was sick of it, all of it, and I instantly stopped crying, looked at him in face, and told him I wanted to go home.

"It felt like time had stopped, everything just stopped. I turned around and walked to the closet to pick something up from the floor. As soon as I bent over, he hit me on my backbone with his elbow. I fell and he started kicking me, stepping on my face, and calling me a stupid bitch. After that, he dragged me down the stars by my hair, stood me up in a corner near a bookshelf and started jabbing me with a pool cue. He was spearing me with it, again and again, in my ribs, stomach, and chest. Why would he do those things to me? To anyone?"

"So in short, he would offer you a way out, but if you ever considered taking it…"

"He would beat me, and keep beating me until I told him that I was sorry. After a while, I started believing there was no hope, no way out, no way home. This was all my life was ever going to be. I had to come up with a way to get out."

"Wait, you figured out how to get away from him?"

"I guess. At least that's what I was calling it." Eliza looks off into the deep beyond, focusing on emptiness. "Recently, I…I don't know what he was thinking, but he kept me in the bathroom for like forty-eight hours."

"*What?*"

"Yeah, that's where I came up with my first plan. While I was in the bathroom he would make me stand in the center of it, naked. I couldn't sit, kneel, or lean against the walls. He would keep the light in the bathroom on. I never knew when he was going to walk in. I remember looking down at the door whenever I thought I heard footsteps coming. I hoped I could see the shadows. He would play games. He would walk in front of the door, and just stand there and never enter. It didn't matter; my adrenaline would skyrocket because I knew what he was going to do to me. On the rare occasions he didn't walk in to beat me, he would come in to cuss me out. During that time frame I wasn't allowed to eat anything. I had to sneak small drinks of water from the sink, each time I prayed he didn't walk in and catch me.

"This went on for about a week. It seemed like the only time I got to lie down was when he was beating me on the bathroom floor. Chris, something happened to me, to my mind. One day he was sitting in the living room watching TV. He made me stand in the corner of the room near the TV. He said I wasn't worth the trouble of him having to get up to check on me in the bathroom. He would make me stand in his eyesight no matter what he was doing.

"I became crazy. I started slipping in and out of what was reality. I subconsciously started pinching myself. Breaking my own skin, hurting myself, became the only comfort I could find. I could at least control that. I had welts up and down both arms. One day, after treating me like a dog, he sent me back to the bathroom to stand. The next time he walked in to beat me, my wrists were covered in blood."

Her rage turns to regret as she breaks down again in tears, "That was the first time I tried to outsmart him. That was my plan on how to get away from him. I thought if I was dead, maybe all the pain would go away. Since then, I've tried to kill myself four times. Maybe Macc is right about me. Maybe I am a fuck up...I couldn't even do that right."

Now I'm the one in shock. I massage my temples. Suddenly, I feel exhausted. "No, sweetheart, he's wrong about you. You're wonderful."

"I'm ruined."

"Oh, girl," I smile warmly, "we are all ruined. All of us are imperfect, but we can aspire to be better, to rise above that, that's when we become beautiful and inspiring. Right here and right now, you are perfect."

Like the sun breaking dawn, a smile rises above her angst and tears, shattering the gloom. There are still more questions I need to ask her, and I will, as we become closer as her trust in me grows. But for now, this is a good place to start closing down this interview. I need to leave her in a good place, and her smile will be my gauge.

Looking over my right shoulder I raise my eyebrows at Al and offer him a slight nod, which lets him know he can ask a few questions. I look back at Eliza. "Eliza you're doing wonderfully. Just a few more questions, and we will be all finished up."

Timidly, she replies, "All right."

"Detective Beas, do you have any questions you'd like to ask?"

Al's strong voice barrels from the darkness of the back seat. "Yeah, I've got a few questions. Earlier you mentioned a quota. Can you expand on that?"

"Um, Macc told us we couldn't come home unless we had so much money. Like one of his girls, she would only break like $300 dollars every two or three nights. She would be out there like for two to three days at a time, because she couldn't make enough money to come home."

"Breaking, what does that mean, can you explain that?"

"Breaking is at least $300 dollars. I remember he would make me quote $500 to $700 dollars when I first started, and I wasn't allowed to go on any 'dates' if they were for any less than that. So it's all that, going upstairs with guys, getting paid by the tricks, and turning over the money to the pimp."

"Okay, one more thing, you mentioned a term. Something about how Macc said you could make money without having sex?"

"Oh, um, 'trick fucking.' "

"Can you elaborate on that?"

"Well, the girls pretty much taught me how to do that. Katie initially taught me when we were upstairs with a guy. There's different positions you can do it in, and you use little tricks so the guys you're doing it to don't catch you. It's like you're creating it. I don't know. You're pretty much making these guys think that you're having intercourse with them. You aren't though, you're, umm, you're creating another hole. You position yourself in a way where it looks like you're having sex, but all they are getting from you is a hand job. You're jumping up and down on your hand, or lying down on your hand and letting them screw your hand," looking slightly embarrassed, Eliza cringes, "I don't know how to explain it any better."

"That's all I have," Al replies, as he leans back, allowing his face to be swallowed by the darkness.

Eliza has done well, but we have more business to complete. Reaching above my head, I flip down the visor and pull out the picture I'd printed off before coming to meet her. "Eliza, I need to show you this picture. Do you recognize the man in this picture as Macc?"

I lift the sheet from my lap and flip it over. Eliza reaches for the sheet. Moonlight bounces from the image. Her eyes widen, and she needn't say anything. I can already tell we have our man.

"That's him," she says, exasperation pours from her voice.

"Does the name Mario Davis mean anything to you?"

"Yes, yes, yes! I remember seeing mail in that name at one of the other girl's houses."

I feel relief flood every pore in my body. "Eliza, you've been amazing tonight."

She looks back, not even attempting to hide her elation. "So what happens next?"

"That's it for the moment. My team has quite a bit of work to do, and we don't want to kill you with questions on the first night. How do you feel?"

"Pretty good. Actually, I feel really good. For a long time I couldn't talk to anyone about this. I mean, how could anyone understand? Thank you for listening and for believing me about all of this. It really does feel like the stress isn't as heavy on me, ya know?" She smiles and peeks over her shoulder, searching out that surly Marine-turned-Detective. "Thank you, too, Al."

I look into the mirror to find Al cracking what looks like a painful smile back. Well, well, well. I guess she has found a chink in his armor.

Leaning forward, his face barely illuminated, Al replies with more of a promise than a statement. "We've got your back now. That *puto*...sorry...he's gonna answer for what he did."

Al's right. Macc...Mario...or whatever he calls himself, is in the crosshairs. Soon, we'll fall on him like a plague of locusts.

8

The Hero Judas

"Where to now?" Al asks while lowering himself onto the front passenger seat. "The Triangle?"

"Yeah, I need to get this transcribed as soon as possible. I get the feeling we're in for a long ride."

Al rolls down the passenger window slightly. The crisp air is a welcome transition from the hotbox the car had turned into. "Chris, you know, when she got out of that truck…it kinda fucked me up, man."

"You, too?"

"Yeah, bro. She… she looked like she could have been my niece or something. Damn."

My mind moves to the matter of Mario Davis. He, at one time, was one of my city's most promising sons. He had the potential to be an inspiration, a light that the little ones might have used to see through the hopeless murk of the projects. He had all the makings of a hero.

But he's a hero turned Judas. He places his poisoned kiss on the cheek of my city while driving a blade into her back. Like a stalker, he roams through our city, snatching up the lives of young women before they are ever given an opportunity to bloom.

As we move closer to the Triangle, I reflect at how just beneath our feet, is a woven fabric, stitched and held together by a common thread — the veins and sinews of abused and murdered women. I know because I see them every day. We stand upon a quilt of their suffering, and the thread, the web that binds them all to each other, is spun from hatred. This is Hell's highway, and it runs from the Golden Coast all the way to the feet our own Lady Liberty.

The gate to the Triangle draws back with its usual sounds of screeching metal wheels and rumbling chains. I hadn't realized how deep within myself I'd fallen until Al's voice rescues me from my dark thoughts. "Chris, before we go in, I need to bring up something."

"Sure," I reply, pulling into an empty spot.

"Look, before I say this...you know I trust you, and I have your back no matter what."

"I know that. Go on."

"This picture of Mario? You printed it before we left the office to meet with Eliza, right?"

"Right."

"We didn't even know who this clown was yesterday, unless I missed something."

"That's right, too."

"So how did you know? You got all secretive on me yesterday, and went to your old neighborhood without me, and, well, it's got me wondering if everything's ok." He pauses before going on. "I'm just sayin', if there is anything about this case, or this bastard you want or need to tell me, you can."

"All right Al, I guess now's as good a time as any to tell you as any. Turns out I know this cat. We pretty much grew up in the same circles."

Distraction is one thing Eliza and my team don't need. I can only hope that this doesn't cause one.

"Are you sure you're good with leading on this case? Was homeboy a friend?"

"No, we were never that close, but I'll admit, I guess in some ways I looked up to him. He was a bit older than me, and a hell of a basketball player.

"Damn. Fair enough, homes, fair enough. You mind if I hang on to this picture for a minute," Al asks as we enter the elevator.

"You want to get started on the work up?"

"I figure the more we know about him, the better. I want to do a little digging, starting with his Department of Motor Vehicles history."

"Al, you know what you're doing...better than I do, so go for it."

In fact, I'm counting on him to be the best. Al must do as fine a job peeling back the layers of this man's life as he ever has. Meanwhile, I need to download Eliza's taped statement for transcription.

Her testimony will be burned onto paper and serve as my blade in shaping a case against Mario. I pull out my recorder and attach it to the dock. I lean back in my chair and glance to my left, where I see Trey has joined us. The show is about to begin.

Al's fingers bounce off of the keyboard. "All right, boys, here we go." The screen flashes a list of Mario Davis's on the screen. Al scrolls down the list hunting for a probable match. "Chris, do you remember his birth date?"

"I think April, maybe 1974."

"Cool, cool," Al murmurs to himself as he moves through the names, page after page flickers across the screen. "I think we've got something."

"Here we are. Mario Merchant Davis, and his date of birth *is* April, 1974. Good memory. So how's about we start off by running down the list of cars this guy has owned?"

Trey nods his approval, while I close my eyes and recount the pieces of this puzzle my past had already provided me.

"Our records show the first car he registered was a Ford, some type of pick-up truck. Following that, a hard-top 1966 Chevy, and a 1994 GMC Utility Vehicle. Finally, he stepped his game up and bought a 2007...stop me if you've heard this before...Mercedes-Benz sedan, an S550. That's pretty much it for his vehicle history."

Through a sneer, Trey poses the common question: "Pimps and these damn 550s...what's the deal with that?"

"No kidding, Trey. Chris, what do you think? Maybe this guy ran into a shitload of money and couldn't help himself?"

"Not likely, Al. Can you run down the years he bought each of those cars?"

"Sure. Looks like 2003, 2008, 2008, and the last one was purchased in 2009. What are you thinking?"

"That pattern. It's too controlled. I mean think about it; this guy started pimping in, let's say, 1996, and this Benz doesn't come into the picture until 2009. That confirms something I suspected but didn't particularly want to hear."

"What?" Trey says, spinning his chair in my direction. "That this fucker is a shitty pimp who hasn't made a dime?"

"I wish, but no. It wasn't luck that helped him avoid us. It was his discipline. Al, did he list an address?"

Al backtracks through various screens and highlights an address at the 1600 block of K Street.

"I'm calling bullshit on that right now!" Trey blurts out. "Al, if this asshole lives on K Street, I'll buy you tortillas for a month!"

Trey makes a valid point. Mr. Davis isn't fooling anyone, least of all us. The geography's all wrong; K Street is nestled in one of the many neighborhoods that nurtured me as a child. It's a short street in what some might politely call an economically-challenged area.

Vexed, I rub my chin as I think. It's asinine for someone like him to list this address because the most common characteristic in any pimp is their addiction to vanity and the need to flaunt their success. A small house in the 'hood, just doesn't fit. I have a few questions needing an answer about his alleged home on K Street. I push away from my desk and stand. "Trey, you up for a drive?"

"Sure kid, what you got in mind?"

"Let's shoot down to K Street and have a look around."

Trey collects his Glock from the top of his desk. "I'm game. Let's check out this man's humble abode." Walking toward the door, he can't resist giving Al a parting shot. "Al, do me a favor, and try not to fuck up the office while Papi's gone."

Al, with eyes still fixed on the monitor, raises his right hand and pops out his middle finger. "Call me if you need anything. Good luck."

As we travel along dark side streets, away from the golden towers that line the strip, I'm troubled by two thoughts. The first is who it is that we're hunting, and secondly what turned him into this. I can't help but question circumstance. Could I really be so different from anyone else on this planet? I am neither wealthy, nor powerful. I was raised in poverty, surrounded by death, drugs, violence, and hatred, and there are things in my life I would rather forget.

Thoughts of my mortality bubble to the surface. My environment had me constantly questioning whether or not I'd live to see my twenty-first birthday. Eventually, I came to believe that I wouldn't. My teenage years were spent expecting death, while fighting to save those younger than I from the evils that would eventually tempt them.

Shouldn't I be dead already? I've lost count of the number of friends ripped from me in my youth, so how is it that fate spared my life? I tried to run from the devil then, yet as I stand here today, I somehow find myself surrounded by the same demons.

Trey breaks into my thoughts, anxious to be brought up to date. "So, you gonna tell me how this interview went?"

"Well, I think she was very honest, and very scared."

"You think? What makes you say that, if you don't mind my asking?"

"I guess everything—her voice, her emotions, even the way she tried to fight them. I just know she's legit."

"What did he do to her?"

"You sure you want to know?"

"Look, I don't need all the details, maybe just glaze over 'em."

"*Readers Digest*?"

"Yeah."

I fill him in, keeping the gory details to a minimum, and finish by telling him that Eliza came up with foolproof plan to escape.

"Obviously her plan didn't work," Trey says. "She tell you what it was?"

It feels like an eternity before I can get the words out of my mouth without choking. "She tried to kill herself."

"Damn," says Trey, clearing his throat.

"Five times."

The truth is heavy, and Trey's semi-calm exterior buckles and then cracks. His hand covers his mouth as he shakes his head in silence. "Jesus…he couldn't just let her go! How much is enough? So that's what we're dealin' with on this one? Do you think we were right on about this fucker?"

"I don't have to think. I know our profile couldn't have been more on point. But this guy *is* different. He's connected. He has as many friends in this city as I do. That could be a problem for us down the road."

"Seems like you know a lot about this asshole, Chris."

"I know enough to know we need to be mindful."

"Mindful of what?"

"Everything. And everyone we plan on speaking with about him."

As Trey peers out the car, "Chris, don't you ever get sick of this shit?"

"Sick of what?"

His head moves from right to left as his eyes scan every window. "This. This city, what people do to one another here. Listen to what you just told me. I know you grew up in Vegas, but the shit that happens here, it ain't normal, kid."

Trey couldn't have been more correct. "Every time I meet another victim, I feel like something inside of me breaks, and by the time I piece myself back together, it seems like it starts all over again. As for normal, what is that, Trey?"

"Fuck if I know, but back in New York, the shit we just talked about was unheard of. People don't even know one another here; neighbors don't even speak. How can you look out for people who won't even look out for each other? God forbid anyone try to raise children here. Hell, that aside, if gangs, drugs, and everyday crimes aren't bad enough, this place crawls with animals who traffic women. I gotta tell ya, I worry about your daughters, kid."

"Trey, don't start that. Just because you didn't see it back in New York doesn't mean that it wasn't there. As for my girls, I'll teach them everything I know, everything this city has taught me."

"Hmmm," Trey mutters, running his right index finger across his brow. "Maybe you're right, kid. Maybe I've just hit my boiling point. I've been thinking a lot, and right now's as good a time as any to tell you what's on my mind."

As always, Trey's timing is impeccable. Based on his lead-in statement, I doubt I'll enjoy this. "Well, it's just me, you, and the city, so let's have it."

"Ever since we left gangs two years ago I've been kicking around the idea that I need to think about my future and where I want this job to take me. I've decided to test for Sergeant. The way I see it, after four years together, you should be the first to know."

The third blow. The coup-de-grace, or the killing blow. It's usually reserved for the mortally wounded, but I suppose there are exceptions to every rule. The first blow is the monster I once knew and admired. The second strike is the weight I'm carrying for Eliza – my promise to protect her and offer her redemption. Lastly, this…one of my closest friends has reached his limit.

For a split second, I take my eyes from the road, and offer him a small shrug. I know I should be happy. I know I should support him. Still, I can't help thinking selfishly. "Trey, are you sure? Is this what you feel is right for you?"

"It is," he says, nodding. "I can't keep doing this shit. Why don't you test with me? We could take this department by storm, Trey G and C-B man."

"You know I can't do that, Trey. I wish I could ask you to reconsider, but I won't."

"Chris, not everyone is like you, man." Trey's head drops down. "Four years together, and I know you won't leave with me. That's the thing about you, you care more about the people in this fucking city than you do your own career. Do you ever wonder that if you fall, would they be there to pick you up?"

"I don't know. I've never really thought about it. I guess I never wanted to."

"We all fall, kid. We all fall." Trey cuts his prose short as he points to a house at the intersection. "There's the house."

I slow the car to a crawl as we both take in the single-story home. From the dimensions, I guess three bedrooms, maybe two baths. The exterior is drab, a brown colored stucco laced with white trim. Even by moonlight the dead grass is atrocious. Oddly enough, the only living grass seems to be the stuff growing through cracks of the driveway. Weeds surround the house, making their best attempt to climb up the stucco. Wrapped around the property line is a rickety chain link fence, maybe four feet in height. Six mature trees have grown wildly just inside the fence line.

"No way in hell this guy's living here," Trey says.

"Agreed. No need to sit on a place we know he isn't living in. It's late, let's head back."

Reclining the seat, Trey makes himself comfortable. "So what do you think the deal is with that address?"

"It's an old trick, kind of an early warning system."

"Huh?"

"Say you're the bad guy. You know you're up to no good, and so do a few others in your circle. You, being the enterprising criminal that you are, list a certain address as yours, only you don't really live there, but your cousin Giuseppe does."

Even without looking at him, I know Trey is firing a smirk in my direction. "Giuseppe?"

"So Giuseppe lives there, and because he's your cousin and you trust him, you've given him some very intimate knowledge of your criminal activity. Are you with me so far?"

"Okay."

"So let's say a few detectives catch scent of your operation and decide to pay you a visit, only after getting Giuseppe's consent to search the house, they come up with nothing other than Giuseppe is a great guy, and you don't live there. Now, as soon as those brilliant detectives wave goodbye, who do you think Giuseppe calls? None other than Old Trey G."

"Early warning system. Damn." Trey gets serious. "Chris, all bullshit aside, I want you to think about what I said tonight, man. I worry about you. One day I may not be here, ya know? You're from this place and understand it better than most. Just don't let this fucking city kill you. I swear to God, man, the devil owns this place, and one day he's gonna come back to claim it."

It's late when we arrive back at the Triangle, and I pull up next to Trey's car. Getting out, he says, "Well, look on the bright side, kid. The sergeant's test is a few months out. That gives us time for one last hurrah. How's about we send this motherfucker to hell in a hand basket?"

I smile watching Trey climb into his car. Rolling down the passenger side window I yell out, "Well, if this is it, let's make this ride one neither of us will forget!"

I drive off into the city with Trey's voice still in my head. *The devil owns this place, and one day he's going to come back to claim it.* Not if I have anything to say about it.

The counter to the violence that breeds unabated in my city lay inside my house. I quietly place my hand on the knob and push open the door. Even when hell rises all around me, here I can find solace. Heaven exists, and the proof is right before me with my two angels, my daughters. At ten and eight, they are sleeping peacefully, cuddled beneath a pink comforter. I tuck the sides into the mattress and deliver two soft kisses, one for each forehead. As I tiptoe out, I pray that they have been given the best of me, and spared any of my many faults.

"I love you."

9

Purpose

I step into the office and drop my backpack at the foot of my desk. Looking over, I see that I'm not the early bird this morning. "Hey, Al, Trey make it in yet?"

"I haven't seen him, but I only got in a couple minutes before you," he replies.

I nod at the manila folder he pulls from his desk drawer. "So, is that the beginning of the end for Mr. Davis?" Al has begun the excavation of every skeleton inside Mario's closet.

"I don't know about the beginning of the end, but we have the makings of a pretty decent case-file. I still have a shit-load of systems to run him through, but here," he says, handing me the file, "take a look."

I run down the list of offenses, but I see nothing that tells the story of his decline. Traffic infractions; I count three. Wait, what have we here? Battery Domestic Violence? Threatening a person? These are pimp starter kit charges. I'm not so naïve to think that every person with a history of those charges is a pimp, but it is more than safe to say most pimps have these charges in their portfolios.

Just beneath his criminal history is an information sheet. Mario Davis, thirty-four years of age. Current city of residence: Barstow, California. High school: Rancho High, Las Vegas, Nevada. I didn't need this paperwork to know that, seeing as how we attended this school together. What in Barstow could possibly capture this man's attention? And if not what, then perhaps who?

"Good job so far, Al. I need to run. There's something I need to handle."

"All right, homeboy. You need back up on this?"

"I certainly hope not. Just keep digging into Mario. What we have is decent, but we aren't even close yet."

"Will do."

As I get into my car and pull out on the road, I think about the duality of my responsibilities. It's my job to make a case against Mario so he can never brutalize another woman, but I can't forget the victim, Eliza. Her bravery in coming forward is the catalyst to this case, and I won't abandon her. I have to find her a safe harbor.

There is no better person for this task than Regina Davis, who heads up Victim Advocacy. Even though we've never met, I have to believe, or at least hope, that she can offer Eliza the type of shoulder to lean on that I can't.

The pain of the abused rests heavily on my soul, and I understand Trey feeling overwhelmed. On this battlefield and in this crusade for lives, we have been gashed time and again. Vanquishing the abusers and helping the victims come at a price, and I wonder just how hideous have I become. With all I've seen, is there still any beauty left inside of me?

Conversely, Regina's office stands as a sanctuary for lost souls, and I find that my heart is racing and my stomach is in knots. Perhaps I've wrestled against this particular evil for so long that I no longer feel worthy of stepping into Regina's light.

As I stand outside Regina's closed door, my nausea won't subside. I wipe a few droplets of sweat from my forehead and knock on the door, wondering only one thing; am I here for Eliza or me?

A woman opens the door with a pleasant smile. "Hello. May I help you?"

"My name's Detective Baughman, out of Vice." I dig into my back pocket and pull out my badge, and flip it open I for her. "I'm looking for a woman named Regina."

Her smiles stays in place, as she opens the door and lets me in. "Well, Detective, you are in the right place. Please come on inside."

Stepping inside, my eyes jog the large room. These walls have soaked up as much anguish as I have. Pamphlets, fliers, and posters hang like decorations in a college dorm. "Domestic Violence Is

Not Your Fault!" "S.a.f.e. House...a haven for the abused," "Shade Tree...sanctuary for battered women and children," "Victims of human trafficking may be living in your neighborhood."

"Right over here, Detective," she says, leading me into Regina's office. "Regina should be back any moment." She points to two chairs on the opposite side of an oak-toned computer desk. "Why don't you have a seat in her office?"

The office is dead quiet, so much so that I can hear my heart pulse against my chest. This experience with Eliza, and all the others before her, have left me drained, exhausted, weak. I place my elbows on my knees and cradle my face in my hands.

"Detective? Detective?"

I hear a voice, tender and compassionate, and look up into her lovely mocha-colored face. Extending my hand, I manage to botch a simple introduction. "Hello, Detective, I'm Baughman..." I fight back the grimace that's spreading across my face. Great. Now, not only do I look like an imbecile, I sound like one, too. This visit just keeps getting better.

She graces me with a soft smile and a laugh. "Oh, Lord," she says, taking my hand, "you *are* having a rough day."

"You have no idea. Here, let me try that again. My name's Chris. Chris Baughman."

"Yes, Chris Baughman. I heard good things about you and wondered when our paths might cross. I remember seeing you a while back."

"I've heard the same about you. That's why I'm here today."

Inching her chair closer to the desk, she places both her hands on it, one overlapping the other. "You've got my attention, young man."

"I have a situation. I'm helping a young woman, but I'm not sure I'm the right person to give her all the support she might need."

As I attempt to paint this picture the world surrounding us melts away. Nothing matters, nothing but Eliza's story. Regina rubs her jaw in thought. "Explain how you aren't the right person, and what kind of trouble is this girl in?"

"She's about nineteen years old, and was sucked into a world she hasn't been able to escape, and she's still falling. It's the whole escort service/prostitution thing. The lies. All she wants is to go home, to have the opportunity to piece her life back together."

"How deep is she in?"

"Deep. So deep she felt her only release was suicide. Where do I start? See, there was this man…" Regina give me a look as if to say, when isn't there? "…this man, who led her to down this road…he…uh, he did things to her. Nightmarish things, for well over a year. Do you think maybe I could bring her by sometime to meet you?"

She smiles. "Chris, it's none of my business, but I have a question for you. Is there something more, something else going on here?"

My head drops and we break eye contact, maybe from the shame of what I'm about to say, or possibly because I know how eyes tell the story. If she were to look closely into mine now, she'd find piles of hatred. "This person who did this to her, to Eliza, his name is Mario Davis. We have history. He's a bit older than I am. It's a long story, one which I suppose doesn't matter now."

She shakes her head slowly. "I can't imagine what you must be feeling."

"You know, there was a time, long ago when I actually questioned whether or not I should be doing this. I felt guilty. For a while, I thought I might have hated myself. I mean most times the men I hunt actually look like me and, in fact, grew up just like me. I know that some people could never understand, but to have to destroy your own brother, over and over. I guess it all goes back to what I experienced growing up. Too many men from my neighborhood were hunted, locked up, and sent to prison, leaving far too many women raising sons alone. The streets picked up the slack the fathers left behind. Back then, I believed it was possible that we could all become better men. I was hopeful then. Now my dreams of that day are all but dead. Now I look at what I've become…a hunter, just like the ones I hated." For a moment it's quiet.

"I want my city back, Regina. There are men here, wealthy, powerful, and evil, and they ruin everything they touch. Each day they get stronger, wealthier, and become even more violent. If all of that isn't bad enough, these men target only one thing. Women. Women like you, like my mother, my sisters. I try not to focus my hatred for this way of life, for these monsters, but instead focus on my love for destroying everything they've built."

Regina sits in silence. I know her eyes blanket me, and even though she says nothing, I can feel her empathy washing over me like warm summer rain. "Oh, Christopher," she whispers.

Clearing my throat, my eyes lock on hers. "You were right about me, so I won't hide anything from you. I realize I can't continue this particular battle without your help. Wherever I move, there's a dark cloud, and it's filled with hate. If you decide to help, you should know who and what you're teaming with."

"Do you really believe that?" she asks. "That you have some cloud of darkness following you?"

"Following me? No, it isn't following me. I *am* that dark cloud."

"Dear Lord, what have you seen? Child, let me tell you something, you have to try your best not to hate. That is a heavy weight, one that could eventually consume you. You've got to see that there's good all around us. Doing what you do is your redemption."

"Don't worry about me. I don't carry this weight alone. I make sure to share my pain with those who've earned it. As for recognizing the good all around us, that's not my department."

I stand and pull out a business card. After jotting down my cell number on the back I place the card on top of her desk. "I told you that I can't be anything more than I am, but I'm hoping because of you, I won't have to be."

I step from Regina's office knowing everything I've done up to now is nothing but a pre-amble, and the real work is just beginning.

From behind me Regina calls out. "Detective . . ."

I turn and see Regina leaning against the door frame of her office. "Yes, Ma'am."

"Before you leave, I need to know if you will be able to accept one thing. The victims are of the utmost importance to me. What I do isn't just some job, and some people, some detectives, don't respect that. I know your cases against these men are important, but the victims always come first for me."

How refreshing! How did I ever work without her? "Agreed, Regina. I promise to never put you in a position that compromises your priorities."

She smiles, "Well then, whatever you need from me, I'm prepared to give."

"I know. Oh, and Regina, welcome to the war."

10

A Las Madres Tormento

I've had a frustrating day. Al and I discovered where Macc has been hiding his money. The facility he's is using seems to have covered all the bases in making the place police proof. A secret bank vault is putting it mildly. We need to see if there's a way to get in, so we developed an elaborate ruse that had Al playing the role of the street pharmacist looking for a safe place to hide his ill-gotten gains, and I, as his compromised accountant. We bought our own box at the facility, so we could get a full tour and see all the safeguards that is guaranteed to keep out law enforcement.

What we learned is that we won't be able get to whatever he's holding in his vault using traditional methods, like subpoenas, which is frustrating. But at the very least we have an understanding of how the security safeguards operate. Maybe this information will help us at some point during our investigation.

Now I'm headed to North Las Vegas, where Eliza lives with her mother. Opposing emotions tug at me. The up side is obvious; Eliza's anger has given birth to empowerment, confidence, and most importantly, the thirst for retribution.

I'm thankful for her progress, and want her to fight back. But there's also a more somber side that involves resurrecting nightmares. I need to unearth Eliza's emotions and memories, which have more than likely been buried in the recesses of her mind. A sad truth of my job is that I sometimes have to cause the most pain in order to do the most good. The thought of what this does to the victims of human trafficking like Eliza destroys me every time.

Of course, Eliza's recollections aren't the only ones I'm after. Her mother's testimony will be an invaluable complement to that of

Eliza's should we go to trial. The interview I'm about to conduct is all part of the long game. The way I see it, what jurist's heart wouldn't be left shattered after hearing the cries of a mother whose daughter was made a victim of human trafficking? I've been around long enough to know that it's one thing for any citizen seated in the jury to hear how a life was destroyed from the mouth of a victim, but it will be another entirely to hear the account of events from the vantage of a mother left powerless to protect her daughter.

I arrive at her home and ring the doorbell.

"Just a minute," a happy voice chirps out. The deadbolt falls backwards, and Eliza's cheerful face peers out from behind the door. "Hi Chris."

"Morning, Eliza," I say warmly. "How are you today?"

"You know, every day gets better than the last. But I still struggle from time to time…my self confidence, it's jacked up."

I walk in with a heavy heart. "Well, you know why I'm here. Did you explain to your mother why I was coming by today?"

Her head drops to the floor. "I did."

"Do you think she'll be able to make it through the interview?"

She shakes her head softly. "I don't know. This was all so hard on her. She didn't deserve this. I feel like I've already dragged her through hell. I still have a hard time looking her in the eye. Guilt, I guess."

"Eliza, this was hard on both of you, and you have to know neither of you deserved what happened, okay?"

"Thanks. Well, I guess I should go get her. Have a seat here." She points to a brown wooden office desk with a glass overlay.

As I sit down, Eliza rounds the banister wearing an apprehensive smile. "She's coming. Um, Chris, I'm not sure how she'll take to you. I just want you to know she's pretty bitter."

"I'm guessing this isn't a police thing?"

"Good guess. The last black man that came into our home beat me and put me on the streets. She hasn't forgotten that."

Rubbing my chin, I take a moment. I understand this is the kind of betrayal, of heartbreak, that festers. As a father, I have my own ideals. But to be a mother, to have brought a life into this world only to see it devastated, I can hardly fault her for her feelings. This attack is far too fresh for me to expect reason to show its face. "It's okay."

Eliza's mother makes her way down the steps slowly, all the while taking me in.

"Mama, this is Chris, the man I told you about." Eliza has a nervous smile on her face.

I stand to greet her. "Hello, Ms. Serra. I'm Chris." I swallow my pride and extend my hand, hoping her hatred hasn't corrupted her every fiber.

"Hmm." She takes my hand in both of hers and presses gently, feeling the wrinkles and calluses. What is she looking for? What does she know, or wish to know? I shoot a quick look over at Eliza, who offers a dumbfounded expression which clearly states, "Don't ask me."

"Eliza, please, leave us." Her Latin accent is rich and thick. "Come, sit." Her penetrating gaze follows me as I sit down. "So, you have come to hurt this man who hurts my daughter?" I'm not sure how to answer, so I say nothing. Her eyes continue to burn a hole into my soul. "Yes, you will hurt this man. How can I help you do this?"

"Ms. Serra…"

"You call me Adelia," she says in a commanding, yet soft tone.

"Yes, ma'am. Adelia, in order to stop him, to hurt him, I need to understand him better. At this point, the only way I can do this is to speak to as many people as possible, people who I can trust, people who have had contact with him. One of those people is you."

"He is a bad man," she says, dropping her head, shaking it slowly. "A very bad man."

"I need to record what we talk about. We can hurt him, but I can't do this without your help."

She nods, her right hand rubbing the fine arches of her eyebrows. "Okay, so at the first time I met with him, she bring him, ah, at my home. She introduce him to me and I did have some conversation with him, asking him several question. What is the relationship with my daughter, and he says, 'Well, I've got to take care of her, she is a good girl. So, I will handle her okay.' Then he smiled this smile at me. Evil.

"I ask him what he's doing for a living. He told me that he got a shop, he has stereos, and tinting cars, and whatever in the shop. He gave me his business card. I tell Eliza to come downstairs. I tell her to give me his address. He smiled and said, 'Yes, Eliza, give the address to your mother.' I walk to the kitchen to get paper and hear him tell her, 'No! You won't give her the real address.'

"I come back into the room and tell my daughter that I want her to be secure, 'cause I don't want her hurt. He said, 'Don't worry, I love her, and I'll take care of her.' And that's it. He took her. She left with him. They left. So that's what happened that time."

Her face is grief stricken. Her hands are balled tightly into fists.

I must be conscious of the fact that with every question asked, I push this loving mother closer to a place that she doesn't want go. "Adelia, I'm sorry, but I have a few more questions. I promise once we're done, I won't put you through this again, okay?"

"Yes," she says wiping her nose with her index finger. She clears her throat. "I sorry, this is hard."

"Adelia, have you ever had circumstances where Eliza contacted you crying or afraid, asking you for help?"

Her voice drops to a whisper as tears stain her cheeks. "Yes."

"Can you talk to me about some of those instances?"

She sniffles, fighting what must be a tidal wave of emotion. "One time she call me. She was crying like she can't talk, and she begged me to come over and pick her up. I tell her okay, I'm going now, where is she? She say something…and then she say she'll call me back. She sounds like she was trying to sneak on the phone to talk, she was very quiet. She's looking...she can't talk. It sound like somebody put a hand over her mouth. I hear her with hand over mouth, she is yelling for help, but I can't help her!" She breaks down.

I reach for the box of tissues, and pull the last few from the box. She takes the tissue, clutching my hands tightly in the process. "Thank you," she whispers.

"If you feel like you can't go on . . ."

"No, I need to help you now. We will finish what we start." She moves her hands from her face. The tears have reddened her eyes, and now they look even deeper into me. "So Eliza never calls me back, and I waiting and waiting. I call her back and nothing. She never answers her phone. I am up all night. I don't know who to call. I don't know what to do. I call her in the morning, and call her, and call her. I want to know where she is, maybe she in trouble, or hurt. Finally she answers.

" 'I'm okay mama,' she say, but she no sounds right, not like my Eliza. But what can I do? I know something is wrong, but I can't even help her. There was another time that she called, but that time she was able to give me the address, so I went to her, I go to this house. She is crying, crying, crying.

"I yell at him, 'WHAT HAPPEN TO MY DAUGHTER?' She comes to me and says, 'Mama I can't talk about this.' So I ask him, 'What is going on?' And he comes to me and says, 'Nothing.' He's laughing. He shrugs and says that's just the way she is. Nothing happen, it's just something she do.

"So I talk to her that time, but she won't leave with me. She says she better stay, and that he promise to give her two thousand dollars in two weeks. Then she can leave him? I don't understand this. Why she cannot leave? So I tell her I want to take her to lunch with me, we will talk there. She says, okay.

"So days later I pick her up and take her to lunch. He was calling her every five minutes, asking where she is, what she's doing. She tells him she's with me, and he yells back at her that she has to come now. I don't want to cause her trouble, so I tell her that I take her home. So I took her back. I didn't know how bad until that time she asked me to take her to the Department of Motor Vehicle for new ID. I think it was about a week later..." shaking her head, she slowly lifts her eyes to the ceiling. "Yes. It was in January. She calls me and I tell her I want to see her, since I didn't see her for Christmas. She tells me she don't want to see me. I ask her why, and she tells me she cut her hair. I ask her why she do this, what's happening to her? I want to see her. So, finally, she comes to my home, and she's not with him."

My mind rehashes how common it is for pimps to take the identification of victims. Without a driver's license, it becomes virtually impossible to escape because rental cars, airplanes, buses, and trains become inaccessible. Even worse, because many victims are left without proof of identity, they may feel their situation is dire because there's no escape. As Adelia continues, I can damn near see the venom dripping from the tail end of her statement.

"I see my daughter. I'm crying, and she's crying. I say, 'Why did you do this? Your hair?' She didn't tell me nothing. It's gone! She had chunks of hair...just gone. She's still crying to me. She says, 'No mama, I—I did this to myself. I want to look like this.' And she don't tell me nothing else. And we cry together."

Adelia wipes the bottom of her nose as a sharp pain runs through me, piercing my heart. "Adelia, when you saw her, do you remember any bruises or marks on her body?"

"No, she covered her body at that time. She was wearing long clothes, you know."

"Did you find that odd?"

"No, I actually didn't think about it then." Her haunted eyes search mine. "Why do I not notice these things?"

"That's okay." I lean in closer. "You said she was covered, so you couldn't tell if she had been beaten, right?"

Her gaze drops and she slowly shakes her head as though searching the corners of her mind. "Yes. No. I—I think I saw something. Something on her cheek."

"Her cheek?"

She closes her eyes. "Yes. Her cheek is red. I'm asking her, 'Why? What happen to your face?' It looks like she got smacked in her face. You know, she just covers it. She hides her face and says nothing to me."

"She covered it. I understand. Adelia, do you know if Eliza has ever tried to hurt herself?"

Her hands cover her face, catching the tears. "Yes."

"Please, go on."

"One night she calls me in the middle of the night. She told me, 'Mama, I gonna die.' I'm worrying, so I say, 'Why? What happened? Can I go pick you up or help you?' I don't know what is wrong with her. She tells me no. I don't understand this. I'm her mother. I supposed to help her, and she, she won't let me.

"So then for like three days she calls me. She's crying…crying and crying. Then I tell her, you know, 'I want to see you, please. I have to see you. I have to take you to the doctor. Crying like this, all the time, this is not normal.' She says, 'Mama, I'm crying because I love you.' I tell her I know she love me, and I want to see her. She tells me she can't see me until next week.

"I want my daughter back, and I tell her I'm coming to get her. She says, 'No! Mama, he's coming back at ten o'clock.' There is a grocery store by the house she's living in. So I go there at ten o'clock in the night, and she comes out to me. She doesn't have a jacket, and she was cold, you know? She was trying to cover her body and says the same thing to me again. 'I'm gonna die, Mama.' She say, 'I'm going to kill myself. I don't want to live because I think I don't deserve this life." ' Then in the car, she falls asleep, and that's it. She don't say nothing else. In the morning, I tell her I have to take her to the doctor because it's not normal, her crying like this. It's too much. She's too sad. She says, 'Okay, mama. It's okay.' When she's getting ready to leave, I see her in the shower."

Another pause, and the bitter taste of hatred settles in on her. Adelia's top lip curls beneath her teeth, she bites it as her eyes well up. Through the tears, she bellows, "SHE HAS CUTS ON HER ARMS! MY BABY, SHE'S TRYING TO DIE!"

I need to keep it together. "Cuts?"

"Yes! Cuts on her arms, cuts everywhere."

"Up until that point, had she ever tried to hurt herself?"

"No! Never! She is a good person. She goes drinking sometimes with her friends, but nothing like this.

"Okay, is there anything else you can remember, anything we didn't cover?"

"Yes, I remember a time where Eliza is very nervous, very nervous, and scared. And I'm scared, too, for her sake. She calls me and says 'Mama, come get me please. I leaving.' So I go to the house. A few girls in the house are helping her bring her things out to my truck. A black girl came home and went upstairs, where Eliza is. Another girl come down stairs and tell me, 'Someone is try to keep Eliza up there.' Then, I hear my daughter screaming, 'Why're you hitting me?'

"I don't know what is happening. The girl downstairs won't let me go up. They're keeping me back. Eliza is still screaming and the black girl comes down stairs and says, 'What do you want?' I tell her to give me my daughter! Then Eliza comes running down the stairs. The other lady, her name is Sadie, I think. She comes and closes the door and locks us inside. Eliza is crying and I'm trying to call the police to help us. I yelling to them that my daughter doesn't have to stay there!

"Then, this guy, Mario, calls one of the ladies. They give me the phone, and he is yelling on the phone to me to get out of his house."

"So he wanted you to leave his house?"

"Yes."

"Did he want you to leave with your daughter, or did he want you to leave her there?"

"Oh, he don't tell me anything. He give me his phone number and said he was out of town, and to call him tomorrow."

"Was he trying to act nice to you?"

"Yeah, like that," she replies, nodding. "I didn't call him! I didn't talk to him! I don't want to! When we try to leave, the other girls try to stop us. They want to make me leave my daughter there. When we're leaving, they get in a car, too, and chase us...they try to follow us everywhere we go."

I pause briefly and then lean back in the chair, rolling my shoulders. "Adelia, I don't have any more questions." I reach for the recorder and send it sliding across the desk, right into her lap. "I'm sorry. Clumsy."

She gently drops it into my palms and places her hands on the back mine and softly presses them closed. These are her prayer hands, and they rest gingerly on the outside of mine. "Chris? Do you speak to God?"

From her single question, several ripple through my mind. Should I be honest? Should I lie? Should I appease her with some generic answers, or tell her I can't talk about faith while on the job. No, as I look back into her eyes I realize this woman already knows my heart. So to be anything but honest with her would be an insult. "I, uh, Adelia I..."

"Shhh," she whispers, powerful enough to command silence. "I know God talks to you. I think you see too many things, too many bad things. I will pray for your soul."

She's right. My soul is battered and scarred, muddied and tattered. Even to me, it feels beyond any cleansing or repair. I wonder that with so many others hurting, so many more in pain, if those requests to the heavens might be best spent on someone more deserving. Still, I manage a cordial smile. "Thank you for allowing me into your home, Adelia. Now, it's probably best if I get going."

"Ah," she says slowly lifting herself from her chair. "*Dios está con vosotros, Christobal.* You wait. I send Eliza down to say goodbye."

My Spanish...terrible. I have no idea what she said, but somehow the words resonate. As I move towards the front door, Eliza comes down. "Well," she asks quietly, "how did it go?"

"Your mother's something else. I think things went well, but it was hard on her. Eliza, you're going to have a second chance, so I hope you take full advantage. That woman loves you so much."

"I know. That's why this is so screwed up. On top of hurting someone who loves me, imagine her embarrassment."

"I get the feeling embarrassment is the last thing she's feeling. If anything, I think she's grateful."

"Grateful?"

"You're home now, and nothing else matters. Nothing else should ever matter. You look to the future. Let me worry about your past." We stroll toward my car.

"You know, Chris, my mother, I think she likes you. When she came upstairs, she told me, *'El es un hombre bueno.'* "

"Phht, of course she did. Hello, what did you think she would say?" Levity feels welcome after all this.

Eliza leans, her back against The Beast and cracks a smile. "Do you even know what that means?"

"Come on, of course I do." She looks at me. Her expression tells me she knows I haven't the slightest. "Okay, okay, I only got through a week's worth of Spanish in high school."

"She thinks you are a good man."

"Well, I didn't feel like such a good man during that interview."

Eliza steps closer and wraps her arms around me. I haven't had a bear hug since I was a child. I smile and reciprocate. I slide into my car and start the ignition as Eliza pushes the car door closed. "Say, your mother said something to me, before she sent you down stairs. 'Adios estan cone bosotrose.'" I give a small shrug, knowing I have fully butchered the Spanish language.

Eliza's shoulders drop and she shakes her head. "That was terrible, Chris."

"No, no, I'm pretty sure that's exactly how she said it."

"No, my mother said, *Dios está con vosotros,* which means, God is with you."

"Yeah? Seems like no matter how badly I screw up all God's rules, He just will not leave me alone." I should feel grateful. "Hey, before I forget, I meant to ask you if you remember any of Mario's phone numbers."

"Of course, even though I wish I couldn't."

She runs down the digits that make up this animal's cell phone number, and I enter them as a text message in my phone. It takes only a moment before it is blasted off into cyberspace. Destination: Al Beas.

ME: See what u can dig up on this number

AL: Does this b-long to dickhead

ME: None other. Compliments of Eliza. I'll b in shortly.

AL: Give her a hug for me. I'm sure I'll have sumthn for u when u get here.

ME: Good man.

I lean out the window and give her a tight hug. "That one is from Al." A quick heartfelt embrace, compassion, and concern can be good medicine when dealing with broken spirits. Human contact has the power to heal, and even as good as this may be for Eliza's spirit, I'd be a liar if I said it didn't help my own.

After a quick smile, she's gone. In the rear view mirror, I see her sprinting up the driveway, back to her mother's side. This morning, this visit, the whole thing is difficult to stomach.

So Adelia is convinced that God is with me. I hope she's right, even though I can't help but ask myself how long? Each new case arrives as a storm, and only God knows how many more I can weather.

11
The Path

I find Trey and Al in the office. Trey is leaning back in his chair, feet kicked up on his desk perusing a file while arguing with Al about the finer nuances of speaking Italian, the "tongue of Kings," according to Trey. So far, Al seems to be dubious of Trey's ethnic purity.

"Hey, my mom's maiden name is Millitello," Trey says, "That's as Italian as it gets, *paisan*."

As usual, I play the role of referee. "I hate to interrupt this United Nations love fest, but were you able to find out anything, Al?"

"I linked that number you sent me back to an AT&T subscriber, and was able to get an address. I've still got a lot more work to do, but I figured you guys would want to go take a peek at the house."

"That *is* good news. How far away is this place?"

He jabs a command into the MapQuest site. "Viola."

Trey picks the freshly printed document from the printer, and we're out the door. "Al," I say, turning before we exit, "if you come across anything of interest, hit me on the cell." He answers with a nod, then dives back into cyberspace.

The Triangle shrinks away in the rearview mirror.

With a new trail to follow, we merge onto the freeway, aiming for the far Southwest corner of the city.

Trey cracks the passenger window to let crisp winter air whip throughout The Beast. "I heard you had an interview this morning."

"I met with Eliza's mother this morning."

"I'm guessing that sucked."

"It was tough. These interviews never get any easier. But this one…I don't know, Trey." I become silent and my words trail off in thought. At the moment, my eyes are on the road, but my mind is elsewhere.

"You okay, kid?"

"I don't know. This dude, he just walked right into her mother's house and took her daughter away. No shame."

"Eliza's mother actually met this asshole?"

I nod. "He walked into her living room and smiled right at her. He had the nerve to tell her he was going to 'take care' of her daughter. How often have we ever seen that?"

Trey shakes his head slowly and massages his temples. "Damn, I bet she wishes she could have that day back. I mean, if she could have known then what she knows now, there's no way he would have gotten out of her house alive."

"I don't know. She didn't seem like that type of person."

"Type of person? She's a parent, isn't she? There are only two types of parents, Chris, ones who give a damn about their kids, and ones who don't. Which one was she?"

"Yeah, maybe you're right."

"Maybe? Ask yourself what you would do to a man who walked into your house with the sole intention of beating the hell out of your girls and renting them to the highest bidder."

I don't answer him. I don't need to. My disquiet is enough. Silence kills, and Trey knows that for my daughters, so would I.

He grabs the sheet of paper from the visor and runs his finger along the thin lines of the map. "Make a right on the next street, then hang a quick left. Time we got some answers."

We pass the house at a snail's pace. It's a standard Vegas house, a modest, handsome two-story on a decent-sized lot, complete with Spanish tile roof and a three-car garage. An extremely dusty, unregistered gray-colored Pontiac sits in the driveway.

"This is bullshit, kid," Trey says. "It's all smoke and mirrors with this prick, isn't it?"

"Looks that way."

"Dead grass. Even the hedges are dying. Look there." Trey points to the door frame where several newspapers have formed a small pile, untouched. The walkway is riddled with piles of dried pine needles and broken blades of grass. It's dusk, so we should see some interior lighting, perhaps a lamp through a window, or the flickering of a TV. Yet, there's nothing.

"All right, kid," Trey says. "Pull up a few. I'm gonna sneak up and take a closer look."

I make the u-turn and park two houses away. He makes his way down the street looking more the obtuse pedestrian than calculating super sleuth. The gusts of wind, piercing and bitter, have a bite, and they seem to be eating him alive. He hunches over, tugging the collar of his jacket higher onto his neck. Further down the block, he moves slower at the front of the house. At that ideal spot, Trey drops to one knee. With his head lowered and canted slightly towards the house, he goes through the motions of tying a shoe lace.

He rises and moves quickly up the driveway towards the seemingly abandoned vehicle. With his hands cupped over his eyes, he leans in against the passenger side window and slowly circles the car. Still peering into it, Trey pulls out his flashlight and puts the end in his mouth so he can write something on the palm of his hand.

He checks out the front patio area before returning to the car. "Crank the heat, kid, it's freezing out there."

I blast the heat and punch the accelerator. "Well, what did you figure out?"

"The place is abandoned, but I was able to get a name, though. There was all kinda mail and shit in that car." Pressing the interior light, Trey reads what he'd written on his hand. "Haley Harrison. Does that mean anything to you?"

"No, not at the moment. Still, it's something, another small piece of this god-forsaken puzzle."

We speed back towards the heart of the city in silence. Our dark streets are painted with the vivid greens and bright reds of pulsating traffic lights. In spite of Mario's elaborate subterfuge, we have come away from this place with the only grain of truth left behind; a name, an identity that he, in all likelihood, didn't create.

William Shakespeare's Juliet posed one of the greatest questions in all of literature, "What's in a name?" To the criminals I hunt, it's everything, and these men go to great lengths to mask their names and those of their victims to make it harder for us to track them.

Identity Manipulation isn't just a mildly harmless term where names are changed. The monsters I hunt cut and stitch pieces of other identities, others' lives and histories, onto that of their latest victim. Eventually, a woman may no longer even recognize herself. She finds herself swapped into an unfamiliar state where families and detectives have much less of chance of ever finding her.

Traffickers don't need a whole system, one or two individuals in key places are just as damaging. A corrupt, low-level employee at the D.M.V., for instance, can deliver an authentic, falsified license; or bribed clerks at a hospital can set aside a blank birth certificate. Those who supply these materials may have no idea what damage they cause. The supplier, if caught, may suffer a demotion or the loss of a job. But this pales in comparison to the loss a family would endure at the prospect of never again seeing their loved one again.

This is exactly how our nation can have hundreds of women murdered each year who apparently have no families, no identities, and no names.

Looking toward the evening sky, the cold front's brought in ominous clouds. They hang over the city and feed the growing darkness. My cell phone buzzes and I momentarily shift my gaze. "Baughman."

"Hi, Chris. It's Stephanie Dirks I'm the new Investigative Specialist for your section. You got a few minutes to talk about this Mario character? The Lieutenant asked me to take a look at his financials. It looks like he is the owner of a business, a stereo shop or something. It's off of Western Avenue, the name of the place is Desert Audio. I'm currently looking at some aerials of this building. It's kinda tucked away in an industrial area. You guys feel like taking a look?"

"Absolutely. Good job, and welcome to the team." I have no doubt that this business is more of a front to explain his illegal proceeds than a legitimate source of income."

I exit the freeway and decide to make our approach from the back roads. For now, we have his scent.

While en-route, I tap the icon for Al on my cell. "What's up, Al?"

"Nada. Still grinding. You find out anything at that address?"

"The house was vacant, but Trey managed to find a name in a car that was left behind. Can you look into it? Her name's Haley Harrison."

"Yeah, give me a second to get into the right program." The sound of the keyboard pops and snaps from behind Al's voice. "It looks like this Haley of yours has had a few issues, bro."

"Issues?"

"Yeah, she's been through it."

"I've got a minute. Elaborate."

"All right, let me just get a count." Beneath his breath, Al takes a running tally. "This girl's only thirty years old. She's been arrested over thirty times and every one's for something vice-related, either trespass or soliciting for the purpose of prostitution. It's a damn shame."

"You're right, it is. Keep at it and see if you can't connect a few more dots from that end."

After a quick visit to the stereo shop we come away with another name, Paul Whittier. I tap my phone screen and highlight Stephanie Dirks's name.

"Hello, Detective," she answers in a bubbly voice.

"You wouldn't happen to be at the office still, would you?"

"As a matter of fact, I was just wrapping it up for the night. It figures you'd call now." After a playful sigh, she continues, "Lucky for you my computer's still up. So what ya got?"

"Another name; Paul Whittier. He's supposed to be the co-owner of Desert Audio. Very interesting place this business is. Thanks for the lead."

"Don't mention it. Thanks for letting me play in your sandbox."

"Sure, hey while it's on my mind, have you had a chance to meet our Latin counterpart?"

"Oh you mean Al? He was really nice…and a little scary looking. Okay, Paul Whittier is listed as the co-owner, along with none other than Mario Davis. If you don't mind, I'm going to take the liberty of checking for more businesses in Mario's name."

"Perfect. If we need to twist Paul to testify against his business partner, we'll have that option."

"I like the way you think. Hmm, well it looks like Mario has been busy opening businesses for years now. None of them really lasted though. Carwash, auto detailing, you name it, it seems like he's tried it."

"Shocker."

"Let me try one more thing before I head outta here. Al told me he was looking into a woman. What was her name?"

"Haley, Haley H-A-R-R-I-S-O-N"

"Bingo," Stephanie exclaims. "Now were cooking with fish grease, and before you ask, no, I don't really know what that means, but it sure is catchy. It looks like this Haley Harrison is an officer in a business. Something called 4 Women, LLC."

"Can you cross reference that business against her name to see if there are any others with interests in that company?"

"I can and I have. Right now I'm looking at four names listed as the principal officers. The first, which should come as no secret, is Haley Harrison. After her we have Sadie Ortega, Laurie Blackmon, and last but not least, Katie Coughlin."

"Interesting. Okay, can you do one last thing? Can you pull DMV records and see where Mario bought his Mercedes Benz? I'll grab it from you tomorrow."

"Sure. You boys have fun tonight. I'll transfer you to Al's desk."

Stephanie's voice fades away as we sit on hold. Soon I hear the fumbling of the receiver, followed by Al's voice, "What's up, fellas?"

Trey replies in his usual manner, "You tell us.

"Okay, so once you gave me Haley's name, I decided to take a closer look at her arrest history. I cross referenced that against receipts from the court system. Once I did that, things just started falling right into place."

Based on what we'd just learned from Stephanie, I couldn't agree more. "What did you find?"

"The court documents show that Haley Harrison, a.k.a. Ally is, or was, linked to a woman named Laurie Blackmon, a.k.a. Bianca. Laurie Blackmon is tied to a Faven...Drazkovich, Faven Drazkovich is linked to another girl, umm, an Alisson Becker."

Trying to lighten the mood, Trey interjects offering his best attempt at a compliment, "Holy shit, Al, it's about time you carried you're weight. Well done, tubby."

"If you don't mind, there's more," Al sniffs. "Okay, try to keep up, 'cause things get confusing here. So, also linked to Laurie Blackmon are two more women; Sadie Ortega, a.k.a. Mya and Marissa Shipley. Sadie Ortega leads us to Katie Coughlin, and back to Haley Harrison."

What has been unveiled to us we will call, for lack of a better term, "The Family Tree." If Mario is the trunk, then the women he controls are the branches, each in some way, shape, or form is connected to the next. "Lord have mercy, Al."

"I know, bro, and I'm not even done yet, it gets worse. So, this Marissa Shipley, she's linked to a Paula Hartley. Paula Hartley leads us to Georgia Andrews." Al pauses, sounding as somber as I have ever heard him, "Who brings us to uh, to our girl, Eliza Serra."

For a moment none of us speak. I think of the lives he's affected, or more precisely, infected, and the number of families he alone has hurt.

12
Broken Souls

Brief intermissions of moonlight weave down through the gray storm clouds. What reaches us can barely illuminate the car's interior. Even in this low light, Trey can make out my preoccupied stare.

"What's on your mind, Chris?"

"I don't know, man. I don't know."

"Come on, I'm looking right at you, and I can see something ain't right." Trey leans back, shifting his body to look straight at me. "So are you gonna tell me what's going on in that head a yours?"

"Is there any way I can get you to leave this alone?"

"Not unless you have an ejector seat in this car."

At this point, if I did, I'd have seriously contemplated using it. "I just…I'm tired, sometimes feel like I'm losing myself. Does that make any sense?"

"Shit, I don't know, kid. Who isn't lost in this world? The things happening in it are so fucked up." Trey adjusts his body once again and interlocks his fingers. "Has it occurred to you that maybe you aren't lost. Hell, the way I see it, you're one of the few sane people left on this damn planet."

"I don't feel sane, Trey. You know, the more we hunt these people, I just look at them and don't even see humans. It's like I… I see something else. Monsters."

As Trey stares at me, I can hear my own words, and I sound as if I'm at my wit's end. "Trey, I sit up nearly every night asking myself the same damn question. I look at my daughters, and I ask myself if what I'm doing is even worth the cost."

"The cost? What do you mean?"

"The cost, Trey! What we have to do, what we see. I feel like it's changing me, little by little. I worry that by the time I'm done, I'll be a shell of who they love, a shell of the man they knew. I take my daughters to parks and watch them play with other children just so I can be reminded of what innocence is." My eyes well up. "That's not normal."

"Fuck that! And fuck these assholes!" Trey's voice is both angry and supportive. "You're the most compassionate man I know, and possibly one of the smartest. Anything you say you're going to do, you get done. Anyone you say you're going to fuck up, you fuck up! Do you even realize that in the five years I've known you, you've never lost a case? Not one. Ever. Who can say that? I'm going to tell you something I noticed about you a long time ago. You're bigger than what you're doing on the force. Anyone who's ever met you knows that. You're destined for something on the big side, brother."

Trey places his arm on my left shoulder and squeezes gently. "The ways you've led this team, and the things you've done for this city—no one's ever seen anything like it. Look, we both know I'd be a fucking liar if I told you I know exactly what you're feeling. I don't think there are too many people wired like you. But I will say this; you're here right now, in this place, for a reason. I know it, and you know it."

Another moment passes and Trey shakes his head and looks down at his lap. A smile has risen on his face. "Those may have been the wisest, most inspirational words I've ever spoken. Sometimes I amaze myself. Aristotle, eat your heart out."

"I do feel a little bit better."

"Good, now, let's focus on this piece of shit."

The Triangle's lot is still covered by a blanket of darkness, and I park beside Trey's car. He gathers himself and opens the passenger door.

"You know, you're one of the best friends I've ever had, Trey. Thank you."

"You don't have to thank me." His face is a mask of sincerity. "Have a good night, kid."

I stand outside The Beast for a moment and watch Trey's blazing red tail lamps move deeper into the city's lights. Closing my eyes, I inhale the night's sharp air. Once upstairs, it's back to work, back to the hunt, and back to the monster.

The office is desolate at this time of night. The lights have been switched off, save for the single fluorescent bulb running above my desk. I nudge the computer mouse and wake up the monitor. The first program I want allows me to track any inmate at the Clark County Detention Center. It's time to take a look at faces of the women both Al and Stephanie have so masterfully identified. Now that we know who they are, all that's left is to figure out where he's hiding them.

I open a tan folder; the very first printout summarizes the police record of the ever-elusive Haley Harrison. My finger traces down the number of arrests she has incurred and, sure enough, Al was right on the money.

I type Haley's name into the computer and less than a second later, the screen shows her to me for the first time.

She is a stunner, even in the harsh light of a dull police mug shot. These pictures usually make people look awful. But not Haley. She seems fully composed and nearly serene.

Who is next on the list? I flip the page and see Sadie Ortega. After noting her address, I take a moment to look at her picture. Utterly beautiful. The tilt of her eyebrows reveal an anger bordering on fury. I can't help but wonder what those eyes have taken in.

I flip to the next sheet and face, and Laurie Blackmon pops up. I punch in another name to see Katie Coughlin's blue eyes staring back at me. A shame. As beautiful as Katie is, her history is just as ugly. Charge after charge, trespassing, followed by soliciting, even loitering.

I continue to move through the list of cases, flipping one page after another, until I get to the last face. Eliza Serra. I know Al, and it's likely he placed her picture at the bottom on purpose.

With her picture now on the screen, I can hear her words in my head as clearly as if I played the recording. "He beat me again and then gave me two options. I could either walk around bald headed, or he was going to bring a group of his friends over and force me to have sex with them, one after the other, or two to three at a time. He didn't care."

In his attempts to command her mind, body, and soul, Mario drove her to the brink. He continued to push her toward that dark void, where she would finally attempt suicide.

I lean back in my seat and stretch away the tension. It's nearly two in the morning. My eyes are heavy, and my resolve is beaten to near submission. I need to rest in order to travel even deeper into this labyrinth of depravity.

13
Hoop Dreams

I haven't slept well since the day Eliza and Adelia walked into my life. I peer into the rear view and a have a hard time looking away from my own reflection and the macabre expression on it. I head to my office in a haze.

Stepping through the office door, I make my way over to Stephanie's work station, curious as to whether she was able to pan any more nuggets of gold from Mario's river of lies.

Spotting me, she gives me a tentative greeting. "Oh hi, Chris."

"Are you all right?" I ask, taking a seat on the corner of her desk.

She lifts her head from the monitor and locked he ice blue eyes onto me. "I started to dig a bit deeper, doing more background work on that Mario guy. I mean...I went back, way back, all the way to what high schools he attended." She sifts through a stack of printouts on her desk. "Did you know he attended Rancho High School? He graduated in 1992."

I simply nod.

"The more I learned out about him, the more I kept thinking about you. It's like your paths kept crisscrossing. I know you went to Rancho as well. Do you know this man?"

I offer another nod before speaking. "You know, Stephanie, that's the funny thing about life. It takes us wherever it wants to with no say at all from us."

"Does anyone else know about this?" asks Stephanie slowly, leaning in closer to me. "About you...about him?"

"Just Al and Trey."

"Well, if it helps, I haven't told anyone. This is crazy, Chris."

"You want to hear something really crazy. Let me tell you a story. Back in 1990, I was a skinny little fourteen-year-old who had dreams of becoming rich so I could send my brothers and sisters to college and buy my parents their dream home. Basketball was my sport of choice, so I wore my quickest pair of gym shoes to basketball try-outs.

"The next day, I returned to the gym, where gaggles of kids surrounded a lone sheet of paper taped to the wall. Some walked away in tears, heads hanging, while others cheered and high-fived each other. I slowly made my way toward the sheet. My eyes worked down the list, until I found my name. I couldn't wait to race home to tell my family the good news.

"I had the opportunity to play against others from all across the city. A few of them were phenomenal. I wasn't one of them, but I gave the coaches my very best. Of course, sometimes our best isn't good enough.

"One evening after practice, I was told to stay behind on the court. As the other's lumbered into the locker room, I waited in the gym, sweaty, tired, and sore. When the coach came out, he told me to stand at the baseline. When the whistle blew, the coach ordered me to sprint from one line on the court to the next, over and over.

"The whole time, the coach barked at me, lecturing about how I wasn't playing to my potential, how I was too 'nice' on the court, and needed to start playing angrier. After what felt like an eternity of sprinting, the coach ordered me in. He stepped closer, moving right into my face and said, 'If you ever want to be anything in life, you'd better learn to take what you want. There's no room for kindness on the court, or in life. You want to see what a true winner looks like. Just look at Mario Davis. That boy's got a fire in his belly. If you're gonna try to be like anyone, or anything, choose him! That kid would kill his own mother to win.' Can you imagine that? Me being told to emulate Mario, a beast who kicks women around when he's not busy selling them.

"So, that's where that story ends," I say, clearing my throat and shaking my head, "and the story of our crossing paths begins. Mario never really knew me, but I knew plenty about him. From then on, our lives would pretty much be separated by no more than one degree; friends, family members, acquaintances and such.

"I can still remember when I heard he was awarded a big basketball scholarship. I was so happy for him, for his family. I thought maybe he'd go pro, or at the very least return to the neighborhood as some type of professional. You know, help make things better."

"Well, that didn't happen. So now what?"

"Now I finish what I started. As I step away I can hear Stephanie whisper beneath her breath, "Unreal.""

Al is leaning over Trey, both of them are concentrating on the screen with their backs to me. "Okay, guys, we've got a lot to cover today. I took the liberty of looking up a few of the addresses from the women you found last night, Al. I think we've done enough groundwork, so it's time to go on the offensive."

"What's the plan?" Al asks.

"I chose the women with the most extensive histories. Since we know Ms. Harrison isn't living at the house on Wheat Grass, we're left with two targets." I hand over two manila folders, one for each of my partners.

Trey reclines back in his chair, feet up on the desk, and opens the file. "Well, hello there, Miss Ortega, so you live off Old Salt Circle, huh? All right, Chris. I'm game."

For a moment Al silently looks over his assignment. "And I got Laurie Blackmon. How do we even know if they live where they say they do?"

"We don't," I answer. "I need you to figure out if these addresses are still viable options for us. If so, take pictures, and we'll meet back here in about three hours."

"Sounds good," Trey says, "but why are we only going after two of the ten girls he's pimping?"

"Based on our conversation with Eliza, we've established that when he's not beating the women, he grooms and brings them along slowly. The way I see it, the ones who have the longest police record for the longest period of time are probably his main girls. My guess is the women he listed on that LLC will be of the most consequence to us. Sadie Ortega, Laurie Blackmon, Haley Harrison, and Katie Coughlin."

"What's the deal with this Katie chick?" Trey asks. "Seems like we should be on her ass, too, unless I'm missing something."

"Remember when Al did that workup on Mario? Well, he listed his place of residency as Barstow, California. At the time, we found that a bit odd until last night, when I was going through all the women's sheets, and I noticed that Katie lives in Barstow. Now we know what, or who, he's been hiding out there."

"Scumbag. All right, so Al and I hunt down the women, do we even want to know what you'll be doing?"

"I'll be paying a visit to the dealership where he bought the Mercedes. I'm hoping they'll have something we can use. You guys ready to go fishing?"

"I'm down," says Al, grabbing his car keys from the top of his desk. "Besides I could use the fresh air."

"Sure as hell beats sitting around this office, see you guys in three," Trey replies.

Wheeling into the lot of the car dealership, I park and grab my case file. Norm Baker Motors specializes in high-end used and new vehicles. As I walk through the midsized car lot, I can't look in any direction without my eyes stumbling across a Mercedes-Benz, BMW, Porsche, Lamborghini, or Lotus. Even under a darkening sky, the rims on each car sparkle.

A man sits near the entrance, pecking away at a computer terminal. "Excuse me, sir," I say, pulling the badge from my back pocket. I'm Detective Baughman. I need to speak with the owner, if he's present."

"You just missed the owner. I'm a manager, name's Donny. Is there some way I can help you?"

"That depends. Do you have access to customer files—records of purchase, service and such?"

"Oh, I can get those for you, no problem."

Donny leads me to the other side of the showroom to a small office. "Have have a seat, Detective. Who are we hoping to find?"

I set the ever-growing binder down on the desk and flip it open to Mario's picture. "We're looking for this man and anyone associated with him."

"Hmm," says Donny, rubbing his chin. "Man, this guy looks so familiar." He leans over the table and closes in on the picture. Tapping the tip of his index finger against the surface of dark brown table he attempts to jog his memory. "That's it! I do know this guy. Give me just a second. I'm gonna grab his file."

Donny exits the room and returns with a manila folder. He sets it on top of the desk and pushes it over to me. "This is everything we've got on this guy. He's something else, man."

"What do you mean?"

"Whenever he comes in, he always has like two or three girls he parades around with. Beautiful girls, too. He seemed like a nice enough fella. I guess when you've got it, you've just got it, huh?" Donny hunches his shoulders and shakes his head.

"Do you think I could have a few minutes to look over this file?"

"Sure. Take your time. Yell if you need me for anything."

I open the folder and it doesn't take long before I pull a few different strands of viable information from the sheets. His credit application lists 1653 K Street as his home. Apparently he's lived there for the last thirty-three years. Under "Present Employer," he lists Desert Audio, no surprise there. He's even given himself the title "General Manager."

Taking into account the deserted location of the audio shop and the lack of traffic flowing on those industrial streets, I'm shocked to learn just how much a general manager earns. One line states that he makes $9,500 a month. For anyone else, this would be a wonderful salary, but to a trafficker, it's a drop in the bucket; one that instantly raises a red flag. I take note of it, and wait to see if a pattern develops.

Under "Personal friends known over one year," he lists Sadie Ortega and Haley Harrison. Friends, indeed. I turn the page and look at the total sales price of the car, which is $115,123.09.

How much did you put down Mr. Davis? I flip a few more sheets, and find that he shelled out $25,000.00. That's interesting, but not as interesting as the payment breakdown scribbled across the sheet of paper. A Bank of America cashier's check lists the remitter, or purchaser of the check as Desert Audio. So, "the company" plans to pay Norm Baker Motors $17,000.00. Of course "the company" will front the money. I make another little note for myself and place it beside the $9,500.00 figure from earlier. I continue moving through the stack of papers. What's this? A receipt made out to Mario Davis for another eight thousand, paid out to Norm Baker Motors in cash.

All these numbers add up to one thing. Structuring. The criminals in my world are always looking for ways to move money, and to do this, they "structure" payments in ways that keeps them from eclipsing a certain dollar amount. The magic number is $10,000. These animals know that if they cross that threshold, the banks, car dealerships, jewelry stores, or any of the other places they filter money through are obligated to notify the IRS. Since Structuring is a federal offense, a state guy like me would need to get a federal agency on board, preferably the IRS. This is will serve as a nice card to play in the event I need to.

Satisfied with what I have learned thus far, I lean out and call for Donny to get his statement. With the pictures I show him, he verifies that Mario came in with Eliza, before he chopped off her hair, and Haley Harrison.

14

The Trishula

My foot drops on the accelerator, flooding the engine with fuel. I look at my reflection in the rear-view mirror. I'd like to think it's an ordinary face, and for a plain-clothes detective, that's a good thing.

The word on the street has made my warning clear. To the monsters and all their friends who feed on the flesh of women, my face has become the razor-sharp spear pointed at their chests. If ever they should see it, it's time to run as fast as possible in the opposite direction.

Soon, I'm back at the Triangle. As I think about our three-pronged attack, the cell phone in my pocket vibrates. It's Al. "How are things going on your end?" I open the car door and grab my backpack from the rear seat.

"Well, I'm at the address you gave me, but it's kinda like a condo set up. There really isn't anything outside her unit that tells me if she's still living here or not."

"All right. Did you notice any kids or adults at any of the neighboring units?"

"Actually, I did. A lady pulled up and started bringing in groceries right next door. She had a couple of young kids with her."

"Okay, that might work for us. Do you still have your file and the photo of Laurie?"

"Of course."

"Do me a favor. Grab the unit number of the neighbor's condo and the license plate off her car if you can still see it. I'm heading to my computer now."

"Let me call you back."

As Al begins the recon, I enter the office and move directly to my workstation. Al's text message contains the neighbor's address and license plate.

On one hand, we need another ally, and quickly. However just because we're moving swiftly doesn't mean we should do so sloppily. One error, one slip, could set off a chain of events which could eventually tip the scales back in Mario's favor.

Before Al calls me back I'll need to have a few questions answered. Who is this woman? How long has she lived there? And the most critical riddle of all, can she be trusted?

Computers aren't crystal balls, however, the DMV, marriage license bureau, and a few other programs should help me to form a decent opinion. In the time allotted, it'll allow a glimpse into the life, patterns, and history of this woman, this Tanya Breckenridge.

I sit silently, patiently, and then my phone lights up.

"Damn, It's cold," says Al, his voice still quivering from the winter chill. "All right, what ya got for me?"

"The neighbor's name is Tonya Breckenridge. It looks like she's a single mother, who works at a casino."

"Hang on, hang on. Let me grab a pen and write this down. Tonya Brec…"

"B-R-E-C-K-E-N-R-I-D-G-E."

"Okay, okay," Al replies, the sound of scribbling and paper being jostled competing with his voice. "Go on, bro."

"From what I can see, there's no real record, but she's had a couple traffic tickets."

"Anything else?" Al asks through a nervous sigh. "Advice, words of wisdom?"

"Yeah, the best advice I ever got was, whatever you do, don't eat the yellow snow."

Just then my cell phone beeps with another incoming call. I peek at the screen and see Trey's name.

"Al, Trey's trying to get through. Let me see what he's got brewing. You'll do fine, take a breath. You're a veteran who made it through a war, I'm pretty sure you can handle interviewing a mother."

I press the answer button and am welcomed by a bit of New York charm. "Hey, you son-of-a-bitch! I'm not saying I'm the most amazing man on the planet, but far be it from me to stop you if you wanna."

"All right Trey, what makes you so amazing?"

"So there I was, minding my own business, spying on…"

"Trey it's not spying, it's surveilling."

"Potato…to-fucking-mato. So I'm sitting out here parked down the street from Sadie's house, and who rolls up but the elusive Haley Harrison."

"You're kidding!"

"Naw, CB-Man. I'm not. Tall, hot redhead. It's her, kid."

This is Karma showing us her favor. My guess is she's come to collect for the blood that Macc has spilled. "Trey, you are amazing. Are you still at the house?"

"No. I left."

Dear God! My breath drops out my chest and settles into my stomach. "Trey," I state calmly, attempting to swallow my anxiety, "we need to figure out where Haley lives. She's one of the main three."

"Yeah, no shit. Why do you think I left? I'm following her right now. What do I look like? A Johnny-come-lately?

Suddenly, I can breathe once more.

"We need to work on your communication skills. Somehow the words 'I left' don't accurately depict exactly what you've got going on at the moment."

"Wait. Okay, hang on. She's pulling into a neighborhood."

"Where are you?"

"Near at the far west-end of the city. I think Spring Valley, maybe. You gotta pen?"

"Yeah."

"Jot these names down: Quinella and Torrence. She's pulling into the driveway of a house at that intersection. Okay now, the garage door's lifting up, and…she's inside. We got her! You heard from Al?"

"Yeah, he's working on confirming Laurie's address. He should be making friends with her neighbor as we speak."

"Al? Making friends?" Trey laughs. "That's not really in his skill set, is it?"

"Let's hope it is today."

Nearly three hours have passed. I wait by our desks for the final outcomes of today's excursion. Al and Trey come barreling in at the same moment, chewing up the once-serene atmosphere. Trey, sounding rather jovial, provides the color commentary. "Al, I kid you not. Haley just rolled up right in front of Sadie's house. After a couple of minutes, Sadie walked her out. It couldn't have worked out any better. From there, she led us straight back to her place."

"Damn, bro," says Al, shaking his head. "That's some lucky shit."

"Okay, okay. So, we know how Trey did, but how did things go with Ms. Breckenridge?"

"It went good," Al says. "She recognized Laurie as her neighbor. Apparently, Laurie keeps some very late hours. But the best part? Laurie has..." Al lifts both hands placing his air quotes perfectly, " 'a boyfriend.' A certain dude named Mario. She told me she wasn't sure about him, something about how he gave her a funny feeling."

"A funny feeling, huh? Gotta love a woman's intuition. Did you both get pictures of the girls' places?" They nod and place their digital cameras on top of my desk. "Thank you very much, gentlemen."

Against a wall a few feet from my desk, Trey leans with crossed arms. "Remember, I took pictures of two houses. Sadie's spot is the first group, and Haley's place is gonna be the second."

There's a long pause.

"So, where do we go from here?"

"Let's get these pictures downloaded. I have some documents from the car dealership I visited this afternoon. I need to read through them to figure out exactly where we go, and what we do from here."

"No problem," Trey replies. "I'll get em' downloaded right now and save 'em to a disc."

I glance over at Al, who is already scrolling through what he shot at the home of Laurie Blackmon.

Just as I open up the case-file to review the documents from the dealership, my phone rings.

"Um, he...hello? I'm looking for Detective Chris," a man's voice asks in an uncertain tone.

"Well you found him. Is, is this...Donny?" I barley recognize his voice over the phone.

"Yes...yes it is."

"I'm surprised to hear from you so soon. Did I forget something?"

"Well, not exactly. But you told me that if anything came up to contact you right away, so, that's what I'm doing."

"Well then, please proceed." I lean back and get comfortable.

"I was walking the lot, checking on cars. I went through the service department and almost had a heart attack. Sitting right there in the lounge was Mr. Davis. I grabbed up his service folder and hot-footed it right on outta there to call you."

I damn near fall out of my chair trying to scramble to my feet. "Donny, how long has he been there?"

"Judging from the paperwork, I'd say maybe twenty, give or take."

Adrenaline surges through me. "Service?"

"Yep, he's here for an oil change. I'm guessing we're pretty close to done though. The mechanics were lowering the lift when I came in to call you."

I ramble around my desk, hurriedly grabbing my backpack, pens, and whatever else I think might be of use. "Okay, Donnie? I need to ask a huge favor of you."

"Shoot, Detective."

"No pressure...no pressure at all...but we have been waiting for this man to show himself for quite some time. I need you to stall him."

With my phone still plastered to my ear, I sprint toward the front door. "Al you're with me, Trey stay on those pics. Mario surfaced!"

Al jumps from his seat. "We taking The Beast?"

"Yeah, it's the fastest thing we have. I'll meet you in the lot."

"Right behind you!" Al's voice bounces off the walls and down the stairwell.

"Donny," my voice fluctuates as I sprint down the steps, "you still there?"

"Yes…yes, sir!"

"I'm on my way. Do whatever you have to, but keep that man in the dealership!"

Running through the lot, I hang up the phone mid-stride and unlock my car. The engine cracks like thunder and the tires chirp as I reverse. Al bursts through the glass doors. Perfect timing!

"GET IN!" I smash the gas. The race begins!

15
The Wolf Hunt

The cold streets melt as we blaze through the city.

"All right, cut left at the next light. That'll put us on Sahara."

"Hang tight!" I veer left, weaving through the sluggish traffic.

"There!" Al's hand rockets towards the windshield. "On the left!"

"I see it." A yellow traffic signal is no match for The Beast's prowess, evidenced by the way its tires carve into the asphalt. Adjacent to the dealership is a deserted lot. I nestle in between a few parked cars. Soon American muscle will challenge German engineering. I dig my phone from my pocket and scroll down to Donny's phone number.

"Hello?" He doesn't answer so much as ask nervously.

"Donny, we're in place. Let him go when you're ready."

"Okay. Just remember, a black Benz."

"Okay, I got it. A black Benz. We won't miss him."

They have many names, the Canis Lupus. Cagey, swift, intelligent, and violent; these are the characteristics of the wolf. As we stare through the swirling dust plumes kicked up from The Beast's V8, I see the nose of a jet black monster creep from the exit of the dealership.

"All right, Al. There he is. Keep eyes on that bastard. I'll do my best to keep up, but I'll have to mind John and Jane Q."

"Damn, he's pushing a V12," Al says. "Let's just hope this goes niiiice and easy. Be a good little pimp and take us home, Mario."

The setting sun gleams from the highly polished midnight black paint on the Benz as he pulls out of the lot and hits the main road. We give him no more than a two-second head start before slowly creeping from our desert vantage and merging in three cars behind him. We want to be close, but not too close.

"He's four cars up, and the light just turned yellow. Move faster!"

"Dammit!" Cranking the wheel, we shift, moving quickly through the center lane and over to the far left.

"I'm losing him!" Al yells out. "Punch it!"

I drop the accelerator once more. The needle on the tachometer kisses redline and the engine screams bloody murder. My body sinks into the leather as we move faster and faster closing in on both the yellow light, and the congested intersection. Click! The yellow light shifts to red just as we cross the intersection. "You got him, Al?"

"Shit, I don't… I don't see. Wait! There, three cars up on our right. Stay in this lane. It looks like his blinker is on. All right, looks like we're gonna be hopping on the freeway. Northbound."

At the freeway entrance, a fresh red light acts as the starter's pistol. Al rakes his fingers through his hair. With a sigh he exhales. "Here we go again. The light's turning green…now!"

The black V12 rockets from the starting gate and turns left for the on-ramp. We lag behind and just beside. On the freeway, he opens up his horse power. We ebb behind, creating just a bit more breathing room between the two of us. Now I match his speed from a few lanes over. He rushes ahead, weaving in and out of lanes without the simple courtesy of ever using a turn signal. A quick glance at the speedometer tells me we are both moving far above the posted limit. His Benz is a black blur streaking against the backdrop of a now glowing city.

"He drives like an idiot," Al says. "We should pull his ass over and write him a ticket just on general principle."

"Don't worry about it, Al. Pretty soon his whole world will go up in flames, and you'll be holding the lighter."

"Hell yeah. Burn, bitch!" Al adjusts his body while peering through the smoked windshield. "He's merging onto the 95. Get

into the far right lane when you can. All right slow down, he's
getting off at the first exit."

We creep up just behind him as he sits in the turn lane. The
crimson stop light glows softly against the darkness of night. He
drives past a few million-dollar neighborhoods before hanging a
right on Alta.

His black sedan moves steadily, oil in a sea of darkness. Its
location is only given away by an occasional glimmer of light
catching the polish. Slowing, he turns into a very exclusive guard-
gated community.

"He lives in the Scotch Eighties." I can hear the slow simmer
in Al's voice, the anger bubbling just beneath his words.

"Let's not jump to conclusions. He may just be visiting
someone," I reply, pulling into a school's dimly lit parking lot.

"Now what?"

"Let's give him a few minutes. We should be able to find out
everything we need to know from the person at the guard gate."
After a few moments of idling, I kill the engine and exit.

The blistery chill of winter sucks the warmth from our bodies
and I can hear the frozen blades crushing beneath our shoes as we
step across a patch of well manicured grass. The Scotch Eighties,
as Al called it, is an older neighborhood filled with immaculate
estate-style homes on oversized lots. Old homes in an old
neighborhood can only mean one thing...old money.

After a brief introduction, the guard inside the shack is quite
amenable when it comes to handing us over a copy of the
homeowners list. He'd even taken the time to highlight a property
for us.

We quickly make our way back to The Beast. I start the
engine and hand Al the papers. "I think we should take a look at
the highlighted property." Al punches the address into his smart
phone and instantaneously gets directions. As we reach the guard
gate, the barrier lifts, and we now see what's behind the curtain.
This may as well be Oz. It's a different world. Immaculate homes
sit on vast lots where mammoth trees line the streets. This doesn't

even feel like Vegas, at least not the Vegas I know. I'm reminded of a fall scene from a Norman Rockwell painting.

"Damn, this is nice. Our street should be the next one coming up."

I kill the lights and turn down the stereo. A quick left and there it is, tucked deeply into the corner of the cul-de-sac. It's more a small palace than a house. The walls surrounding it bring to mind the Alamo, and not just because of the Spanish tile roof. The front yard is large, and leads to a gated entry way. Behind that sits a vast courtyard with decorative shrubbery. No palace would be complete without a large fountain. Ambient light from the porch glows against it.

"Al, you think you're tall enough to get a peek into the garage?"

"I don't know. We should probably play it safe. You're a bit taller than me."

"I'm going to pull forward and park on the side street. You hop in the driver's seat. We'll want to get out of here fast when I get back."

"Good luck," Al replies unlatching is seat belt.

I use the darkness as a tool and stay close to trees. The howling winds mask the sound of my feet as they crunch on the decorative rock and dead leaves. I'm just few feet away from his garage and sprint from the shadows into the light. With no trees to conceal me, I scramble up the driveway towards the garage door. A light sensor at the edge of the garage clicks and triggers a floodlight which blasts the immediate area with illumination. I quickly stand up on my toes and look through the dingy rain pelted glass panels nearest the top. There it is, his demonic ride, aka the black Benz, parked alone inside.

I smirk and dip back into the shadows. Now we have you!

As I round the corner and hop in the passenger seat Al fires up the engine, "Did you see anything?"

After fastening my belt and dropping my head into the palm of my hand, I can finally exhale. "We've got him."

"It's about damn time. So what now? Back to the office?"

I look around at the homes in this beautiful place as we head back into the cityscape. If only they knew there truly is a monster among them. "I'll be in early tomorrow to start drafting the warrants. Right off the top, I'm thinking five different locations."

"Five, at once? Do we even have the manpower to pull that off?"

"We may need to beg, borrow, and steal bodies for manpower, but we'll have to hit at least four houses simultaneously. I want to hurt this man, and I want to do it on every conceivable level."

The reasons we're cast into this hell will never change. Wherever there is a daughter lost, we'll venture to find her. In the end, all that will ever be remembered of us is that we fought for even one shot, one single opportunity, to make a difference in the life of one family. Today, that family belongs to Eliza Serra.

16

Hell Freezes Over

Trey spins around in his chair, and the springs creak as he reclines. "Based on the fact I heard nothing from you two for the last couple hours, I'm guessing it went well."

"We got his ass," Al says. "It's only a matter of time now."

Trey beams. "Okay, that leads me to my next question. How soon can we blow him up?"

For a moment I sit quietly, thinking on logistics for the upcoming operation. Task one: Break down every criminal act, all the evidence we've gathered, and the role each person played in this case. Task two: Fuse them together into one set of easy-to-follow circumstances. That means the warrants' details must be tied into five different properties, linking no less than eight separate individuals to at least five different criminal acts. Seems simple enough.

"I'll start writing the warrants tomorrow and finish over the weekend. I'm going to need to catch up with the lieutenant. I'll see if she can get us some help. If I can get the warrants signed by Tuesday—that'll be the 16th—we'll need another day to get S.W.A.T. on line and brief our task force so they can recon the properties. I say D-day for Mr. Davis is December 18th."

"It took us months to get this close," says Al with a smile, shaking his head. "Now we gotta wait a whole week before we Shock-and-Awe him."

I look over the photographs Trey had left on my desk, "Be cool, Al. Trey, this would be a good time to give us a quote about the benefits of patience."

Trey crosses his arms, still leaning back in his chair. "Patience… is like a fine wine, kid. A fine, fine wine."

Al and I look at each other, then back at Trey, confused, waiting for him to deliver the punch line. "What the hell you two clowns looking at? That's it…that's the quote."

Yet another gem from the mind of Trey G.

"All right, guys I'll be here first thing in the A.M. to get cracking on the warrants. See you tomorrow."

Traveling along the freeway I look to the sky. Behind a thick sheet of white clouds the sun glows softly. I press the power button on the radio just in time for the weather report. "A cold front is moving in over the weekend. Buckle down and button up, Vegas! Come next week we're going to be looking at snow in the desert, and lots of it."

Snow in the desert. Under any other circumstances, even I'd be surprised, but not this time. I move through the heart of my city, all the while envisioning Mario screaming from his throne. "I'll stop pimping when Hell freezes over!"

Well, get ready, son.

My life is somehow bound to the lives of the women he destroys. I am held captive by the same flaming, soul-searing thread that runs through their lives. Hell on Earth is no metaphor. There is such a place, and I've found its gateway. Of course, the trick isn't knowing that it exists, or even how to enter, but rather, figuring how to get out alive.

At the office, Lieutenant Karen Hughes sits at her desk toiling over reports and accounts. I peek in and speak to myself beneath my breath. *"Now is as good a time as any. All I need is a miracle."*

"Excuse me. LT?" I wrap softly on her opened door. "You mind if I bother you for a minute?"

She lifts her head and adjusts the fashionable square-framed glasses resting on her face. "Good God, Chris, what are you doing here so early?"

"I'm getting ready."

"Getting ready?"

"Yeah. We found him," I reply taking a step further into her office.

"Him," she asks? Swiftly leaning forward, she nearly jumps out of her chair. "Wait…him…you mean Macc?"

"That's exactly who I mean."

"How?"

"We had some help." I lift my gaze to the sky.

"So what's next?"

"Well, that's what brings me into your office. We're going to need some help."

"You already know my stance on this issue. It's my job to make sure you have whatever you need to hunt these criminals down."

"I know, I know. But I've got a feeling no one's ever asked you for what I'm about to."

She releases her hands, opens her palms to the sky. Across her face, the proverbial "try me" look.

"So like I said, we've tied him to several women, but we're going to hedge our bets. There seem to be three main constants; Sadie Ortega, Laurie Blackmon, and Haley Harrison.

"And…?"

"When we hit them, we need to do it simultaneously. Anything other than that and we run the risk of losing cars, money, jewelry—but most importantly, we risk losing him."

Lt. Hughes sweeps aside a lock of her blond hair. "So what are we talking about, Chris?"

"We're talking about a strategic service, four teams, one for each of the four premises"

"Damn," she says, shaking her head at the thought. "You're asking me to throw everything I've got at this man?"

"Aww, come on, LT.," I chime in with my sweetest smile. "I'm not asking for *everything* you've got. More like eighty percent of everything."

Looking rather stone-faced and, dare I say, unimpressed by my charming wit, she replies, "Very funny. So how soon do you want to move on him?"

"I'd like to go next week. I'll get the warrants started today and hopefully completed by Monday. I'll sit down with a judge on Tuesday. Wednesday we can have the massive briefing with whatever and whomever you can wrangle up. That leaves…"

"Thursday. Thursday is the day we drop the bomb," she interjects with confidence.

"And there you have it. At least that's the plan on paper."

"All right, Chris, I'll get you what you need." Grateful, I rise, grab my bag, and bolt for the door before she has a chance to change her mind. Extra resources are a luxury, and I'm grateful.

Back at my desk, I attend to the task at hand—writing the warrants. After some time, I peek at the clock. What felt like a moment was nearly three hours. Across from my desk, Trey sits silently. My mind is clear, but the facts of this case have left my heart a twisted mess.

"So how're those warrants coming along, kid?"

"Making sense of all the evidence is just as hard as finding it. But I'm preaching to the choir, aren't I?"

Trey leans back and kicks his feet up on the corner of his desk and looks at my cell phone sitting on my desk. "Your phone's blowing up."

I flip it open and run down a string of texts that all came from Eliza.

"Chris r u there?"

"Hello Chris?"

"Text me bac as soon as you can."

"It's my sister's birthday; I'd luv it if u could come by n say hi."

I punch the dial button. "Hello, Miss Eliza. How are you today?"

"Today is a beautiful day!"

"Oh, is it now? Well, I don't want to bring you down, but I'm not sure I want to crash your sister's birthday party."

"You have to come by. Please? I even baked her a cake. It's my first one. You gotta come see it."

"All right, All right, how about a compromise? I'll pass on the party, but I'll come by to check out this cake. How's that sound?"

"You've got yourself a deal, mister."

I look over at Trey. "So, how about we get out of the office for a few minutes?"

"I'm game. Where we headed?"

"We're going to take a look at a birthday cake."

"What? A birthday cake?" A look of befuddlement crosses his face. "What is that…slang for a dope house or something?"

"No Trey." I shake my head while chuckling. "It's English for 'We're going to take a look at a birthday cake.'."

Winter's wind slams against the frame of The Beast as we make our way towards Eliza's house. Our heater improves the climate inside as warmth billows from the floor vents.

"Did you hear that shit the mayor's talking?" Trey asks, obviously indignant.

"I can't say that I have."

"The shit is all over the news. Let me get you up to speed. If that man gets his way, this precious city of yours is going to become an even bigger shit hole."

"Okay, what are you talking about?"

"The mayor thinks we should legalize prostitution in Clark County. He wants to make it a damn red light district. The whole city's in on the debate."

"Yeah, right," I chuckle, but Trey's facial expression doesn't change. "Wait, he didn't really say that, did he?"

"Do I look like I'm smiling? He was all, 'We can tax it. We'll require health tests for the prostitutes. We'll regulate it. We can make it safe. It's a win-win, all-around. Everyone wins.'"

"*Everyone* wins?"

"My ass," Trey growls. "I swear, the people running this city find new ways every day to make it just a little worse than it was the day before."

I envision images of Hell rising. A hundred-thousand women lined up like cattle, waiting to be funneled into clinics. By day, they walk in through the front door to be poked, prodded, and tested, only to be shoved out the back door, pushed into these so-called "legal brothels."

What about the women who are assaulted, brutalized, and victimized by the by those I hunt. Do they simply expect these monsters to vanish because city wants a cut? Who could be that naïve?

"Damn." It's the only word I can push out of my mouth.

"Could you imagine us throwing in with the fuckers we're trying to stop?"

"Was there any public outcry?"

"Actually, there was a mixture of opinions. Some people said that since it's here, we may as well benefit from it. Of course, other people said they wouldn't stay to raise a family in a town like that."

I shake my head and veer over into the next lane. "It's bad now, but if that happened, every trafficker in the country would flock here."

"I know, kid. Imagine what they'd bring with them."

"I don't need to imagine. We'd be flooded by a sea of violence, victims, and murder."

Trey turns to the passenger-side window to stare out at the passing streets, "You gotta wonder what world these people live in. Everybody in such a rush to be so damn 'progressive.' They can't even see what's right in front of their faces. I mean, the mayor is a grown-ass man, he's got to know better."

How foolish of our government to think they can regulate or even control an animal they don't understand.

"Heads up, Trey. We're here." I pull up just past the driveway of Eliza's house.

When Trey slams the car door, an echo rides the wind all the way down the street. "Nice place."

"It is, isn't it?" I step up to the front door, but have to add a special request at the last second with a whisper. "Hey buddy, do me a favor and be on your best behavior. It's your first time meeting Eliza and the family."

"Come on, man. What do I look like, a seven-year-old? Relax." I look over to see his most recent statement is accompanied by an angelic smile. One I don't trust.

The scent of herbs and spices seeps from behind the closed door. "You smell that?" Trey asks, licking his lips in the process. "I hope you planned on staying for dinner."

"No, not tonight. We'll be in and out."

I knock on the door and moments later Eliza emerges in a tee shirt and shorts.

"I'm so glad you came. Thank you!"

I can't help but laugh. "You say that like you left me with any other option."

"What's that supposed to mean?" She smiles coyly.

"Well, allow me to introduce you two. Trey…Eliza, Eliza…Trey."

Trey just smiles. Eliza pushes the door back and asks us in.

"So where is this amazing birthday cake?" I ask as Eliza ushers us inside.

"Oh," she smiles. "Well, before I show you guys, let me just say it's kind of a work in progress."

"A work in progress? That sounds like a disclaimer."

We follow her around the corner into a dining room that's separated from the kitchen by an island. "Okay, you guys. Wait right here while I go grab it." Our hostess dips into a side room.

"She's a nice girl kid," says Trey, breaking the silence. "Fucking shame what she's been through."

Not a second later, she exits the room. She looks over her left shoulder as she walks backwards, using her body to shield the masterpiece from our line of sight. At the opposite side of the island she stops, and prepares for the big reveal. "Okay, boys." She spins around slowly, "Here it…"

"Oh dear God!" Trey blurts it out as if he'd tripped over a mangled corpse.

"What," Eliza asks, allowing a gigantic grin to cross her face.

"Umm…that's, uh, that's…that's a cake?" Trey asks, doing his best not to stare. There is a pronounced sagging on the right-hand side, making me think of a sinking ship.

"I told you guys it's a work in progress."

"Yes, yes you did. I mean it's not bad for your first cake. I guess."

"Okay, okay, so maybe this IS the worst looking cake in the history of cake baking, but I made it, and I'm proud of it."

I do my best to stifle a laugh. "Girl, you should be. And just so you know, I'm proud of you, too. Thanks for wanting to share it with us."

"Are you kidding? There's no way I was going to let you miss out on seeing this baby."

"I really appreciate that, and I hate to put an end to the fun, but we have quite a bit of work to do if we're going to make our target date."

Eliza's eyes widen. "Really? We're that close?"

"We are. I'll let you know once we've made our move. You just stay near your cell phone."

"Okay," she replies through a sigh. "I sure don't want to be the one to mess up your timing. Let me walk you guys out."

Driving back to the office, I can't help but reflect on Eliza's glowing face and the horror she's lived through the idea that my city could even contemplate legalizing prostitution is revolting. Victimless crime? Try convincing Eliza of that.

17
The Needle

Back at the office, I step towards my lieutenant's door and hear her voice. "Ahh-*hem*."

I lean against the frame and peek in. "Good afternoon."

"*Is* it, Chris?"

"Well, it's shaping up to be that way. The warrants are signed for all the properties. Care to take a look?"

"Don't mind if I do. Come on in." I set the manila folder down her desk and make myself comfortable in a chair. "No complaints from the judge, but he did have one request."

"What is it?" she asks, lifting the folder and reading through the pages.

"He basically wants us to spank the hell out of Mario."

"The next time you see him, tell him we love him over here."

"I will. I'm sure the feeling's mutual."

"Good." Our conversation trails off as she reads the full details of the warrant. The next time she speaks, it's to ask the exact question that stumped His Honor. The same damn question I vowed not to burden myself with while preparing for the showdown with this monster. "So Chris, any ideas on how you're going to handle this secret vault yet?"

The vault. The one thing that has frustrated me ever since I discovered its existence because there aren't any laws that will allow me to get inside to see what Mario is hiding. The retinal scan all but decimates any hopes for a paper trail, and the cameras intricately placed on both the interior and exterior walls limit my ability to get a close look without drawing too much attention. Hell, even once we're in, we still have a huge problem…which lock box is Mario's?

"I'll be working on that tonight. All night if I have to. Did you have any luck finding us help for Thursday?"

"Actually, I did," she replies, closing the manila folder and handing it back. "I managed to scrape together about thirty detectives for you. It's the best I could do on short notice. I set the briefing up at a location big enough to accommodate all of us. We're going to hold it in the briefing room at South Central Area Command. I already sent an email to everyone involved."

"Perfect. And *thirty* detectives?" I'm elated. "That should do."

"Well, I want you to remain a success."

"When you come through like this, you make it hard to fail."

"Chris, I want to take him down as much as you do. Just be ready for the briefing tomorrow. I need everyone clear on what you'll expect."

"I'll be ready."

"All right, then. Good luck figuring out that vault. If I were a betting woman, I'd put my chips on you."

I step from her office with a smile and am soon back in my element, surrounded by my crew.

"Well," Al asks, "are we looking good on the warrant, bro?"

"We are. It's signed. Now we need to get ready for tomorrow. The lieutenant got us about thirty bodies to help with the various targets around the city. We'll need to put together instructional and target packets for each team. Since we don't know who our people are as yet, designate the packets by target address. In them, we're going to need a list of names and pictures of any of the people our detectives are likely to come across during the warrants. Anyone want to volunteer?"

"I'll take it," Al says, raising his arm. "How about five packets per property?"

"Sounds good, Al. Okay, Trey, you drew the short straw."

"I didn't know we were drawing straws." Trey chuckles and shakes his head. "What do you need?"

"Would you mind putting together the search warrant kits for each of the properties?"

"Oh. Is that all? No sweat."

"Great. Al, before you get started, pass me our keys to the vault. I need to figure out how we're going to get into this damn place."

"Sure." Al digs into the top drawer of his desk and tosses me the keys. "Good luck."

Trey cringes, and gives me a look I've become very familiar with over the years. It's a perfected glare that says, 'I wouldn't want to be you.' As they launch into their assignments, I settle into mine.

To drown out distractions and any background noise, the volume goes way up on my headphones. I need to think, to clear my head. I close my eyes to meditate and in less than one minute, I'm transported far away from the office and back into my mind. I imagine that I'm sitting alone on an old oak chair in a quiet room. I look at the door. There is no knob, only a keyhole. I rise from my seat and check the door, only to find it is locked.

I turn and walk to a desk that's in the middle of the room. On it sits two keys. I grab them from the desk and walk to the door and attempt to jam them into the keyhole. It makes no difference which angle I tilt them—be the teeth up or down—since they simply will not fit.

What these keys are trying to tell me?

I exhale deeply, and toss them onto the desk. Maybe...maybe there's more to this. Perhaps I'm not looking at all the pieces of this puzzle. Mentally, I take one step back, hoping this'll allow a broader perspective.

The challenge at hand is that this vault—Mario's vault—has a one-of-a-kind security system, complete with specially designed keys, a secured vault, no-associated-paperwork, microphones, surveillance cameras, retinal scans, access codes, and customized boxes... hundreds, if not thousands of them.

I'm still too close to the forest to see the trees. What makes this vault so special, so different from any other? What was the vault employee's big selling point when Al and I posed as interested buyers and bought our own box? I can still hear his voice, "We don't know your names, and hell, we don't wanna. That way we can't spoil the trust our clients put in us. Each of our boxes is uniquely engineered. When you agree to the terms, we will hand you a very special set of keys. Inside the vault, no one key holder can get into any other box except their own. You're only going to get two copies of the key, and well, they're damn near impossible to duplicate. And we're the only place in Nevada that uses this system. Now mind you, if you lose 'em, there's gonna be a hefty fee in order to get that box up and running again. We would need to have both new keys and locking mechanism machined. See what I'm sayin'?"

Wait! I press pause on my inner conversation. His words are as much a part of this puzzle as the keys are. Is the problem actually the solution? I laugh out loud, grab the keys from the desk and stand. This riddle has been solved.

I glance over to find Al staring at me curiously. "Bro, sometimes I worry about you. You were zoned out for a bit. Your eyes were closed, the next thing I know you're laughing out loud."

"Al, Al, Al. Do you know what I'm holding in my hands?"

"Yeah, the keys to the vault we can't get into."

"Catch!" I stand and quickly toss Al they keys. "What if I told you these keys were the answer to all our problems?"

"They're keys, Chris. I'd say maybe you do need some rest."

"Maybe one day, but not today."

Al's face wears a cross expression. "What the hell are you talking about?"

Trey interjects, setting down one of the search warrant kits. "Is Chris talking in riddles again, Al? Be careful, when he speaks, he's like a damn snake charmer."

I invite Al And Trey to sit down. "All right, boys, you're going to love this. What do we know about this vault?"

Al makes the first contribution. "We know they have surveillance cameras all over the damn place."

"Exactly," I say. "But at the moment those cameras are the least of our worries. Trey, care to give it a shot?"

"I can only go on what you guys have told me about it, but didn't someone mention a retinal scan and no supporting documentation? I guess the lack of a paper trail could be an issue."

"Could be, but it isn't. Think about it; what makes this place so special? Remember what the salesman said?"

Al, scratches his goatee in thought. "Well, other than the retinal thing, there's the twenty-four-hour access."

"Keep going."

Trey chimes in, "Al, weren't you telling me something about the boxes in this place being specially made or something?"

"Yeah, but how does knowing boxes are customized help us? Are you thinking about contacting the manufacturer or something?"

I shake my head. "No. Come on guys, what is the one thing that every client who walks out of that business leaves with?"

Trey laughs. "From the tone of your voice, I'm gonna have to say a false sense of security."

"Fellas, we know everything about this place. We have the advantage now. Remember what he said about the keys?"

"Not to lose them, because they're expensive?"

I stand up straight, cross my arms and being pacing. "Exactly. They're so expensive because the keys are customized as well and damn near impossible to duplicate. He was so busy bragging, he didn't realize that he was telling us everything we need to know in order to defeat their safeguards. When we go in, we defeat the cameras by wearing balaclavas. Even if they act like they don't have the ability to let us into the vault, it won't matter."

"It won't matter because our retinal scans are already entered in their system," Al says, warming to where I'm headed.

"Exactly! We don't need them to get that first door open. And since their policy is that no documentation is signed, there's nothing to link our names or pictures to the retinal scans. Boys, they'll never know what hit them, or who the hell we are."

"That's all well and good, Chris," Al replies, lifting his hands in the air, "but how do we get the warrant for the box?"

"This is the best part," I reply smiling. "The salesman told us the only thing linking their clients to these boxes was the retinal scan, and he was dead wrong."

Al and Trey exchange confused expressions while leaning into the conversation.

"Two keys are given to the patrons because of the fail-safe on the boxes, which is the double locking mechanism. Now if that weren't enough, we also know the keys that the patrons are given are very rare. They're so rare that no other vault company or bank in this state has them. For the purposes of our warrant, these distinct keys can only lead us to one place...their facility."

Al's smiling as well. "Damn!"

"It gets better. In order to have a warrant approved, we need to be sure that the box we're targeting belongs to Mario. The fact that each key is specifically machined for each locking mechanism on each box helps, but the fact that the keys are impossible to duplicate is the clincher. The way I see it, those keys place our percentage of opening the wrong box at zero. We have our warrant, gentlemen. Furthermore, Mario's keys to that lock box are one of the keys to shutting him down. Now, if we know anything at all about pimps it's that, like squirrels, they hide everything. I don't know if the keys will be on him when we find him, but I'd be willing to bet they'll be someplace where he has access to at all times."

"Hmm," Trey ponders momentarily. "In one of the four houses?"

"That would be my guess. Trey, let's wrap it up. It's late, and we have a hell of a day tomorrow. Let's meet at the area command around five."

I staple the freshly printed pictures of the keys onto the backs of each packet as Al and Trey gather the search warrant kits.

With reservation, Al asks, "You think we'll find the keys, bro?"

"I think if we have any hopes of finding them, it's going to be up to the others. The least we can do is let our detectives know exactly what the needle in these haystacks looks like."

~~~

South Central Area Command is based out of a new multi-level building. It could be mistaken for any of the other modern offices in town, with its stucco walls, earth-toned paint, and desert landscaping out front. The important distinction, though, is that this place houses all the police officers who safeguard the Vegas Strip, along with many of the surrounding neighborhoods.

The blizzard's subsided. In its aftermath, mounds of gray snow make Vegas feel more like Cincinnati. I turn into the small parking lot out front and find that it's already packed.

Clutching the stack of packets Al created, I throw my backpack over my shoulder and hopscotch over the slush and snow, trying to land on as many dry spots as possible.

There are upwards of forty detectives waiting expectantly inside the spacious briefing room. There are no less than five sergeants, and my lieutenant leaning against a wall in the rear of the room. She gives me small nod. Trey and Al huddle near the front. A few of the other cops greet me with smiles and hellos.

"What's up, boys?" I ask, stepping into the huddle.

"We were just waiting on you, kid." Trey looks out onto the crowd, "Lieutenant did a hell of a job recruiting, didn't she? It looks like we've got at least four squads here."

Lieutenant Hughes owns the room as she approaches the front of the room. The room is now dead silent. "Thank you all for coming. I'm Lieutenant Hughes. I've asked you all here today because we need your help. In a few minutes, Detective Baughman will be briefing you on the individual we're targeting. Pay attention. To date, this man is one of the biggest we've gone after. All I'm going to ask is that you use your heads and stay safe. Chris, they're all yours."

"Thank you, Lieutenant." Al and Trey immediately start handing out the respective packets to each squad. "I appreciate you all coming. These packets you're being handed list which addresses each of your squads will be responsible for. They contain the pictures and names of individuals you may come across during the service of your warrants. Feel free to leaf through them while I give you a brief overview of our target, Mario Davis. Birth place: Nevada, Las Vegas.

Black male. Height: six feet. Weight: one-sixty-five. Black hair, brown eyes. Occupation: Pimp." The only sound in the room is the shuffling of folders and flipping pages. "Al, your turn."

Al steps out of the background and onto center stage. "Flip to the last two pages of the packets. You should be looking at a set of keys. Memorize what they look like. As you can see, they're sorta funky looking…very thin. Chris thinks they're gonna be hidden at one of the four properties. These keys are important, so if you find a set like them, put them somewhere very safe.

"As an added incentive, aside from the satisfaction of being the one who finds the keys to this piece-of-shit's nest egg, I'll throw in a case of your favorite beer, or whatever you drink." I spot a few grins circulating through the crowd, which are followed by chatter and a few sporadic hand claps. Al looks back at me. "All right, Chris, that's all I've got."

"Detective Gethoefer prepared a search warrant kit for each squad." As Trey hands out the stack of folders, I wrap up the briefing. "Are there any questions?" I wait briefly. No one raises their hand. "The last order of business is our start time. We are crashing the doors at ten o'clock sharp, people, come hell or high water."

Each team disperses. I drop my head in thought. This has turned from checkers into some serious chess. While juggling the "What ifs," I feel a hand on my shoulder. Trey's beside me. "Come on, Chris. We've covered every possible angle on this thing"

"You're right."

No more than two seconds pass, and up walks Al, clapping his hands and licking his chops. "All right, fellas, tomorrow we put this motherfucker down."

Al – always succinct and always willing to break the tension. It's the perfect balance to the seriousness of this mission.

I add my final comments. "We rally tomorrow at nine a.m. in the church parking lot, the one on the edge of his neighborhood. "

Lieutenant Hughes steps forward. "I just wanted to say thanks to all of you. You've raised the bar, along with all of the quality of work I expect from this unit. I'm very proud to have you under my command. Good luck tomorrow, boys."

Today has been but a prelude. Come tomorrow morning, another type of storm will roll in and we'll be riding on top of it.

18
Worlds Collide

09:58 hours. Standing just around the corner from our target, I look up to the sky towards the burning sun, which does its best to penetrate the gray storm front. For now, only a silver edge of backlight manages to define each cloud.

For Mario, our four squads present an even darker kind of cloud. Dispersed across the city, we're only moments away from letting loose. I look forward to dragging his ass back to the light and stand before the people of this city.

09:59 hours. We cautiously step forward in a single-file line. Trey leads the way as we round the corner, just outside the cul-de-sac. We step closer. Quietly. Trey takes the path of least resistance as we near the neighbor's house, avoiding shrubbery, boulders, and even the small decorative rocks. Like trackers, we mimic his every step, moving silently.

After crossing the neighbor's property line, we lurk outside the Davis house. Trey crouches for a moment, then quickly leads us past the garage. The pace heightens. Trey checks the gate leading to the courtyard, and is greeted with slight squeak as he pushes it back. Al ducks in behind him. The fountain and shrubs in the courtyard provide just enough concealment for us to stay hidden from anyone peering out the front window.

Trey raises his left fist, the universal signal for 'all stop.' The adrenaline spewing through my body burns my veins. Everything is moving slower. The seconds tick down like minutes. This is that moment, the one before any warrant is ever served, when a man's heart stops beating and Father Time sees fit to forget all laws of physics. The one just before impact, the odd disquiet before two worlds collide.

10:00 hours. "SEARCH WARRANT!" Trey screams, his fist pummels the front door. The small glass window inset starts to rattle as he bellows once more. "SEARCH WARRANT!"

Trey's next command will, for our present purposes, be the last we need. "Breach up!"

From the middle of the pack, a detective designated as "The Breach Man" steps out and charges the door. He grips a ram powerful enough to shake the foundations of Mario's crumbling empire. In only a second, he's at the door, but before destroying it, Trey quickly and quietly checks the knob.

Unlocked!

The breach man steps aside as Trey pushes open the door and enters. As he does, the morning sun leaps ahead and overwhelms the darkness.

Our team floods one room after another. From my vantage near the front door, I quickly count five. I look to my right hoping to see the rest of my team, but they're already gone.

The entryway leads straight into a massive great room. Hanging on the wall is a ridiculously oversized frame. Encased behind the glass is a basketball jersey that I instantly recognize as coming from Rancho, my old high school. He has saved this one keepsake from the wonder years of his life, and it is one that undeniably has ties to my own.

Far in the background, I can hear the voices of different detectives as they enter and check each room for threats. "Clear! Coming out!"

"I got two," yells a detective who rounds the corner from the left side of the house. Walking just ahead of him are two young women. I only recognize the first. Alisson Becker. The detective follows her into the living room. All of our intelligence leads us to believe that that the young Alisson is the newest on his list of victims.

"Hello, Alisson. Sit down right here please." I gesture toward the couch.

"How…how do you know my name?" she asks in a trembling voice.

"I know a lot more than just your name. Try to relax. I'm not here for you."

"Then why are you here?"

Footsteps. The sound of shuffling comes from the darkness of the hallway. From out of the blackness emerge Al and Trey. "Anybody order up a pimp?" They push Mario towards the front of the house.

His face shows concern and confusion, at least the parts of it that aren't covered with ragged stubble. He shuffles up the hallway looking a hot mess. This is not the vain man the photographs had captured. There's no freshly shaven head. Instead, small sprouts of hair have grown in, emphasizing the fact that he's balding. He walks past me with hung head. Ashamed? I doubt it. If he could feel any shame, I wouldn't be here today.

He sits down and looks around the room, begging for anyone to speak to him. "Whaa…what's going on, officers? I haven't done anything. This must be a mistake."

He wants answers. They all do, every pimp we have ever hunted has asked *why me?*

I'm sorely tempted to spit on the ground where he walks. "Mario, I'll get to you soon enough. In the meantime, think about everything you've done, and who you've done it to."

"What?" he whimpers, breaking down into tears. Now he wants to cry. His tears are wasted on me. If he were engulfed in fire, the only thing I'd offer would be another log to keep the flames burning.

"Al," I turn to my partners, "care to join me for the interview?"

"Hell, yeah," Al answers looking over my shoulder at the huddled crying mess.

"Give me five minutes. I want to take a quick walk through."

"No problem. I'll keep eyes on this him 'til you're ready."

I stroll through what must close to 4,500 feet of home, five bedrooms, three and one-half baths, kitchen, dining room, laundry room, great room, and den. By then, the text messages from our other squads start rolling in: "Chris, we have Haley Harrison in custody. We're conducting the search now. We've recovered money, a ton of jewelry, and, so far, I think about three or four guns. I'll get back to u later."

Then the report comes in from Sadie Ortega's house: "Hey Chris — tons of evidence over here: money and jewelry, pretty much a treasure chest."

As I make my way back to Al, I peek inside the laundry room. There on a hanger is a rather pristine-looking shop shirt. The name tag says Macc. The business logo on the shirt reads none other than Desert Audio. Things just keep coming up roses.

"All right, Al. Let's get started. Mario, follow me. It's time we had that discussion you've been begging for."

"I…I'm a little dizzy," says Mario, standing and slowly staggering out of the house, leaving young Alisson and her friend behind. "I'm sick. I have an ear infection."

I agree, you are sick, Mario. And the infection you have has affected much, much more than your ears. "We're almost there," I answer, without any hint of compassion. "The car's just around the corner."

"Have a seat." With his cuffed hands behind him, he slowly leans down before plopping onto the leather seat. I secure his door and move to the driver's side, pushing my seat forward to allow Al entry.

Two binders filled to capacity with documents rest on the dashboard. The name printed on the spines reads Mario Merchant Davis ID# 1183673. I can be sure he's already noticed them. After all, I left the spines facing out for a reason.

Initially, I don't say anything. He's in a mental tailspin, and soon he'll be stumbling over his story. But more than anything else, I want him to go crazy wondering what the hell we know.

To my right, less than twelve inches away from me sits the very thing I'm determined to destroy. "Why the tears, Mario?" My tone is as cold and callous as my heart.

"This…this is crazy. Someone tell me what's going on. Please!" His eyes beg for answers as he frantically scans the car, looking towards Al and then back to me.

"You're an intelligent man. I really can't tell you anything you don't already know."

"Look, I don't know what's going on. Can you tell me why I'm in this car? Why you raided my house?" He is behaving like a wounded mouse trapped in a corner. That must make us the cat.

"You think we raided YOUR house? Oh, that's funny, Mario…" I lean in just a bit. "We're not just here, we're everywhere."

After a few minutes of silence, I continue to poke at him, hoping to provoke him. "Mario," I say with a grin, "you must know why we've come for you."

His eyes are still running through the cab of the car, but come to rest on the two thick binders sitting on the dash. "Everywhere? What do you mean? What are those folders? Why is my name on them?"

"Those files? Well, those are what we're going to use to destroy you."

Mario is the consummate showman. He promises–he even swears on the life of Christ—that I must be mistaken. "Destroy me? I…I work every day. You've got the wrong man. I own a business. I…"

"Really? Those binders sitting right there in front of you, with your name running down the spine, tell me that I am exactly where I'm supposed to be, and we both know I don't have the wrong man."

19
Untold Truths

I already know what to expect before I begin. Mario's lies have taken on a life of their own. He's wrapped himself in them and, like a second skin, they've become the largest living organ on him.

As long as he's frantic and in tears, his emotions should hurt his ability to reason. The first thing we will attack are his proclamations of innocence. Next, we'll have to deal with Mario's commitment to his own unique version of events. Somewhere deep beneath that, I expect to find what I've come for. Truth.

"So, you want to talk, Mario?"

"Yes, yes I do!"

"All right. If you can convince me I've got the wrong man, I'll let you go. It'll be my mistake. I'm man enough to admit when I've made one." I look in the back seat at Al who shakes his head and smiles. "But before I start, I'll need to do a few things. First off, I've got to read you the Miranda warning."

I grab a small note book from my visor and note the time when I officially spell out his Constitutional rights.

"So, there are a couple of important things we have to make clear, Mario. Once I start the recording, I'll tell you why I'm here. I won't lie to you about anything. I don't need to. I hope you understand at this point I can bury you even if you and I never speak. Secondly, I don't have the time or energy to waste listening to lies. Do you understand?"

"I do, and I wanna talk to you guys."

With that, I hit the red button and place the recorder on the center console between us. "Do you want to speak with us?" I ask once more to capture his answer on the recorder.

"Yes."

"All right, Mario, why don't you tell us how long you've been involved in the pandering of women?"

He looks at me for a moment, his face now turned into a blank mask. My guess is he's weighing his options, debating whether or not he will dive straight into his lies. Maybe he'll test the waters by dipping his toes in first.

"Uh, I've been around prostitutes for...since I came home from college."

"How long has that been?"

"Six...going on six."

"Six years?"

"That's as long as I've been back home. I've just been around."

"Why don't you tell us how you got involved in this?"

"Uh..." His tone is feeble.

"Speak up a little bit, please."

He adjusts his body, and slumps his back. "So, when I came home from college, I had a girlfriend that, um, worked in a strip club and, uh, she used to give me money, ya know. Then she was like, 'I don't want you anymore.' Everybody else is out there trying to sell drugs to get money, so I went and got a job. I had a job at this place called The Dive. I was making a little bit of money with the tips. So around that time, I ended up meeting another girl who worked as an escort. So it was really like...I guess I just like them kinda girls, 'cause you know, they take care of you. Ya know, them kinda girls are sexy. That's just what I like, the strippers and stuff like that."

As he finishes speaking, I make a mental note. He really hasn't told me a damn thing. "Okay, so how long ago was it that you had this girlfriend?"

"Well," he lowers his head in thought, "it's a long time ago. Say about six..."

"...what was her name?"

"Her name was Christine. I don't know her last name."

"Okay, why don't you tell me the last job you worked?"

"I work now."

Oh, this is about to get good. "And where do you work now?"

"Desert Audio."

"How often are you there?"

"Umm, it all depends. Sometimes I'm there…I mean, one week I might be there every day, you know what I'm saying? Then one week I might, ya know, it just depends on how busy it is. Like lately, it's been horrible because of the economy, so you know, I only go down there when it's time for uh…uh…him to pay people. I just go down to check up on stuff, ya know?

"Who is *him*, Mario?"

"Um…my manager."

"Manager…interesting. What's his name?"

"It…it's uh, Paul."

"What's his last name?" I ask as I scribble away on the note pad.

"Um…Paul Gant."

As he tries out another lie, I place another check mark in the Do Not Trust column. "How long have you worked at Desert Audio?"

"Um, for like five years." He still scans the interior of the car and begins to rock his left leg. A nervous twitch, he probably doesn't even know he's doing it.

"How much do you make a month working there?" I keep my voice calm, level, and smooth.

"Um…monthly? Like I say, it all ranges, but I claimed fifty or sixty thousand…"

"Last year?"

"Yeah, and also I'm entertaining."

Pathetic. I constrict my stomach muscles and bite my bottom lip just to keep from smirking. "How do you entertain?"

"It's…it's like I got my own business. So basically like, ya know, like girls like that, you know what I'm saying?" He stumbles over his lies like a stooge. "If they want to…it's the same as their business. If they want me to go out with them and take them out, um, it's like I'm a gigolo."

A gigolo. Well this is a first. I look at him and can't help wondering if he thinks this is working. "That's news to me Mario. A gigolo? What's your definition of a gigolo, if you don't mind my asking."

"Well, it's an escort. It's a male escort, isn't it? A male escort with a license. I pay my taxes on it. I did the bank statement, the whole thing. My tax people told me how to file if I was going to be an entertainer." He shrugs his shoulders, which draws my attention away from his face and the woe-is-me expression plastered across it.

"Mario, you're an intelligent man, college educated. What do you think the word pandering means?"

"I...I don't know."

"All right, let me rephrase. What do you think a pimp is?"

Be very careful, Mario, answering this question. It might feel like a trap...because it is.

"Uh, a pimp is somebody who sends girls out there and takes all their money."

"What about a person who facilitates another individual going out to get money by selling themselves?"

"Well, that could be a friend?"

"A friend? How so?"

"Because I'm in a similar lifestyle to what they're in 'cause that's what I like. I like being around strippers and whores." His tears have subsided. His indignation grows. "I like being around them. That's what I like, I mean, I'm sorry, but that's what I like."

"So you're telling me that you are nothing more than a gigolo?"

This is an unexpected turn, he's gone from whimpering to angry in mere moments. "I'm an entertainer. I'm an entertainer...so it's like that. They just don't give me their money! It's like whatever they do, however they get their money, that's how I get paid. So if they want to go out with everyone, yeah they got to give me some money."

"Who has to give you money Mario?"

"Whoever takes me out. Whether she's a working girl or not doesn't matter to me."

"So you're saying you go out on dates with working girls, and they have to pay you?"

I reach towards the dash and grab the first of the thick binders from it. After setting the binder in my lap I open it to show several disks. All phone conversations placed to Mr. Davis by his troop of victims after various arrests. I'm always curious to see the inner workings of a monster's mind. How will he navigate through these? "I'm showing you some disks right now. What these CDs contain, Mario, are conversations between you and certain young ladies. That disc says Mario Davis, July 2008. Here is another, Mario, October '08, another September '08…November '08. Are you starting to see the pattern?"

He doesn't answer. His Adam's apple moves like an elevator as he swallows. I know he can he feel the noose tightening.

"Mario why don't you tell me about the women you know and your relationship with them? Why don't we talk about that?"

"Well, you know…it's um…"

"Just the ones you see and contact regularly."

"Well…there's…there's Katie."

"Katie? Katie who?"

"Katie Coughlin. Her daughter's name is Katalina. "

"Her daughter? An interesting choice of words. What does Katie do for a living?"

"Um…she uh, has her own, like, coffee service. She's also enrolled in school."

"What did she do before that Mario?"

"She was an entertainer, man."

"An entertainer? You keep using that word."

"Because that's what she is! That's what I call her. She pays her taxes!"

"What did she do? How did she make her money…or your money?"

He's silent.

"Mario, right now we're at an impasse, and you aren't being up front."

"Yeah! She's been a prostitute! But she's an entertainer now. She has her license to be an entertainer."

"All right, let's move on to some other people."

"Okay." He answers coolly, seemingly haven gotten his anger under control.

"Who else do you know?"

"Um...Sadie. She has my three-year-old daughter."

"Where? Where does she live?"

"She lives in Summerlin."

"Where?"

"Off Sahara and Ft. Apache."

That would be helpful if there weren't thousands of homes in that area. Of course we don't need him to answer anything honestly, because we already have Sadie and that house in our custody. "What's the address?"

"She lives...I, I don't know the names of the streets. I mean...I mean..."

"Let me help you. Old Salt Circle. Does that sound familiar?" His eyes widen and his jaw falls open momentarily. That's right, old friend, I know her address. "Tell me, what does Sadie do for a living?"

"Same thing, man."

"What? Another entertainer?"

"Yes."

"So, this Katie has your child?"

"Yes."

"Has she ever been arrested for prostitution?"

"Yes."

"Sadie Ortega?"

"Yes. I have a three-year-old daughter with her, and yes, she's been arrested for prostitution."

As we strip back the layers of lies, his patience wears thin.

"Who else?"

"Laurie Blackmon. She's pregnant now."

"And has she ever been arrested for prostitu..."

"Yes!"

"So we have three women, Mario. They all have a few things in common. One of them is you. I know you call them entertainers, but what I see is that they *all* have been arrested for prostitution."

"Right," he nods, and quietly answers, "Look, I don't go out there and follow them around."

"I didn't say you did. So are you trying to tell me that you don't know what they do behind closed doors? And they don't call you when they get caught up?"

"Yeah! Yeah, no. I mean, I would know. Yes, I would know. But I'm not out there following them around! I...I...you don't see me out there behind them in casinos."

His voice climbs an octave.

"Calm down Mario. Take a breath. We're just having a discussion."

"I'm sorry. I'm just saying I don't know...I don't see what they do."

"Who else?" I flip over a few pages to a picture of Haley. He shakes his head in weariness. "Who are your other 'friends'?"

"Um...Haley, Haley Harrison. She...she's pregnant, too."

"So four different women either have been, or are pregnant with your children." I've seen this before. It's another method of control. "What does she do for a living?"

"Same thing."

"Same thing? She's a prostitute, or is she an...entertainer?"

"An entertainer! She also...they all pay their taxes as entertainers."

"We're back to that entertainer thing again, huh? When was her last prostitution arrest?"

He hangs his head once more and then tilts it. His pitch black eyes dig into the floorboards of The Beast. *Oh yes, Mario. I come bearing gifts...every bit of dirt you've done I carry with me.*

"Probably about a week ago."

"What happened?"

"I don't know! She just told me that they have a lawyer. All that kind of stuff. Man, look, they handle they own business."

How sad, he isn't even trying anymore. Now he relies on short blunt answers. So much for a battle of wits. I look behind me momentarily to see Al's face is red. He looks to be growing tired of this little game.

"So they handle their own business, you say?"

"They handle their own business!" he says, spitting the words out with rapid fire pacing. "They pay their own bills! They lawyer up...they do all that themselves."

"Meaning your name is not on any of the bail paperwork?"

"Yeah, right! Nothing, period! None of their house stuff, nothing. Like I said, what they do with their money is their business. But like I say, if we go out..."

"Have you ever been to any of their places...taken money from their houses?"

"From their houses? No, oh no. I haven't taken money from their houses. I may go to there to mess around, you know." He flashes a sick smile.

"Any other girls?"

"No. That's it, except for their friends."

"Really? There are no other girls that you can think of?" His mind is such a wreck, he's forgotten about the most obvious one.

"That I can think of?" Fine wrinkles form between his brow as he scrunches his face. "Um...those are the main ones."

"How about I name a few others for you? Maybe I can help refresh your memory since you seem to have forgotten so many of the others."

"Well, everyone else is just a friend. Not like these right here. Them are the ones I've dealt with for years now. I'm saying deal with like go to their houses."

"Riiiight. So, what about Alisson Becker? The woman that's inside your house right now?"

"I just kinda met her. Yeah. See I've only known her like two, three months."

"Who is she to you?"

"Just like a friend."

"Like a friend?"

"As far as I know she's never been arrested for nothing."

"Is that so?"

"As far as I know."

"Would you be surprised if I told you she, too, was involved in prostitution?"

"Hang on...wait. Listen to me...listen to..." He blurts out franticly. "Okay...okay. She told me she got arrested because of a warrant."

"Let's try this again. What does Alisson do for a living?"

"Uh..."

"Mario, there's a common theme here that you apparently don't see, and it's not 'she's an entertainer and pays her taxes.' "

"Man, those are just the type of women I like to associate with."

"So basically, we've already linked you to one, two, three, four, five women, all of which have been arrested for prostitution several times over. You understand that no one would ever believe the things that are coming out of your mouth. We'd crucify you in court."

My last statement knocks him on his heels. Al uses the opportunity to attack. "Look, from the beginning you said that you didn't want to lie to us."

"Right."

"We know a lot more than you think we do, so you can lie to us if you want to, but we already know the answers to the questions we're asking you. We know when you're lying."

It's time to call it quits, at least for the moment. Now we let his mind marinate over all the little details and intricacies we have dragged into the light. "Al, you're right. He's useless. I'm glad he didn't talk. At least now I don't have to go into the DA's office and tell them he cooperated. Mario, you need to understand that you can only help yourself by falling on the sword. If you choose, we can talk later. Of course, if you choose not to, we never have to speak again."

His glossy eyes and awestruck expression say it all. Still he manages to utter more deception. "I'm just so overwhelmed right now. I mean I didn't think I was doing too much. Dealing with these women basically has me guilty by association? That's why I'm like…"

I start the car engine to pull around to the front of the house, but not before I cut off his next fallacy. "You're not guilty by association. Not even."

20
Game of Wits

The garage door is wide open and the search is well underway. Standing just inside, Trey flashes a sly grin.

"Al, you mind keeping eyes on him 'til I'm done speaking with Trey?"

"Not at all. Go handle it. We'll be right here. Just come back with some good news."

Trey cracks smile as I walk over to greet him. "So how'd the interview go? Did he fall on the sword?"

"Do they ever?"

"Right. Okay, let me give you the rundown of what we've got so far. Follow me, kid." Trey steers me into the spacious three-car garage, and to the jet-black BMW sitting inside. "Take a look inside."

"Just look inside?"I ask, looking through the window on the driver's side.

"Just take a peek."

I duck my head inside the sedan, but initially, nothing seems unexpected. There's a strong new-car smell. The dashboard and center console have lustrous wood-grain panels. Still nothing. On the dark leather seats, exquisite stitching runs down the seams. Matching Mercedes-Benz floor-mats lead my eyes to…oh, what's this? Standing up straight I look to Trey and nod.

"See?" Trey smiles. "I told you, you couldn't miss it. This son of a bitch has the same fucking gun I use. I hate to say it, but at least he knows what a quality firearm is. Also, I've been getting calls from all the other teams. It looks like that gun is going to be the fourth one we've found between all the different properties. Several hand guns along with a pistol grip shotgun."

"Four? Not a bad haul."

"Nope. It's really a shame, us having to take guns away from such a fine citizen."

I shake my head. "What else we got?"

"The usual, loads of jewelry, cash, a little weed. You know, all the pimp essentials. Oh," Trey asks innocently, "did I fail to mention that we got his set of keys to the vault?"

My eyes widen. "Uh, yeah, you hadn't mentioned that."

"Sorry. I gotta lot on my mind, considering I'm managing four search warrants at one time. Anyway, we found them at Laurie's house. I guess they were taped underneath the big king-sized metal frame in the master bedroom. Hell of a hiding place, if you ask me."

"Oh, he's already feeling a little sick," I reply, my smile glowing, "but when he finds out we've got the keys to his vault...mmm. Painful."

Trey leans against the edge of the garage door. "We're making it real hard for a pimp to earn an honest living in this city. So what's next?"

"Next, I finish breaking him down. I'll talk to him a bit more, then book him in."

"All right, I'll get this warrant wrapped up and get the evidence back to the office. I'll make sure I grab the keys to his vault."

"Perfect." I offer Trey a smile and a pat on the shoulder.

As soon as I turn, Al steps out of the car and closes the door behind him. "Well, what's it looking like?"

"It looks good, really good." Al drops his head slightly. "These warrants are going very well. Why the sad face?"

"I keep thinking about Eliza. The things that piece of shit did to her, to her mother. I wanted to kick the back of his head in when he was giving his interview...fucking liar. I don't want to leave this motherfucker anything! I swear, if I wasn't a cop..."

"I know, Al. I know. But we're here right now. Try to remember everything, so when we call her and tell her that not only did we take his ass down, but we took him for everything he had, including whatever is in that safe deposit box. We don't want to miss sharing one detail."

"Wait!" Al lifts his head. "You mean we found those keys?"

I nod. "And we've got someone in the car who, as of yet, isn't quite convinced that we own him." Al's stone face melts away, and underneath it is the grizzly smile of a Marine.

Al gets into the back seat once more and makes himself comfortable. I resume my place beside the monster. He's stopped his crying maybe because it didn't do him any good earlier. I'm sure he's trying to re-calculate, re-assess his strategy.

"Mario, you look like you have something on your mind." He doesn't reply. I look over to see him peering out the passenger window.

"I'll meet you at the jail, Al."

"No prob, bro." His voice drops to the sound of a whisper. "I hate that sorry piece of shit!"

"I know, I know. Let Trey know he's got the reigns."

"All right. I'll be a few minutes behind you. Ya know, I wouldn't hold it against you if that bastard never made it to County."

I smile. "I'll see you there."

Peering from the corners of my eyes, I can see Mario well enough, that is, enough to know he's looking at me. I wonder whether it's coming back to him. Has it struck him yet that the same neighborhoods that made him also gave birth to me?

"Hey, man. Do I know you from somewhere?" he asks, cutting his eyes in a sidelong glance.

"I doubt it, Mario. I doubt it highly."

"Naw," he replies with certainty, "I know you from somewhere. I've seen you before."

"Mario, you don't know me. But I know you. I know you very well."

"Huh? What? How do you…"

"Let's just say for as long as I have been in this city I've always been just a few steps behind you."

For a moment, the only sound filling the Mustang is our breathing. He shakes his head and turns to look out the passenger side window. "Man, did you go to Rancho?"

"I did."

"When did you graduate?"

"A bit after you."

"What the fuck!?" he blurts out, his eyebrows wrinkled, his faced scrunched up.

"You have to understand, Mario. What's happening here is bigger than you or me. No one can save you. Not your lawyers, and not your lies. I know everything. I know what you were and what you've become."

"What the fuck? I…you…you went to my…"

I look over at him, the expression on my face as solid as stone. "Come on, Mario, do you really think I *chose* you? Do you think I asked for this case? You're fucked."

"Wait, wait. What if…what if I wanted to talk?"

"We've been down that road, remember? You're an entertainer, and I'm just a guy who's got it all wrong."

"Look…uh, if I talk to you…what happens?"

"What happens? I'll tell the district attorney you cooperated." I can't keep the sarcasm from my voice, "That you're 'sorry' for that you've done. How's that?"

"How can I trust you? Like, how do I know?" He's still trying to hustle, trying to get one over, even as the jaws of fate clench down, tighter and tighter on his neck.

"You don't."

We pull into County, and I wait for the massive rolling garage door to lift upwards. Once parked, I grab all the files and unfasten his seatbelt. Mario drags his feet as we pass through heavy glass and metal doors. Perhaps things are settling in on him.

"Sit right here." I point to an open seat in the booking area. A corrections officer is kind enough to switch out the cuffs that bind Mario's hands and replace them with a tattered pair of belly chains.

"In here, Mario." I push open the door to a nearly empty interview room. "Have a seat."

The soft sound of his feet shuffling take me back to my first meeting with Eliza, nearly four months ago, but now things have changed.

The heavy door slams closed, and sound of the latch popping into place echoes from the bare white walls. "Mario, we've done a couple of interviews today in which you have been less than forthcoming. I'd like to try once more and get the whole story from you as far as pandering is concerned."

"Okay," he nods his head and adjusts his arms, resting them in his lap.

The clatter of the chains couldn't sound more beautiful. I start the recorder once more. "Do you wish to talk to me?"

"Yes."

"All right. Tell me how long you've been selling women, and tell me who."

"I've been pandering. I've been having dealings with four…four women who…" He struggles to spit out the words. For an evil man, the taste of truth holds a wretched flavor. "…who, uh, got considered, was, is considered to be pandering. You want names?"

"Sure, Mario."

"And the names are Katie Coughlin, Sadie Ortega, Haley Harrison, and Laurie Blackmon."

I have been waiting for this moment. *Now here, take this blade I've honed for you. Place the cutting edge at the side of your throat, apply pressure, and slowly drag it across.* "Tell me how it is that you pandered them?"

"Well, they all, they all have been arrested for prostitution, and I give, I help them make decisions about what they do on a daily basis, you know, with their lives, and even their money."

"Have you ever taken money you knew these women made while acting as prostitutes?"

"Uh...yes."

"When was the last legitimate job you held?"

"I...I...I'm holding one right now."

"Oh, really? Where?"

"Desert Audio."

"Have you ever mixed or used monies from your pandering activities for Desert Audio?"

"Um, yes."

"Can you elaborate?"

He lets out a sigh, and looks to the ceiling before answering. "Um, it's like, you know, if I had my own money, but if I needed more, I would just get it from the girls."

"Which of these women has been with you...I mean, have you been selling for the longest?"

"Sadie and Katie have been with me, the same time. And both Laurie and, um, Haley, yeah...met me at the same time."

"How long for the first two?"

"For, um, the first two, uh, probably five, six, like six because my daughter is five. They were pregnant back then, so...like I say, six."

"And what about Haley and Laurie?"

"Uh...four...say four."

"Do they give you the money they make, with no questions asked?"

"No questions asked."

"Have any of them ever referred to you as Daddy?"

"Yeah, all four of them call me Daddy."

"Why would they call you that?"

"Well, it's two reasons why they call me that," he manages, still writhing uncomfortably in his chains. "The, you know, the first, um, I'm their dude, and on top of that, we have kids, so, you know, they call me Daddy."

"And by being considered their dude, you mean to say..."

"You know…I'm they representation."

"Meaning?" I close the distance between us by leaning in. *You will own this Mario, no more sly talk, or minced words.*

"Meaning that, um, uh, I mean, I guess you could say that I'm their pimp."

Progress. Finally. He looks sick, and not just from his festering ear infection. I think more than anything, he's sick of me. "And what about these other women, the ones I have linked you to?"

"Um, look, like I said before, I'm just friends with them. Sure I spend time with them, but it's different with the four I told you about."

"How so?"

"We're like family…we're what you'd call family."

"Family?"

"Family!"

"In the game?"

"In the game, and out of it! When I'm done with this shit, they are going to see who my family is. They might not do this anymore, but they'll still be my family."

"How did you get involved in this? What happened to you?"

Slouching slightly, he leans back in his chair and kicks his legs straight forward. Go ahead, Mario. Make yourself comfortable, because I'm just getting started.

"It was always just like, you know, the girl. Well, like I say, it all started way back when I dated a stripper. She didn't want me to, um, you know, I used to be in the streets doing the wrong things. She didn't want me in the streets no more doing wrong. She said, 'Well, since you're helping me, why don't I just go ahead…' Well, she got fired from her job, so she said 'Why don't I go ahead and strip, and take care of both of us.' So, I was fine with it. Then I was like a magnet, you know. That's all I would meet. That's all that would come up to me; those are the only kind that would approach me. Eventually I started dating Katie and Sadie. They was sort of already doing it, so it just went from there."

I sit quietly, allowing him to cut his own throat.

"I would, like, you know, I would ask them for money every now and then, and they would just give it to me. After we had some kids, I had to start thinking of how to make it safe, you know. So I had them get their entertainer's licenses. I got mine, too. And did it like that. The reason I didn't pay taxes on the money they were giving me was because they had already paid on it. Why pay on it twice, that's why I didn't."

"Have you any idea how much money they've made you since you began?"

"Man, I couldn't even guesstimate. You know, they got me some little shit, initially, cell phones, you know, the extras. I guess that's where the pimping comes in. Why? Because I could go to these prostitutes and ask them for anything. They're not going to deal with anybody else but me! Why? Because I'm their babies' father, and we're family!"

"You make it sound like all this was just a natural progression. Are you asking me to believe you couldn't say no? The girls just kept coming to you…asking you to be their pimp?"

"I, I don't know how I could have dodged them," he says with a gleam in his eye, even the crack of a very slight smile. "Honestly, sir."

So he is the victim. A slave to the siren's song. It's too bad for Mario that I've heard this story before.

He hunches his shoulders, "Maybe I could have said no. I don't want to…I quit! I'm done…it happened so fast."

"Tell me about Laurie."

"Well, Laurie was like, you know, my girlfriend on the side for awhile. She saw me spending more time with the other girls, you know. One day she was like well, 'I'm just going to strip.' So she went and started stripping. She said she wanted more money, so she got into it, too. She wanted me to spend more time with her, so to make more money she started working. I mean, that was never my deal for her to do that, but she said, 'You never come over here to see me, maybe I need to start doing what they do because I want to be with you.'"

"Hmm."

"See, and that's how, kinda how our family came…"

"…came together?"

"Came about. Well, they all know I'm sleeping with all of them. Shit, y'all might as well be cool with each other because I let you all know that I'm trying to have a, straight up, you know like a…"

"…a what? A monogamous relationship, with three different women?"

"One-on-one. Yeah, a relationship. So, you can just love me for who I am. That was the motto. This, this is me! I'm…look, I'll fuck the next door neighbor if she'll let me, you know what I'm saying?" As he chuckles, I can sense the sickness oozing from his pores. "So to tell the truth, I'm a sex addict. I like to fuck. I'll fuck any pretty girl out there you put in my face. I don't care if it's your sister. I'm fucking going to tell them, though. I ain't gonna lie about it."

Right, why would a pimp be dishonest? "So, that's how this all came together, Mario?"

"That's right."

"Do you have any nicknames, or monikers the women, or other people call you?"

"Everyone just calls me Macc, but that's not from the game. They call me Macc from, if you remember, way back in high school."

"What about Boss Macc?"

"I call myself that."

"Why did you put the word Boss in front?'

"Because I just feel like I'm a boss. You know everybody wants to be a boss."

"You're the Boss, huh?"

"Right that's what I'm saying." He chuckles after lowering his head. "I want to create my own legacy. I want to have something to pass on."

"All right, operator, we're done with this interview." I stop the recorder and offer him a few words. "Two things, Mario; soon you're going to forget how scared you were today. Your lawyers are going to tell that they can get you off, that they can beat me in trial. What you need to keep reminding yourself is that you are exactly what I say you are. Secondly, take this however you want—as a promise, a threat, I really don't care—if I so much as hear about you beating or hurting any other women, I will hunt you down again and do everything in my power to destroy your name and finish off whatever part of your life I haven't already ruined."

"I...I understand, but I'm telling you, that ain't me. I don't hit women."

I escort him back to the booking area and look out across a sea of inmates to find Al leaning over a counter near a booking window. He's already filling out the paperwork. Sick of my current company, I step over and pat him on the shoulder. "Need a hand?"

"Well," says Al expectantly while handing the booking processor a stack of paperwork.

"He talked."

"Really? No more bullshit?"

"Oh, no. There was tons of bullshit. He's still denying pimping all of the others. For some reason, though, he was comfortable admitting that he pandered Sadie, Haley, Katie, and Laurie."

"I wonder why."

"My guess? He's had these women so long and put them through so much, he probably believes they'd be the least likely to turn on him. A question of loyalty, I suppose."

"Makes sense."

The processor flips through the paperwork, checking to make sure everything is in order. Then she takes a moment to read over the arrest report. With a repulsed look on her face, she shakes her head before handing back to us a complete set of copies.

We exit County to find that darkness has taken the city. As the doors close behind us, we turn to take one last look at our most recent prisoner. I hate what he became, but what's even sadder is the idea of what he could have been.

"Chris, the son of a bitch had it coming," says Al, offering his best advice. "Fuck him."

I don't speak. My mind is visited by the faces of those I've hunted in the past, faces that look like mine, faces of would-be heroes who turned into villains. I squint, focusing on Mario through the smudged glass doors, one more face to add to the pile. "Let's get out of here. We've got a hell of a night ahead of us."

"What do you mean? We're done with the warrants, all the houses are secured, and the evidence is already at the Triangle."

"You know what else is at the Triangle, don't you? The keys to Mario's vault. We can't wait to hit it; we can't take that risk."

Al opens his car door looking slightly deflated. "Damn, it *is* going to be a long-ass night."

21
Raiders

According to the clock it's been close to fourteen hours since we served the warrants, and four since Mario was arrested. With him in custody, Al and I make our way back at the Triangle, where bags of evidence line the walls. Trey sits in his chair at a desk literally buried by documents, jewelry, guns, drugs, and money.

"Jesus Christo!" Al bellows. "What the hell were you doing while we were gone? Napping? News flash, Trey. You're a cop, not a Teamster."

"It's about time you got here. I'm up to my neck in evidence. How's about you two offer an honest Italian boy a little help?"

I can't help but smile. "Trey, you got the keys?"

"Yeah." He stands and pulls a crumpled envelope from the side pocket of his BDU's and tosses it in my direction. "Here's your golden ticket, Charlie."

"Thanks. Now, about that help you were waiting for, uh, we need to talk."

"Talk, but let's do it while we're getting this evidence impounded. The night's still young, and I wanna get outta here. I got plans, kid."

"Trey, listen…" This won't go over well.

"Oh, hell no! Don't, Chris. Don't even think about starting your sentence with 'Trey, listen.' I know where the hell that leads. It leads to working all night long."

Al interrupts, "I told you he'd have a fit. He's a rich Italian from Buffalo. One of these days you'll realize guys like Trey aren't used to working hard."

I can almost see the heat rising from beneath Trey's collar.

"So, you're with us then?" I ask, placing my right hand on his shoulder.

"You suck."

"I'll take that as an enthusiastic yes. All we need you to do is keep doing what you're doing. For now, the most important things to get impounded are the guns, drugs, money, and jewelry."

"Okay, so now that we know what *I'll* be doing, where will you guys be at?"

"I need to draft another warrant. We'll get it signed tonight and hit the vault while you're here. Sounds simple enough, right?"

"You make everything sound simple," Trey grumbles.

"Al, I need you to go down to the vault. Find an inconspicuous place to park out of the line of sight of the cameras. We need to make sure none of the girls show up with a locksmith. You've got all their pictures right?"

"Sure do."

"Good, I'll need at least an hour."

"All right bro, I'm out the door. I'll shoot you a text if anything looks strange. What if one of the girls shows up?" shouts Al, walking backwards towards the exit.

"Improvise. Whatever is in that box belongs to us."

It shouldn't take me long. The computer screen lights up, and I begin by spelling out the success of the warrants. I note how something very special was seized that has led us to our next target. Next come all the fine details of the vault, the special locking mechanisms, retinal scans, metal detectors, surveillance cameras, and most importantly, custom keys fashioned for the most secure vault facility in our state.

I print two copies of the document, along with sealing orders. I want to keep as much of this from Mario and his attorneys for as long as possible. "All right, Trey, I'm out. If you come across anything interesting call me."

"Good luck, kid. I'll be right here, handling the secretarial."

In less than ten minutes I'm back in Henderson and tearing through the streets of Green Valley toward the judge's home. In a matter of minutes, His Honor opens the front door and is back-lit by the soft warm glow of his home's interior lighting. "Get on in here. It's freezing out there."

He invites me to take my customary spot on the love seat. "You know, I was on the way home today when I heard a commercial for the vault you're here about. They were going on and on about how safe it was. I can't wait to see how you figured this one out."

"Well then, I won't keep you waiting any longer." I hand him the documents and he begins reading.

"Mmm." He places his hand on his chin, gently massages. "Mmm-mm-mm."

· After finishing each page he places them on the table face down. "I bet old Mario was surprised to be getting that early morning wake-up call from Vegas' finest." He shakes his head, "Oh, to be a fly on the wall today at the Davis estate." He moves to the next page and pops it stiff. "Ah, finally, here we are…the infamous vault."

He reads without a word, but the grin across his face says enough. He finishes the last page with a chuckle. "Christopher, that was brilliant. Well written and perfectly explained. All right then," he leans forward, lifting his pen from the tabletop. "Let's get these signed."

I can see the vault just up ahead. The lot is a wasteland; desolate and dark except for a single flickering light post. I round the corner to find Al tucked into one of the deep corners of the complex. Before entering the lot, I kill my lights and pull up beside him. "What's up?"

"Nada, homie, just waiting on you."

"Wait's over."

We exit our cars still dressed for war. Green fatigues, black boots, and gun belts are set off against black tactical vests that are clearly titled "Police."

Al zips up his vest and jams his Glock into his holster. "Man, I sure hope this goes as smoothly as you say it will."

"Come on, buddy. We're about to make history. Just like Robin Hood." I smile and pull a black hood from the side pocket of my pants. I stretch the mask over my head so that everything except my eyes are covered. Next, I tug on my black gloves; the word "Police" is plainly visible across the top of each one. "

Al matches my pace, step for step across the field of asphalt. By now we're close enough for the cameras to pick us up. A good rule of thumb, if we can see them, they can see us. I look in through the glass door. It seems as dead on the inside as it is out here. Of course, we both know they're already watching.

Al steps to the front door, lifting his left hand to his eyes to cut the glare from the glass, and peers in. "This is bullshit, these motherfuckers know we're out here."

Bam, bam, bam. Al's knuckles crash against the glass. "Open up! We have a search warrant for this business! Open it up or I'll kick in the damn door!"

Not quite as covert as I might have chosen, but I can't argue his effectiveness. The door latch pops almost instantly and, once again, we enter the small corridor. "Click," and the second door is unlatched. Al leads the way, pushing open door number two and stepping into the lobby. I trail him and take a quick look around. There in the corner of the room near the ceiling I spot it, the ominous all-seeing eye in the sky. Everything's still too quiet. What's the man behind the curtain is doing?

Al reads my mind. "What's the plan?"

"You remember your access codes?"

"Yep. Got 'em right up here." Al taps his right temple with his index finger.

"Let's go. I'm right behind you." I expect we'll force their hand once they see we don't plan on standing around in the lobby.

Al walks over to the retinal scan and pulls the lip of his hood down. He places his chin in the proper spot and opens his eyes wide. As soon as their digital registry confirms him as being one of their clients, another latch pops. Al stands upright and pulls his hood back into position. I push the door open and wait as Al walks through. Just then a voice comes over the speakers. "Uh, hang on. I'll…I'll be right down."

Of course you will. After all, we are customers, although of the most unlikely kind.

I hear footsteps. The night watchman who hesitated to grant us entry sprints from around the corner. As he closes in on us, I take a quick second to size him up. He's a gangly man that looks to be somewhere between the ages of twenty-three and thirty.

"Excuse me." The kid's chest is heaving. His face is flushed, and he trips over his words. "I… I, I called the owner. He'll be here in…in a few minutes. Could I ask you guys to wait on him?"

Al opens the final door and steps through it. Before it can swing closed, he jams a pen between the door and the frame, keeping it from locking. "I'll meet you inside, bro."

"First of all," I say, turning to the guard, "calm down. We're not here to hurt the business, or you."

"Wha…what do you guys want?" His Adam's apple drops to the bottom of his throat.

"We're here because one of the lock boxes in your vault belongs to a very bad man." I hold up the warrant once more. These papers say that whatever he's got in that box is ours."

"But…but…," he manages to stutter. He looks at the floor and starts scratching his head.

"Listen," I take a moment to explain, "we aren't waiting for the owner. We don't have time for that." I place my hand on his shoulder. "How about we make a compromise? My partner and I have work to do in that vault. You have a com system that runs throughout this whole facility, correct?"

"Um, yeah."

"Then it's simple. Contact me through the intercom once he gets here. I'll be happy to come out and speak with him then."

As he makes his way back to the control room, I pull the pen from the door and walk in to a maze of silver boxes.

"Albert?" The acoustics in here are ridiculous. My voice pings off the metal lined walls.

"I'm back here, bro."

I make my way past hundreds of boxes to find Al waiting for me in the deepest corner of the vault.

"Well, we're in. What's the plan from here?"

This place is lock-box hell. I look left, then right, and sigh. "Al when you were a kid did your mom tell you that patience is a virtue?"

"Yeah," he says, hunching his shoulders and raising his brows.

"So did mine. I'd like to think they said that to prepare us for this moment." I dig into my pockets and retrieve the keys. "I'll take the first shift." I drop to one knee and begin testing each box against the keys.

"Man ain't this a bitch! Now I know exactly what you meant. We really are in for one long-ass night."

We're nearly forty minutes in and only halfway through the first wall.

"Hey bro, how about we switch up. Go on and take five."

After checking one more box, I gladly oblige and pass the baton.

Hunched over and working the lower half of the wall, Al rolls his neck. I lift my wrist and look at the dial of my watch. An hour's passed, and we still have eight full walls to get through.

Just then, my cell phone begins to vibrate. I look down at the glowing screen. It's Trey. "Hello?"

"What's up, kid? You guys having any luck?"

"Not at all. We've been twisting locks for over an hour and all we have to show for it are sore backs. This place is ridiculous."

"Looks like you guys pulled the short straws after all," Trey laughs. "So how'd you boys like a little help?"

"At this point, I'm open to almost anything. What ya got?"

"So I'm over here sorting evidence, making photo copies of documents and what-not. I'd just finished the stuff we recovered from Laurie's house. Keep in mind that's where we found the keys that are kicking you and Al in the ass."

"I remember where the keys were found."

"I'm finally down to the last house, as far as the impounding of evidence goes, which is Sadie Ortega's."

"Okay."

"You're gonna love this. Apparently there was a safe inside her room. It was hidden under the bed. You wanna guess what I found inside it?"

"If you tell me another set of keys, I'm going to vomit."

"What I just found is way better than keys, my man. Inside the safe was an envelope. Inside that envelope was some information about a certain vault company."

"All right."

"Go check out box number 1777."

"Trey, if you're joking…"

"Do I sound like I'm joking?"

"All right hang on." I call for Al, "We need to find box number 1777. Trey might have found something."

With a grunt, Al stands from his kneeling positions and walks to his left, lumbering down one of the long hallways. His eyes scan the number placards on each of the boxes. I take the right hand side figuring we'll meet up somewhere in the middle.

"Any luck on that box yet?" Trey asks.

"No, I haven't found it yet."

"Keep looking, this has to be it. It's gotta be there somewhere."

From a few aisles over, I hear Al's voice now infused with a spark of energy. "Chris! I found it!"

"Trey, he found the box!"

Al stands at the center of the aisle and looks over shaking his head, "You ready?"

"What do we have to lose at this point? Let's do it." Al inserts the guard key, and follows that by placing the access key into the secondary lock.

"Here we go." He pulls the keys back and the small door on the box swings open.

"Trey, that was the right box."

"Good! What the hell's in the damn thing?"

Al sets the box down to be photographed. Once I take the pictures he begins his count. Stack after stack is counted and re-counted before he's satisfied and confident of the amount. "Okay. We've got a total of $26,600 in cash, bro."

"All right, let's get that documented on the return, and list the jewelry we're taking so we can get the hell out of here. Trey, we'll see you in a few minutes."

"Wish I could see his face when he comes to collect his shit," Al says with a snicker.

"All right, man, one thing, when we get out of these doors I imagine the owner will be waiting on us. You keep going. I'll handle him."

Al nods.

We exit the vault stepping back through both of the security doors. In the lobby beside that tattered wooden desk waits a man who looks to be nearly seventy. The thin gray stubble on his face hides the wrinkles and blemishes that come from a life well-lived. Standing quietly behind him, is his counterpart, the ever-nervous night watchman. I slow down to greet them as Al dips outside, where he vanishes into the dark.

"Excuse me," says the older man, his voice doused with salt. "Are you the detective in charge here?" He's not aggressive, rather assertive.

"I'm Christopher Baughman, pleased to meet you." I extend my right hand.

"Sebastian." As we shake hands, he wastes no time getting to the matter at hand, a quality I can appreciate. "I'm not sure how comfortable I am about talking to a man hiding behind a mask."

"I understand, and I apologize that it has to be done this way."

He smiles, the whiskers on his face stand on end. "All right then, can you tell me what's going on here?"

"We are here for one reason, for one person. It just so happened, he felt his property would be safest in your building."

"Hmm." He gently rubs the plush stubble on his face. "Well, this certainly is a first for us here."

"Can you tell us anything about him?"

"I really can't go into details"

"A bad man, huh?"

"I guess that depends on how you feel about people who profit from the trafficking of women."

Sebastian's long frame and lanky arms support his torso as he leans over the desk. "Well, I am most certainly not the one to argue on his behalf. So what am I supposed to tell this man when he comes to collect his property?"

"Tell him it's too late. Tell him that you couldn't stop us." As I stand before this man, I don't get the sense he is anything like the salesman who works for him. "I really am sorry that we had to meet this way, you seem like a good man, but I'd be lying if I told you I didn't think I'd ever be coming back here."

"I've lived a long time, son, and I appreciate your candor. I'd be naïve to think everyone who came through here had noble intent."

"I can promise to keep things quiet. Only a few people outside of you or your staff will ever know I've even been here. I know how important discretion is in your line of work."

As I pull the door back to leave, he shouts out, "Detective! I want you to have something." He digs into his breast pocket pulls out a business card and jots a number on the back. "It's my personal cell. The next time you need to come back here, you call me first."

"I will."

As the door to the facility slams shut behind me, I step back into the darkness with renewed vigor.

22
The Front

By now, one day later, the aftershock from the assault on Macc's shattered empire has coursed through the underworld of my city. With him busy scrambling to figure out what comes next, I can tend to matters of a more personal and delicate nature.

I make for Eliza's home. Who can she talk to, who can help undo the twisted memories of the nightmare she fights to survive? Who... but one person?

Regina.

She is the healer whose spirit mimics cleansing water, the perfect medium for a re-birth. As I move along the freeways, I find Regina's icon on the cell.

"Well hello, Christopher," she answers, her voice as warm as the sun. "I was beginning to wonder if I'd ever hear from you again."

"You can rest easy," I answer light-heartedly. "I haven't gone anywhere. At least not yet."

"That puts a smile on my face. So, how can I help you?"

"I'm glad you asked. I have someone, a very special young lady that I'd like to introduce to you."

"Can I ask her name?"

"Eliza Serra. I guess I was just kind of hoping that you might be able to..."

"Don't say another word," she interrupts in her own soft way. "Can you bring her here soon?"

"Of course I can bring her. Let's say between nine and ten o'clock?"

"I'll see you both, then."

The next call is to Eliza, the bubbly young Latina that danced her way into the hearts of three warriors.

Eliza answers, but I can barely hear her tiny voice over the roaring engine. "Good morning, Eliza."

"Oh hi, Chris, how are you?"

Well, I'm better today than I was yesterday. So, I have someone I'd love for you to meet. You have any plans today?"

"Actually, I don't. Who do you want me to meet?"

"A friend. Her name's Regina Porter. She's one of our victim witness advocates." The phone falls silent. I know why. Nobody wants to share the darkest parts of their life with a stranger. Of course, once she meets Regina, she'll instantly know that she's no stranger. "I'm not saying you have to tell her everything, or anything. But, will you at least meet her?"

"Do you trust her, Chris?"

"I do."

"All right. When do you want to go?"

"In about three minutes. I'm just down the street from your house."

"Chris, I'm not even dressed!" she laughs.

"Well hurry up, I'll be there in a few."

I round the corner before parking in front of her home, knowing that Eliza's about to have one of the most amazing days of her life. I reach into the car and press the center of the wheel. A few minutes later, the front door opens, and she steps out. Tee shirt, jeans, gym shoes, light make up, and a purse. Beauty unfettered. Simple. But more than anything else...free.

"Shall we?" she asks, hopping into the front passenger seat.

I can barely contain my smile as she sits beside me. Her eyes jog from left to right as she looks out the passenger window at the shifting scenery. "So, what's new?" she wants to know.

It's not every day I get to share moments like these. Under most circumstances, I'd rush to tell her we'd just crushed Mario. But today, I take my time. "It's all technical stuff. You wouldn't be interested."

"Well," she says with a giggle, shaking her head, "I'm asking. So...?"

"All right, if you're going to twist my arm, then I'll tell you. Al and Trey have been working on this particular case for about four months now. We hit the guy last night."

"Another pimp?"

"Yes, ma'am. We served four search warrants. It was crazy. I think I might have gotten three hours of sleep. And now I'm back up chauffeuring you around the city. I hope you plan on tipping."

"Well I appreciate it. Really, I do." She bites her bottom lip and her face cringes as she asks the next question. "Was he a bad one?"

I pull my eyes from the street and glance at her momentarily. "Yeah, he was. But he's on ice for the moment. You should have seen the look on his face. Snot was hanging off his upper lip, and he was crying like a baby. It was pathetic."

"Are you serious?" She cracks a warm smile. "God, I wish there were a million Al's and Trey's."

"Me, too. You want to hear something crazy?"

"Sure." She fixes her deep brown eyes on me.

"One of the women he was pandering was named Eliza."

"What?" she manages as her jaw drops.

"God as my witness," I say, lifting my right hand to the sky. "But that's not all. It gets even weirder."

Eliza scoots to the edge of her seat and twists her neck so that she's looking me dead on.

"It turns out Eliza was introduced to this dude by a woman she met in jail."

"Chris! Are you serious?" She's in awe.

"As a heart attack."

"Is...is she okay?"

"Yeah, she's fine. She's back home with her family now."

"Oh, thank God. So what's next for that guy?"

"Well, we hit his lock-box last night. He had one at a vault company that uses retinal scans for access."

"Chris, are you making this up? This sounds way too close to…"

"Eliza, why would I make up a story just like yours?" I smile and reply softly. "Now if you can keep from interrupting me, I'll be happy to finish telling you the rest of the story." I think she's finally catching on. "Hey, I'm just telling you what we did yesterday. Don't kill the messenger."

"Mmm-Hmm!" She crosses her arms in silent protest.

"So, as I was saying. Once we took Macc down, we went to the vault later that night, and took close to thirty thou…"

Eliza's head pops back as if her neck were spring loaded. She snaps to attention, and starts yelling. "Wait! Wait! You said Macc! Did you say Macc?" She balls her petite hands into a fist and punches me on my right shoulder. "I can't believe you didn't tell me! If I wasn't so happy, I'd be so mad at you!"

I offer her a happy grin.

"He cried?! Oh, my God, I can't believe it. You guys actually did it! Wait, you said you served four warrants?"

"We hit his main girl's spots."

"I bet they were freaking out." She lifts her left hand to her forehead and massages it.

"I don't know what the girls were thinking, but I could see it in his eyes; his whole world was falling apart. It was beautiful."

"He cried! Bastard! I wish I could have been there." Her smile slowly fades away as it all starts to soak in. "He put us through hell. He acted like he was God. I never told you, but there were times, when if he wasn't happy with us, he'd make us lie on the floor naked beside one another and then he'd walk over us, beating us with a belt." Looking at her, I'm unsure whether the tears she's shedding are of joy, sadness, or a mixture of both.

"Hey," I ask softly. "You okay?"

"Yeah. There's just so much going on in my head right now. That man…he raped me of my innocence. I want him to suffer like me made me suffer. Like he made all of us suffer."

"Well, he will, and we aren't done yet. In fact we're just getting started."

"Okay." Eliza inhales deeply then exhales slowly. With a quick swipe of the thumb, she wipes away the extra tears gathering along her bottom eyelids. "So now what happens? What do we do next?"

"Next? Well, each of us has our own 'next' to deal with. Mine is getting you into the hands of Regina. Speaking of which," I enter the parking lot of her office building and pull into a spot near the front door, "we're here. What comes next for you, young lady, is figuring out whether or not you're gonna trust her to help us."

"You said trust her to help us. Don't you mean me?"

"No, no I don't. This is our journey, together."

"You think that much of her?"

"I do. You'll see." I smile and cut off the engine. "So, you ready to meet one of the city's Angels?"

She doesn't use words, but the electric smile sprawled across her face says it all. I walk towards her side of the car and open it. "Come on girl, you have an appointment to keep."

After dropping off Eliza, I meet Al outside the audio shop. Thus far, we've gotten Mario to admit he's pandering women, but of course, he will still maintain that he is a hard-working man, serving as both owner and manager at this audio shop.

This is what's called the Front. Criminals like to have one so they can fabricate false images of legitimate success. There are a million ways to do this, and Mario has chosen to go the route of audio shop owner. This benefits him because he can now file taxes, open bank accounts, accrue lines of credit, and even get loans from the government. The Front is a mirage which alters the way both everyday citizens and the courts see these animals. They seem like legitimate business owners with real sources of income. This is yet another knot in the ball of lies that is The Game.

At the shop a sign's visible through the clear glass door with the words "Open" spelled out in bright red letters. We enter to find Mario's right hand man. "Hello, I'm Paul. Can I help you two?"

"You can, Paul. I'm Detective Baughman. We have a warrant for your business."

His eyes quickly shift from mine to Al's, and back again. "I, I don't understand. A warrant?"

"Paul, this could be bad for you, bad for your business, and very bad for your family. Of course there is an alternative."

"I don't even know what's going on. You said bad for my family?"

"Do you really want to talk in the lobby?"

"No. No I don't, please come on back." He leads us down the hallway and into a small office that looks to double as a stock room.

Paul enters and plops down on a seat at the desk. He drops his head into both hands and talks through them. "Can you please tell me what's happening?"

"This is all about you and your partnership with Mario Davis."

"Damn! Look man, I have a family. A wife and kids. I'm not mixed up in that shit. I'm just trying to work, trying to keep my head above water."

"I'd like to believe you. Paul."

"I'll tell you everything I know, but I can't lose this place. It's all I've got."

I take a seat in a chair opposite Paul, while Al looms behind me. "I'm going to give you a chance to convince me." I pull the recorder and the conversation begins. "Why don't you tell me how you came to be involved with Desert Audio?"

"Well, I had a stereo shop on Spring Mountain which wasn't doing too good. I have some mutual friends who tell me about a guy who had a business down here. Auto Shine Detailing, and he thought it would be a good spot for me to open up a stereo shop."

"Okay, so what happened after that?"

"I opened up the stereo shop, and it took off from there. Well, it started to take off, but it slowed down quite a bit."

"Who was the person you were introduced to?"

"Mario Davis."

"How long have you known him?"

Paul leans back and looks to the ceiling, apparently working the math in his head. "Um, I'm gonna guess four years, or so."

"What was your impression of him?"

"He was a pretty cool dude. Quiet."

"So then what?"

"I told him there was no money in detailing, that we need to do car stereos. So he said, 'Cool man, let's do it.' Eventually he wasn't coming by as much. I guess he had other plans and was focusing on other things. So I told him why don't you just let me run this, and you can focus on whatever you've got going."

"And that was that?"

"Yep." He nods. "From then on out, for the last four years."

"Interesting. At what point did you begin to realize there might be something else going on with your business partner?"

Paul shakes his head and looks to the floor. Paul has to choose…family or friend, preservation or annihilation. "I noticed he had a lot of nice cars and not making any money out of here. But I didn't ask questions. I mean, that's his personal thing, you know? I don't want him asking about my personal things."

"Do you keep track of payroll allocations?"

"Not really. We got a running agreement where it was fifty-fifty. So if we did make some profit, we'd just split it. But we hardly make any. The store's just been running itself."

"You mean it's just staying afloat?"

"That's exactly what I'm saying."

"So if Mario stated that he made $9,500 a month working here as a general manager, what would you say to that?"

"Man, look at our records," he says, biting his bottom lip and massaging his temples. From the cluttered desk, he grabs up a book entitled Payroll Ledger and hands it to me. "This goes back two years. If you look back at this thing, you'll see me making payments to myself here and there. But those payments are few and far between, and they are us usually never more than three to four hundred dollars."

"So what are you saying, Paul? That's he's lying?"

"We make just enough in this shop to get by. My whole thing is my wife believes in me, she has a good job and basically pays all the bills. What I make here and there, I help out. She's very understanding about all that, but she's getting sick of it, and so am I."

I peruse the book to find several names and dollar amounts paid out to various individuals. Nowhere inside of it do I see the name Mario Davis.

"When did you realize what the girls he sent around were doing?"

"Um, not at first. I thought they were all stripping. That's all I knew about when I first started this place with Mario. Of course, later on, I found out they were doing more than that."

"When did you find out?"

"Come on, man, some things a man just don't want to see, so he doesn't look. But other times, you didn't have to look. It was just fucking obvious."

"Has Mario reached out to you recently?"

"Yeah, he called me the night he got arrested, I asked him what the hell happened." Paul leans forward and exhales with a sigh. "Mario said, 'They got me man, you know? I fucked up and shit, I got pegged. I'm going to plead guilty, 'cause I'm guilty. So I gotta do what I gotta do.' "

I close out the conversation, stop the recorder, hand him a copy of the warrant, and take the ledger. As Al makes for the exit, I turn and offer Paul a final thought. "Paul. If I find out you lied to me about anything…"

"Sir," he says, while escorting me to the front door. "I don't have shit to do with what that man is doing in the streets. I got my own problems trying to keep this place from going under."

As we pull away, both Paul and the business become an afterthought. I have what I need. Paul's testimony will neutralize any lies Mario may try to feed the court about his legitimacy.

23

Namaste

"Good afternoon, boys!" Trey blurts out, sounding well-rested and in good spirits as he tosses me a stapled packet of papers.

"What have we here?" I ask, slowly sinking into my own seat.

"That's the appraisal report from this entire operation. It lists all the jewelry, cash, and casino chips. A pretty lucrative hit if you ask me. On top of the guns, we're talking a total seizure of about $300,000."

"*Three*? Ouch. You think Mario's going to miss any of this?"

"I hope that *pendejo* misses *everything* we took," interjects Al, "including his Benz."

"I'm sure he will," I add. "Nothing matters to them more than their diamonds, gold, money, and cars."

"Oh," says Trey. "Stephanie was asking about you earlier. You might want to swing by her desk. She said something about a message for you."

"Thanks." I hop up from my desk and cross the wide office space to find her.

As I approach she greets me without looking up or breaking the pace of her keystrokes. "Hey, Chris."

"So, I heard you were looking for me."

"I was, as a matter of fact, for a couple of reasons. First, I wanted to say good job! Trey tells me Mario was crying like a little baby." She looks up with a smile that stretches the width of her face. "Strange, isn't it? These guys are so tough when they're beating up women, but as soon as someone as big as them steps up, they break down." She shakes her head. "Okay, the other thing is one of the girls has been calling all morning, nearly every hour on the hour. She's looking to speak with you about something." Stephanie scans around her desk and plucks up a sticky note. "Haley Harrison. She's one of the girls he was trafficking, right?"

"Yeah, she is." I'm genuinely puzzled. "Did she mention why?"

"No, she wouldn't tell me anything. She just said it was important. Her number's right here on the sheet. Would you mind giving her a call back?"

Is this a trick? Has Macc sent her into my camp like some Trojan horse? I've got to mind every step I take, and here I am again in front of a terrible choice. With Eliza now safe, should I continue sneaking through Satan's playground, stumbling across hot coals and flame in search of one more?

I step out of the office and dial the number. The phone rings softly, and everything in me cries out, "This is a trap!"

"Hello?"

"Hi. This is Detective Baughman. I'm looking for Haley."

"Hi, Detective," she replies lightly. "This is her."

"Well, it's nice to finally meet you, Haley."

"Finally?" she chuckles. "Oh, yeah, right. I've gotta remember who's talking. I guess by now you know everything about me."

"Well, I wouldn't go that far. My office told me you've been calling all morning. So, how can I help you?"

"I really don't even know how to say this…"

"Well, just start talking."

"Okay, well, when all the detectives came to our houses, they took a lot of stuff. Some of the things that got taken were…were really important to me."

"Haley, I'm sorry about much of what had to happen, but if these items you're talking about came from Mario…"

"No, no, they didn't. That's just it. The stuff I'm talking about was given to me by my mom and dad. It's just a few pieces of jewelry, none of its expensive, but it still means everything to me."

"Your mom and dad, huh?"

"Yeah," she replies with a very heavy heart.

"All right, I'll tell you what, let's meet. I'll bring pictures of all the jewelry we seized. We'll talk about what I can and can't do for you then. Deal?"

"Thank you, Detective." Her spirits skyrocket. "Thank you so much."

"You can call me Chris. And remember, we're only going to talk about what I might be able to do for you. Don't get all crazy on me. I'm guessing Mario's already bailed out?"

"Um...uh, yeah. He got out this morning."

"Does he know you're reaching out to me?"

"No, he doesn't."

"Well, let me give you a little advice. Don't tell him. After yesterday, he won't be happy to hear about this. This is a safe phone for me to call you back on, right?"

"Yes it is. He's got so much going on right now, that I'm the last thing on his mind."

"Okay then. I'll call you soon with the location."

"Thanks, um, wait! Before you go, there's one other thing."

"What else?"

"Well, there are things, keepsakes that some of the other girls would really like to get back, if that's possible."

"What are you? The spokeswoman? And just which girls do you mean?"

"Well, Sadie and Laurie. Would it be all right if I brought them with me when I came?"

"That's fine. I guess I'll see all three of you in a bit."

Even as I prepare to meet them, I have a terrible feeling. I'm concerned about this meeting with Haley, Sadie, and Laurie. They are the closest to Mario, and he's desperate, and that desperation is the fuse that could easily ignite his explosive nature.

Initially, this was about one young lady adrift in a sea of fire. With her now safe and back on solid ground, I can't help but think about the others. Shouldn't I be happy with the one?

17:45 hours: I arrive in the parking lot of a well-chosen coffee shop. The parking's limited, and it allows me to see everyone either coming or going. In fifteen minutes, the three women should be pulling up. I've left myself with enough time to take up the best defensive position. For now I sit still, simply watching.

At six sharp, a pearl-colored Cadillac Escalade turns right and creeps into the lot. I have no trouble looking through my windshield into theirs. Sadie Ortega, the fair-skinned Latina, cranks the wheel. Beside her sits the red-headed Haley Harrison; and peeking from the rear seat is the creamed-coffee complexion of Laurie Blackmon. They park unknowingly right across from me.

The first one to step out is Sadie Ortega, about 5'4". A baseball cap tries to hide her face, but I can still make a mental photo of her face.

Seconds behind her, Haley exits the Escalade's passenger side. Matched beside Sadie, she's maybe an inch shorter, though hers is a lean, slender frame. A sudden gust of desert wind whips Haley's red hair into the sky where it shimmers like a flame. She turns her back to me and waits for the final member of their expedition.

Laurie is the last to make her way out of the car, and now I see why. Even with a loose-fitting blouse, she's obviously showing. The bump in the center of her body is not so small, after all. Another child will be born to this man, one more way that this woman's life will be held hostage, should she ever choose herself over him. Nonetheless, Laurie is a beautiful woman, and a wave of her jet black hair blends seamlessly into the night sky.

Haley taps on her cell phone, and moments later, the chime on mine announces her incoming text message.

"Haley: We're here."

They glance a bit nervously around the lot, and eventually decide to walk through the shop's front door. I'm not comfortable, not yet. I take a few more minutes, making sure that no unexpected guests slink in behind them.

I step out of the car into the night, and walk inside.

Haley's eyes lock onto me. She slowly tilts her head and raises her brows, wordlessly asking 'Are you Chris?' I answer with a smile, and step over to their table. "Haley, hello."

"Um…hello," she replies softly.

I turn my head slightly. Laurie leans back in her seat and places both hands on her stomach, barely offering a smile. "Hello," I say looking directly into her eyes. "I hope the pregnancy is coming along well."

Lastly, I turn to Sadie, the young woman who recruited Eliza, pulling her into a culture that would forever change — and nearly destroy — her life. Her eyes are as cold and biting as the wind outside. Is that soul-chilling stare even her own? It is the same way Mario looked at me.

"Sadie," I say as warmly as I can. "Nice to meet you as well." She lifts her head and crosses her arms. Above her bicep I notice a tattoo. The words 'Loyal Bitch' are etched into her olive skin. "Sadie, why don't we start with you. Let's see what we can do about these keepsakes."

Sadie stands up and looks at her friends. They shrug suggesting, 'well-someone's-gotta-go- first'.

Because of the inclement weather and the need for privacy, we use my car as an office. "Hop in." Sadie sinks into the dark leather seat of the mustang. I reach to the back seat and haul the case-file into my lap. "Now, you were at Old Salt Circle, right?"

"Yeah," she answers, her voice still cold.

I flip open the binder to the appraisal section. "So, we're going to look at all of the items we seized. You point out the ones with the most significance. I'll make a note and see what I can do about getting it back to you."

"That'd be really nice," says Sadie, lifting the brim of her hat slightly.

"Here's the thing, though — don't waste your breath asking for items in the high thousands, or anything that is designed for a man."

"I won't. The stuff I'd like back belongs to our daughter."

I set the binder on the armrest and begin flipping pages. Sadie is true to her word, selecting only items fit for a child; a broken Mickey Mouse charm and necklace, a small bracelet, as well as few children's rings.

As the final page turns, I hear her chuckle faintly. I look over just in time to see her shaking her head. "Did I do something?"

"I don't know, I...yeah, I guess," she offers, still smiling. "It's just...I didn't expect you to even consider giving us any of our stuff back. I figured you were just lying to Haley about helping us, and that all you really wanted was to get us down here so you could grill us about Mario." She lifts her hands from her lap and flips her palms to the sky. "I guess I should say thank you."

"You don't have to thank me for doing the right thing. As for Mario? That's your own business." She nods in understanding. "So, I guess, we're done here?"

"I guess we are. Well, thank you, anyway." She cracks open the car door and much of the warmth from inside is instantly sucked out into the night.

"Would you mind asking Laurie to step out?"

One down, two to go.

Laurie waddles her way to the car, plops down in the passenger seat, and everything runs smoothly. It doesn't take long before we've worked our way through the entire inventory from Tuscany Rose Court. She points out a few items, thanks me, and excuses herself about as quickly as an expectant mother can.

Now I await the ring leader, the woman who arranged this whole opportunity.

Haley's eyes zero in on me as she gets in. "So, what do you need me to do?"

"We're just going to look at some pictures. You'll point the jewelry out, and viola, we're done. Sound good?"

"Sounds really good, but I can tell you, the only thing I really care about is a ring my mom and dad got for me. There's an inscription on the inside of it from them, saying they love me."

"That's it?" I'm blown back by the very small but extremely sentimental request.

"Chris, I told you, I need to have that. Everything else is just stuff."

"All right, consider it done."

She drops her head into her hands. Several seconds of silence go by before she speaks. "Thank you." Her voice is cracked with emotion.

"Don't don't thank me. I'm sorry about all of this. I wish I didn't have to do these things."

"You shouldn't have to apologize, Chris." Her voice is still thick. "Just...just, thank you." Haley breathes deeply and regains her composure. Do her parent's know how much she adores them? Soon she smiles. "Oh, I thought you'd be happy to know we all have real jobs now."

"That's wonderful."

"We're dancing, so you won't have any more problems out of any of us."

"I never had a problem with any of you. You know who my issues are with."

"I know. He thought it would be a good idea if we all went to work in the strip clubs."

"Is he...behaving?"

"Well, he's just trying to figure out where to go from here."

I bite my tongue. "I meant, he hasn't hurt any of you, has he?"

"No, no, he's calmer now. He knows you're watching him, so he's being better."

At least those are the words coming out of her mouth, but there's something in her voice, something hidden deep behind her eyes that's a warning.

All I know about these animals is what my life has taught me. Pimps don't deal very well with shame, and they easily turn. Like a feral dog when backed into a corner, they become more dangerous, more vengeful, and less predictable.

I want to open up to her, but I fight myself the whole way. Instead I offer a promise. "Haley, I don't know exactly what's going on with all of you. I'd never ask you to turn on him, but I want you to know that if he snaps, or hurts you, I'll come for you. Wherever. Whenever. If you ever need me."

"Thanks, Chris," she smiles, wiping a small tear from her eye. "Things are just a little crazy right now, but don't worry about me. I'm sure there are other people who need you more than me. Besides, Mario's not that like that."

I keep my expression plain. I only listen. Of course she still thinks that, and if I was to throw all the facts back in her face, who'd benefit? Not her, nor I. So I swallow my pride and keep them to myself.

We sit quietly for a moment as the wind hums. Bits of debris from the street fly down the sidewalk, past the coffee shop. I don't know if she believes a single word I've said, but she hasn't left yet, and that has to mean something.

"Well," she says pensively, "I guess I should get going. Thanks for listening and caring."

"I'm glad I got to meet you. Try to be patient with me. It may take two to three months before I get back to you, but I promise, I'll call you when its time."

She opens the door and places one foot out. "Okay, so I guess I'll see you then."

"'Bye, Haley."

I can't say with certainty why melancholy spreads over me. Perhaps it's because Mario is out and still so close to all of these women. Maybe all I've done is prodded the monster, leaving him on edge and making him even closer to lashing out and attacking those nearest him. I worry about them all, but as Haley walks away, she is foremost in my mind.

I focus on a lone word with two meanings which has left me feeling empty. Life promises each of us a beginning, an ending, a birth and a death, a hello and a goodbye…Namaste.

24
The Serpent

Five more months have passed, and Winter's chill has given way to the normal heat of springtime. The whining blade beneath my mower kicks up small bits of grass into the sky, and the crisp scent transmits instantly in the dry Vegas air. This is Sunday morning, what in theory should be my day of rest. I glance behind me and notice my youngest daughter peeking out from the sliding glass door. "Daddy?" she yells out over the sound of the mower.

I release the power switch, and wipe the sweat from my forehead. "Yeah, sweetie?"

"Hurry! It's almost time to go. It's only three hours 'til the movie starts."

"I'm almost done. Let me finish up back here, then I'll get ready, okay? I promise."

"Okay, daddy!" She's still a twig, barely strong enough to push the glass slider closed.

She's only seven, and already her eyes and her smile cast enough energy to rival the warmth of the sun. She scampers off, and moments later another beautiful face peeks through the glass door. My eldest daughter. "Dad, come on! I don't want to be late. We're gonna miss the best part."

"Honey, I'm almost done. We still have hours before the show even starts. We'll be fine."

Who would have called this one? Me? Pushed into a corner by a ten- and seven-year-old. After putting away the mower, I kick off some minced blades of grass from the bottom of my shoes. Hitting the shower and getting dressed only takes me fifteen minutes.

When all this is done, waiting at the hallway door is the woman who blessed me with these daughters, my most-prized possessions in the world. She holds the phone out to me while wearing a look of grave concern.

"Who is it?"

"I don't know, maybe another detective from Vice? He said he needs to talk to you."

I drop my head as I extend my hand. I already know this can't be good. "Thank you."

With a gentle smile, she hands me the phone and closes the door behind her. "Hello?"

"Hey, Chris. It's Joe Lardomita. I'm sorry to bother you on your off day, but there's kind of a situation." Joe's a veteran of Vice, a day shift enforcement detective who'd been there long before I ever walked through the door.

"Don't worry about it. Can you tell me about this situation?"

"Didn't you do a case recently on a guy named Mario?"

"We're waiting for him to either take a deal, or for the trial to start. You have a question about that case?"

"Not exactly," he answers. His tone of voice leaves me even more anxious. "I uh, I just got a call from the watch commander, and Mario's name came up. He had some questions about him, so I told him what I knew, which wasn't much. Anyway, he told me that the family of a young woman was calling and calling, demanding that we do something."

I take a seat at the edge of my bed, "Do something about what?"

"Apparently, she's missing."

"All right, give me the rest of the story."

"This girl's uncle's a retired homicide sergeant out of Orange County, California. He's been calling all morning. They haven't been able to reach her, and she isn't answering her home phone, or her cell."

"Joe, did you happen to get her name?"

"Hang on, let me check my notes. I know I wrote it down." I can hear the paper flipping as he scrambles through his note pad.

"Okay, got it. Her name's Haley. Let me see if I can find her last name."

I close my eyes and lift my head toward the ceiling. "It's Harrison." For a moment I sit still, slumped over the edge of the bed.

"You still there? I've got the uncle's name for you." "Um, yeah," I answer, grabbing a pen from my nightstand.

"It's Mark Harden. Just be prepared, he's probably going to be irritated. I think he might have been getting the run around."

"What do you mean?"

"Look, you didn't hear it from me, but the way it was presented was, oh well, she's a hooker. It's probably just a pimp/ho thing."

"What…really?"

"I think whoever was dealing with her uncle wasn't taking this seriously because of her record. But once I heard the name Mario, I remembered what he did to that other girl, and how violent you said this guy was at the warrant briefing."

Closing off our conversation, I hang up and look at the clock, thinking of my own daughters. In less than an hour, we're all supposed to be sitting in a theater watching a boy wizard, empowered by noble intent, ward off the darkness and slay fire-breathing dragons with a wand.

Rising from the bed I lock the door. For the time being, I feel I must keep her family from knowing the whole story. I drop the house phone and pick up my cell, reluctantly punching in Mark Harden's number. The phone rings for less than half a second before it's answered. "Hello!" A man answers frantically. His voice is full and burly.

"Good morning, sir. I'm Detective Baughman. I was asked to respond to your call."

"Well it's about damn time!" I can hear both desperation and exasperation rippling through his voice. As he continues, I settle in for the long ride. "I've been calling your department all morning, begging anyone who would listen to help us. Are you with Missing Persons?"

"Not exactly, Mr. Harden. But I'm here, and you have my word I'll do everything I can to help you. I need you to tell me what's happened. All I have are fragments of the story."

"All right," he takes a moment and breathes in deeply, "let me calm down a second. I need to have a seat." Mark moves his mouth away from the phone briefly and yells out, "Trudy, what time did we get the call from Betty and Mike?" He's silent, but behind him I can hear a soft, faint voice. "Uh huh, okay, thanks, honey. We got a call about three hours ago from Mike and Betty. That's my niece Haley's mom and dad. They said they got a phone call from Haley's sister, Tina. She was screaming when she called them, something about Mario. They told me she called them in tears because she thought Mario was killing Haley." As the pitch of his voice climbs so does the tension inside my body. "Apparently the two of them were on the phone having a conversation when Tina heard something like a loud crash. She could hear Haley screaming. Then she heard Mario. He was yelling at her...something about 'I'll kill...' " Mark stops speaking. His voice cracks with emotion. "He... he said 'I'll kill you, bitch!' "

"Take your time."

"Sorry." Another grumble and he clears his throat. "So, she hears Haley begging him to stop. A little after that, something falls, she thinks it must have been by where the phone was dropped. Eventually, Haley just stopped making any noise. After a while, the only thing Tina could hear was Mario cussing, and the sound of something...something like a pounding noise. Then the phone went dead, no answer. No nothing. Then Mike and Betty tried calling her house, but the number was disconnected. That's when they called the police. The police told them they had to call back in 48 hours, if they still hadn't heard from her. Then they could file a Missing Persons Report. That's why I thought maybe you were from Missing Persons."

"We'll talk about where I'm from later, but for right now, let's stick with what happened next."

"Sure," he sighs. "They, uh, they called me hoping I could get something done. You know, kind of a professional courtesy, brothers-in-arms kinda thing. They told me the story, and I, uh, I couldn't believe it. We've met Mario before, he's been to our reunions, eaten with our family at Thanksgiving. I have a picture of him. I can send it to you so you'll know what he looks like."

"I already know what he looks like, Mark. I know who he is."

"How…how do you…?"

"I'm in Vice. I specialize in Human Trafficking. I hunt down pimps."

"Dear God, what did Haley get herself mixed into? I knew something wasn't right about that man, but I thought maybe drugs, or something else, not…not this."

"Think for a minute. Was there anything else?"

"Yes, there was. Tina got a text from Haley's phone about two hours later. It said something like, please come get me. Help me."

"All right, that's good. That's a very good thing."

"Detective, if I can make a suggestion? I say you go beat on her door or her friends' doors and say that you want Haley back! Spread the word to everyone that you're looking for her!"

"Mark, I don't doubt you're an exceptional investigator, and probably one hell of a homicide sergeant, but this is a different world, and the rules that you play by don't work here. I'm sure you're probably wishing I was from Missing Persons. Trust me, I'll find her, but the one thing neither of us can afford to do is waste time arguing about how to do it. Agreed?"

"Agreed."

"Good, because I won't be able to pull this off without you. You're going to be the central hub for all information coming in from the family. How much do Mike and Betty know?"

"They know everything I told you. But nothing about this Vice stuff, it's going to kill them to find out what he had her doing."

"I've already got a case pending on him. He's desperate right now, and if you couple that with a volatile temper…well, I can tell you that Haley is in real danger. The reason I can't go knocking on doors and making a scene is because just like I know who Mario is, he also knows me. We can't afford to let him know I'm coming for her. There are at least four or five houses he could be holding her in. More than likely he has connections to other men just like him all across the country. They trade women, lock them in basements, and send them to places where I don't have reach. We have one shot to get this right. If we misfire, we could lose her."

The depth of our situation has hit him. I hear the urgency even as he whispers his reply. "Oh my God."

"I need you to contact all of the family members and tell them to stop trying to call Haley's cell phone. We know she's still alive. What we don't know is where she's hiding the phone, or how much power's left in it. That's her lifeline to you, to all of you. If that phone rings or even vibrates, and he finds it...we're all in trouble."

"All right, Chris. I can do that. Can you at least tell me what happens next?"

"Next, I keep my promise to Haley."

"Your promise?"

"I'll find her, Mark."

"Thank you, and, Chris, please...bring her home."

With a heavy heart, I unlock the door and step downstairs to my family. This won't be easy. I accept the sacrifices I'm called to make, but the two little girls patiently waiting for me on the couch didn't ask for this. Everything I do has an effect on everyone else around me, not the least of which comes in the form of my own children. As I move closer, my wife looks at me with sympathetic eyes. This truly is a family affair. I drop to one knee and ask for both permission and forgiveness.

"Are we about to leave?" asks the eldest.

"Honey...I can't. Something happened."

"What happened?"

"Someone needs our help."

I can see the disappointment in her face, and it shoots to the center of my heart. "Is it another girl?" she asks softly, her eyes tearing up.

"I'm sorry about the movie, baby. Yes, it's another girl and her family."

"Where is she, Daddy?" my youngest chimes in.

"I don't know, sweetie. Somewhere in the city, I hope."

With tears now streaming from her eyes, my ten-year-old asks a question that I'm not exactly sure how to answer. She stammers and stutters out the words. "Why does it always have to be you?" At the sight of her, now my youngest can't stop her tears.

"Oh, come here." I wrap my arms around the both them and squeeze tightly. "I love you two so much, and I always want to make you happy. There are people on this earth that hurt little girls, just because they're girls. God put me here to stop those people."

"And find the girls, and bring 'em home?" My youngest can finish the sentence even before I can.

I bury my face between their shoulders, and pray they don't see how wet my eyes have become. I clear my throat and try to blink away the salt. "Yes, baby, and bring 'em home. Can you two give me your permission? I'd like to find her."

"Yeah," answers my seven-year-old. "We can go to the movie later."

I turn my body and look into the eyes of Big Sis. She nods, and kisses me on my cheek. "It's okay, Dad."

This was supposed to be a day for my two girls; one spent marveling at the power of imagination. In places as special as a theater, our dreams can turn real. This afternoon, though, all the monsters that flicker on the screen will have to wait.

Mario has shed his skin again, turning back into a man-serpent whose very words are injected with venom. Knowing that he's said, "I'll kill you, bitch!" and that he has the means, the motive, and the opportunity to do so rings every alarm in my soul.

So how many sacrifices must be made, and how long is the list of those who have been forced to suffer? There's Eliza and her mother, Haley and her whole family, and now in such a smaller way, me and mine. The darkness I've fought to keep from my daughters has found its way into my home. Now their tears, as well as those of another family, will fuel me on my ride.

The engine purrs as I speed west towards the melting sun, giving chase to the darkness with two thoughts seared into my mind: First, find Haley, and then turn this snake inside out!

25
The Keep

I race through the city knowing that Haley's in a fight against the clock. With every passing minute, the pain of this family grows exponentially. All of their hopes in redeeming her now rest in me—the boy who never expected this life, and a man who never asked for it.

They believe he'll kill her. I know that if I don't find her quickly, her family may never know what became of her. Mario keeps four strongholds, each one a kind of castle. He shuffles among them to stay even safer, so that no one on the outside can ever be sure where the man makes his home on any given night.

I keep this in mind as I head toward Haley's last known address, Quinella and Torrence. Exiting the freeway I weave through one sleepy neighborhood after another.

A few houses east of the target I slow to a halt and kill the engine. My .40 caliber gets tucked it into the waist of my jeans. I clip my badge onto the front and un-tuck my tee. I'll approach on foot.

The small sweat droplets bead up on my forehead and nose from the desert climate. I slowly make my way past the front of the house. Every window is drawn shut, blacked-out. I'm not surprised. Pimps are also nocturnal, just like the bloodsuckers I grew up fearing as a child.

I creep up to a side wall only to find more black-out curtains over the back windows. I move back to the front of the house. The front door's slightly ajar. My stomach churns and my knees buckle as nausea washes over me. Finding that the door has been left open certainly lends credibility to the family's concerns. I hate to imagine what I might find inside. I fall back to my car, call dispatch, and grab my tactical vest from the trunk.

After a few minutes, two patrol officers arrive. With no more than a whisper, I bring them up to speed. "I don't know that she's here, and I don't know that she isn't. But this may very well be the house where everything happened. The front door is still open. Let's not forget to be careful. We can't help her if we're dead.

"Crime scene preservation is our next most important concern. If the beating happened here and Haley is gone, we'll need to be very careful not to trample on any evidence DNA or otherwise. No one moves until I break the threshold. Understood?"

They both nod, and yank their firearms from their holsters. Single file, we round the corner and move up the driveway. My heart pounds. Stress. Adrenaline. Fear. A killer cocktail. We pause at the door. "Police! Open the door!"

Even though it is already ajar, the door seems as heavy as a boulder, and doesn't budge. From the other side, a small dog, maybe a Chihuahua or a terrier, sounds the alarm as I pound the door. "Metro Police!! Hello! Police!" The door swings open, and the pooch sprints into the darkness of the house. Sunlight floods the entryway.

I take the left-hand side of the house. My eyes dart around in a frenzied search, scrambling to adjust to the lack of light as I descend into a sunken living room. The two uniformed officers go right and vanish. I can't see them, but I can hear them.

"Police!" Their voices ricochet in the background, "Is anyone here? Police?"

I move further into the dark cave. The air's become dense, tainted by the stale scent of gym socks, old pizza, and dank marijuana. From the upper levels of the house come the voices of the two patrolmen.

"Clear!"

"Copy that! All clear up here! Coming down!"

My eyes are still trying to penetrate the gloom. Reaching for the flashlight compartment on my vest, I illuminate the void, painting the walls with light. Wandering deeper into the pit, I steer the beam of light to my left. A sofa's set against the back wall. On it, bed sheets, beneath them the figure of a body.

From around the corner comes the pooch. He's back for Round Two, crouching behind an end table and barking non-stop.

"Police!" I have to bellow even louder, just to hear myself over the dog. "Haley?"

From beneath the sheets comes the groan of a male voice. "Hey, man. It's cool. It's cool, bro. Twix! Shut up!" I shift the beam, and coat the figure in light. The sheets slip away just a bit, revealing a disheveled-looking, twenty-something-year-old male. He catches the sheets at his waist. "Whoa man! Is everything okay, officer?" He rubs his eyes clear and notices the two behind me. "Oh, I mean officers."

"I'm Detective Baughman. I apologize for waking you. We were looking for a missing woman, and your door was left opened. We thought maybe she was taken from here. Her name's Haley. You know her?"

"Man," he grumbles scratching his scalp through a mass of matted hair, "I, I don't know, bro, no chicks live here, man. It's just me and my bros. We're DJs, so our hours all crazy, man. So…what happened?" He asks with a befuddled expression.

"How long you've been living here?"

"Like a month and a half or something. We got a sweet deal 'cause the landlady was kinda desperate. She said the last people that lived here just up and left, no warning, no nothing. They just disappeared. You guys are welcome to look around if you want."

"No, there's no need. Lock the door behind us."

My hopes for a breakthrough at Quinella have fallen far short of expectation. This is the worst-case scenario. Mario has reshuffled the deck. I step away from the house and head back towards The Beast. The officers follow. "Is there anything else, Detective?"

"No, there's nothing else." They nod and radio in, clearing themselves from the call.

I can eliminate one property from the list. I'd like to think that one less target means the probability of finding her increase, although not greatly. Still, what condition will she be in? How long can she endure? And exactly what more was happening to her while I stumbled through that house? I can't move fast enough, minutes fall off the clock in chunks.

As I mash the gas pedal a text message comes through from Mark, with an image attached. A grainy picture, shot in a dimly lit room. It's Haley, but not the Haley I know. Her once lovely face is destroyed. Lips bloodied, split open. Her brown eyes aren't even visible. Both the eyelids and the soft tissue surrounding them have been pulverized into swollen masses. We are at odds with a monster, and Haley clings for survival.

Moments later, the phone rings. "Chris? It's Mark. Did you get that picture?" His voice trembles, wrought with fear.

"I did."

"Well, tell me something. Please! You saw her! You see what he's doing to her!"

"Mark, I'm working as fast and as hard as I can. How long ago did that picture come in?"

"Just now. I... I sent it to you as soon as I got it."

I can hear him fighting back tears. "Mark, I'm narrowing down the possibilities of where he's hiding her. Remember what I told you. We can't make any mistakes. Or we could..."

"Lose her, I know. I feel powerless. I just want to get her back home."

"If we're going to find her, we've got to keep our heads. Haley's keeping hers. She's letting us know she's still alive. We still have time."

"Okay, okay." His heavy breathing makes my pulse quicken. "So, what now?"

"We continue with the plan. You keep me in the loop, if she sends any new texts, pictures or emails, forward them to me right away. I'm heading to a few more properties. There's got to be something somewhere."

"Right, the plan. Haley's a fighter, and we know she's still alive. You're right, Chris, we have time. If I get anything else, I'll contact you right away."

"I know you will, Mark. I have to go now."

"Right, right."

I drop the phone and head to my next two destinations, Sadie Ortega and Laurie Blackmon. I don't need to look at my clock to know that I'm losing. The sun moves across the clear blue sky and settles into its late-afternoon resting spot, perched just above our western mountain peaks.

The next two stops are a blur, both homes are unnaturally quiet. No traffic coming or going from either, and there are no sounds coming from either structure. Everything has fallen silent. Everything is dead. Of the four homes, I've come up short on three.

The city begins to glow as darkness falls. I pull off to the side of the road and look to the golden sky. I have tracked despair, hunted torment, and chased loss. These are my three demons, and I hate them. It seems no matter which path I walk, they've already been there, wreaked havoc, and left families torn to pieces. I drop my head and mutter a soft prayer. "If you're listening, if you can hear me, please help me. Light my path. Lead me to her."

Before pulling back onto the road I take a quick look at the green display on the dash of the Mustang. It's close to 7p.m., and I'm nearly out of options and out of hope. The only place left to go is the source. The Keep, Mario's home.

I sit across the street in silence; my eyes are locked on his house as my hands wring the wheel. The phone chimes again, this time with another text message from Mark.

Mark: Chris we just got another text. I'm going to forward it to you now.

Me: Ok

Forwarded message: Please, tell Daddy to come get me. I'm scared.

Mark: It just came through, Chris, less than a minute ago.

Me: I'm working on it, Mark.

Mark: I know."

The texts stop coming.

I know why Mark didn't call. I grew up believing that men weren't supposed to cry, and I can barely hold back the moisture building up in my eyes; He's her uncle, and there is no downplaying the cries of his niece to her sister. "Please, tell Daddy to come get me. I'm scared."

My heart grows blacker, abhorrence leaks from my eye in the form of a tear. I speak to the cosmos hoping that Haley finds the message. "Your father won't be coming tonight. He's sending something else instead."

Just then a car rounds the corner and passes me. I move my head closer to the windshield. It's Laurie. I see her, and everything in me tells me that she's seen me. She knows The Beast. She's been in it. She slows just a tad before continuing past her turn at the cul-de-sac. Dammit! She suspects I'm here. I start the engine and jam it into reverse, slipping back into the dark night and eventually out of sight. I still don't know where Haley is, and if Laurie did see me, then I may have just signed her death warrant.

I race away from their neighborhood left with one option. I just hope I can make Mark understand. I lift my phone and call dispatch, which transfers me to T.A.S., our Technical and Analytical Section. They might best be described as gadget gurus and computer whizzes.

I'm forwarded to Sergeant Fabian, to whom I quickly run down the details of my predicament. "Sarge, I need your help. I have a cooperating witness who is missing, likely abducted by a bad guy I already have up on charges. She has been able to sneak out a message every few hours, so we know she's still alive. The problem is we don't know where. I need you to get a GPS locator on her cell phone signal."

"In order for me to do what you're asking this has to be an emergency situation. You need to be able to articulate that in a warrant without a shred of uncertainty. Do you really believe her life is in jeopardy?"

"On one of the last messages, she was able to get out was a picture of her face. It was destroyed. Her cell phone's dying, and when that goes, my hopes of zeroing in on her go with it. I need those GPS coordinates, either that or at least that signal triangulated."

"Listen, Chris," he manages, clearing his throat, "even if we get it, a triangulation won't give you an exact location. We're talking anywhere from a twenty- to two-hundred-yard radius."

"Just get me in the ballpark, Sarge. I'll find my own way from there."

"Dammit! How much time are you giving me to get this set up?"

"Time is the one thing I don't have."

"It could take hours before everything is online."

"Well, you'll just need to be very persuasive. We have, *maybe*, one more shot at catching her signal. You'll have that warrant signed and on your desk come Monday morning. Sarge, right now, I need you to make a miracle happen."

I can tell he's frustrated, maybe at me, or maybe by the parameters in which he's forced to work. "All right, I've got a few friends at some of the cell phone providers. Maybe I can pull some strings. I'll contact you at this number once I've figured out what the hell I can do."

"I'll be waiting. Thank you."

Now comes the hard part. I'll have to explain to Mark that we'll need to wait...again. His phone chimes only once before it's answered. "Chris, where are we? Have you found her?"

"No, I don't have her yet. We know where she isn't, but unfortunately that doesn't tell us where she is."

"So what's the next step?"

"I'm working on something," I manage with a sigh, offering a tone which begs for understanding. "But it's going to take a little more time to develop. We need to wait."

"Wait? What do you mean wait?" His voice cracks with pain. "What is going on out there? You've been looking for her all day, and nothing! We're trusting you...you told us that you could..."

"Mark—"

"No! No, it's almost eleven at night, and you still don't have her!"

"Mark, we're close!" I have to raise my voice an octave just to get through to him. "I know the family is terrified." I drop my voice back to a calmer level. "I just need you to keep them strong, keep them together just a little longer. I'm not asking that you trust me...but trust that someone or something out there bigger than me wants Haley home with you."

"I'm sorry...this is...this all just, it feels like a nightmare none of us can wake from."

"I know...a little longer, Mark. Please."

"I'll see to the family," Mark answers in a whisper. "Do your best, Detective, but we can't keep waiting. We just can't."

I have no words. Besides, what would they be worth at this point? I press end on my cell phone.

Drained by the sun, and beaten by the stress, I pull into my driveway, park and flop back in my seat. My head bounces off the headrest, and I exhale.

It's after eleven. I unlock my door and step into my now silent home. It's dark and everyone is sleeping. I don't bother hitting the lights. Instead, I sit on the couch, placing my gun, badge, and vest beside me. I pull my phone from my pocket and look at the screen.

One new text. "Chris it's Fabian. Good news and bad news. Good news, we're up and running on that number. They've approved your request for the triangulation and bumped you to the top of the list. We're just waiting for the GPS to come through now. I've listed your number as a recipient, you should receive any coordinates that they pick up. Bad news. Either her cell phone is dead, or she turned it off. There's no signal, which means there's no way for us to key in on her. Good Luck!"

I crank the ringer on the phone and sit in the darkness. With heavy eyes I drift in and out of sleep. My nerves are shot, my body is depleted, and now, even my confidence is waning. I wake sporadically throughout the night, jumping to my feet and grabbing the phone, fearing that I'd missed her. Eleven turns to twelve, twelve to one.

My dreams are the kinds that wake children from slumber screaming that monsters exist. I can no longer tell the difference between my nightmares and my reality. The only thing I know for sure is that in our darkest hour, like a whisper from an angel, comes a sign from my city, my queen.

The phone vibrates! The coordinates! MOVE YOUR ASS, CHRIS! NOW!

26
The Last Bastion

At two in the morning, not even the birds chirp. The only sound comes from my tactical vest, as the zipper's teeth interlock. I clip my badge to the waistband and toss my backpack into the rear seat. Lastly, the sword, the black German is sheathed. Into the vest holster she goes, close to my heart. Well, at least what I have left of it.

I leap into the driver's seat, tense up my legs and summon The Beast to awaken. The engine breathes fire as I peal out the driveway.

I look to my phone and enter the longitude and latitude. The coordinates place her last transmission less than two blocks away from 120 Stonewood Circle.

The sound of soft static comes from my police radio. I lift it and request that two patrol officers meet me at the guard booth outside his neighborhood. The dispatcher copies and sends them in that direction. I hit the freeway and peek at the speedometer, now already on the red line.

I once met a holy man who asked me, "Christopher, do you know the way to Heaven?" I didn't have an answer for him then, and I still don't to this day. What I do know is that there's a back road heading straight into Hell. The drop in is unrelenting, furious, and fast. The engine snorts and the fans kick on. The temperature's rising.

My ears catch faint whispers. The closer I draw to the demon's neighborhood, the clearer and more pronounced they become. They are the voices of the dying, the lost, and the damned. Their moans and pitiful wishes alert the devil's gatekeeper. I can all but feel his sulfuric eyes on me. "We welcome you, boy! But the pretty one named Haley is ours. You'll never leave here with her."

There's no need to welcome me. I won't be staying long, and I don't plan on leaving here alone.

I exit the freeway and just ahead, the guard booth shines like a lighthouse in the darkness. Already parked beside it are two patrol cars with the officers standing sentry and awaiting instruction.

"Thanks for getting here so quickly." I extend my hand and shake both of theirs. "I'm Detective Baughman, we're here looking for a missing woman. Her name's Haley Harrison." I quickly run down the events that led us to this point before laying out the plan.

"So, we start off with a ruse. You two knock on the door. It doesn't matter who answers it. You tell them that a 911 disconnect came from this house, and we need to make sure everything's okay. Any questions?" With a tight nod of their heads, they both seem ready to go. "All right then. Turn your portables down and follow me in. No headlights, let's keep them in the dark as long as possible."

Under the cover of night, our advance begins. Soon we come upon it–The Last Bastion. On the outside, this estate home looks warm, comforting, but the façade doesn't fool me. I know well who lives here. At this distance, I can even feel it. There is darkness here; this is a house of horrors.

At the far corner of the intersection, I roll to a quiet stop, exit, and softly push my car door closed. My dark jeans, black shoes, shirt, and vest should render me nearly invisible. As the patrol cars fall into place I turn and raise my finger to my lips. "Shhh."

We move along the side of the street, crouched, then use the grass in the front yard. The sprinklers have dampened the soil enough to muffle the sound of our feet. The exterior, along with the interior lighting, is all turned off tonight. Fortune smiles upon us as we sidestep through a half-opened gate into the courtyard.

After motioning the two officers to move ahead of me, I take a step back behind them. If Mario or any woman other than Haley should see me too soon, this could quickly escalate from a rescue into a hostage situation. I fade further into the deep corner of the courtyard. For the moment, I submit myself to the shadows and become invisible inside the darkness.

The officers move into position near the front door and I give the command. My voice pierces the shadows. "Let's go."

The officer closest to the door slowly raises his right arm and simultaneously balls his fist. Bang! Bang! Bang! The wooden door rattles. "Hello! It's the Metropolitan Police Department! Please come to the door!" Bang! Bang! His knuckles smash into the door's dense wood. "Hello! We just need to make sure you're okay! There was a 911 disconnect. Please just come to the door! Hello?"

From my darkened perch, my eyes roll from window to window. A bedroom light flickers. Seconds later, another light illuminates the hallway, and finally, a lamp spreads light throughout the living room. My eyes move to the frosted glass at the center of the door. I can just make out the image of a figure moving towards it.

The dead bolt draws back, and the door is cracked open. From behind it peeks the pregnant Laurie, her belly showing from the other side of the door. Her bug-eyes, clammy skin, and stutter tell me she's terrified. Oh Laurie, if you only knew what lurked in the blackness.

"Um, can… can I help you?" she asks, her timid voice is barely audible.

"Yes ma'am, you can. We had a 911 disconnect from this address. We're just checking to make sure that everyone and everything is okay."

"Oh, um," She takes a quick glance behind her. "No, we're uh, umm, none of us called the police. But thank you for coming by to…"

"You said 'none of *us*,' ma'am? Is there someone else here with you?" The officers perform masterfully. That's right gentlemen, use her words against her.

"Waa…um, well, just…just my boyfriend. He's sleeping in…in the back."

"Well, do you mind if we come in, just to check things out?"

"No, I mean I don't want…let me, let me just go get him for you. Wait outside for a minute. I'll be right back."

The officer slyly sticks his foot at the jamb to keep the door from closing. Laurie waddles down the hallway, eventually fading into the background. That's right, run to him. After all, he *is* Daddy.

I see through the frosted glass two, silhouettes moving closer. The door's joints creak as it's pulled back wide. He steps forward, wearing a charming smile. Careful, my friends. This man is not what he seems. He stretches his arms to the sky, "Oh, it's late. What seems to be the problem officers?"

"Well, it's just like we were telling the lady. We had a 911 disconnect from here."

"Hmm. I wonder if it could have been some kind of mistake on your end. We were both sleeping. Are you sure it couldn't have come from one of our neighbors' houses? There's no one here but us, and as you can see…" Mario looks back at Laurie with a smirk. She still looks ill. I'd venture it's not from morning sickness. "No one's hurt here."

He's perfectly calm. Me, I've fallen victim to my darker side yet again. I look at Mario. No, I look through him. There are times when we can't express odium through words. It's in these moments that this hatred, this energy, transforms itself into matter. It leaks out through the windows of our souls. Mine becomes a tear, which I wipe away while waiting in the dark.

Bury yourself, motherfucker. I'm watching you!

The wood from the door frame bears his right shoulder as he leans casually against it. He opens his mouth again; his demeanor is arrogant, confident, and petulant. "If you don't mind, I'd like to get back to sleep." He masks his disdain with more smiles. "So, unless there's something else you officers need…"

"Actually, there is," Dead leaves crackle beneath my feet as I take one step forward. Mario's head snaps toward the shadows.

That's right, you piece of shit, look deeper into the black.

27
Angels

With another step, I shed the darkness like a cloak. "I want Haley NOW!"

His brow furls, his eyes bulge. The arrogance, charm, and self confidence built up through a lifetime suddenly evaporate. He has no more arrogant smiles or quick quips. Like a punch drunk boxer, he stumbles out the front door, staggers past the two officers, and makes his way towards me. My jaw is cinched, and my fists clenched. *Give me one reason, just one, to drop your sorry ass.*

He gets closer and, in a way none of us expected, explodes. Tears stream from his eyes and snot drips from the tip of his nose. "Jesus! C...Chris. I...I, it wasn't me. I, I didn't do it. You gotta believe me, man."

He can't stand up straight, nor does he dare look me in the eyes. Instead he grovels, hunched over, half-curled, half-standing. Half-man, half-maggot. "It... it was, it was some John who hired her...a trick! Yeah, a trick did it. He beat her. He beat her, and left her. She, she called me! I, I had to go get her, and, and bring her here! I couldn't take her home looking the way she does. Her parents don't know what she does. It would have destroyed them." He leans forward, placing both hands on my chest. "Please...help me. Help me help her."

My eyes shift from the Mario to the woman carrying his seed. She's stands just inside the doorway frozen. *Take it in, Laurie. This is the true measure of the man that played God with your life.* As I look at Laurie, there's movement just behind her, something in the hallway.

"Jesus!" A patrolman bellows, pushing his way past her, and moving down the hallway into the shadows. "We've got you, Haley. We've got you."

From where I stand in the courtyard, I can hear her. Haley's soft whimpers are somehow strong enough to drown out Mario's lies. But still he continues pleading. "Ask her...bring her out here right now, and ask her. Ask Laurie. She'll tell you it wasn't me. That's not my style, that's not what I do. I...I, just need you to...."

I look past his contorted face, into the house. My mind mutes out his voice. The officer emerges with Haley, his body engulfing hers. I can only make out the few parts of her left exposed. Bloody knees, raw elbows, scratched skin, and a face...a face I can barely recognize. The second officer moves in to make sure Laurie doesn't become a threat.

Haley is carried from the hallway towards the kitchen. As they pass the doorway, she looks over her shoulder. One eye has been reduced to a pulp, and the other is barely open. Still, somehow she sees me. For less than one second, our eyes lock. Haley's emotions bear down on her, her body goes limp, and tears once held captive run freely.

She's taken from my line of sight, so now all attention turns back to Mario. He's still rambling, with his mouth moving, blabbering...blabbering. He once said he was ill, and that I can help him.

But I'm not myself. In this moment, my vision can only see red. I could wrap my hands around his neck and squeeze the sickness from his body. Who would care? Who would fault me? But then I'd become the monster. How would that play out? Eyewitness news: "Officer attacks alleged suspect...more police brutality. Details at eleven."

To calm myself I look to the sky, in search of my guiding star. Where is Vega? Soon I find it, shining in a sea of black. I drop my gaze back to him and close the distance between us. He's still going on about Haley's misfortune with a violent client. "She called me. This guy beat her, and...and took all her money...he, he robbed..."

"Shut up."

"Chris…I'm trying to tell you…"

"SHUT YOUR FUCKING MOUTH! Turn around…give me your hands." I place him in cuffs and direct him to a small chair in the courtyard. "Sit down. I don't want to hear another word from you. You won't speak again, to anyone. Just shut your mouth." He collapses onto the chair with slumped shoulders.

I step over to the officer who stands outside with Laurie. "Can you call the crime scene analysts? We need to get pictures of Haley as soon as possible, and please, keep tabs on him. If he moves, or says one word, come and get me."

I walk through the living room and stop just outside the kitchen, reminding myself to walk softly. Haley is perched on a dining room chair and has her knees pulled up to her chest. My eyes tally the damage. Small droplets of blood seep through the fabric of her pajama pants. Her face is buried between the damaged skin on her knees. Deep purple bruises cover her shins and ankles. She wraps her arms around them, trying to comfort herself while trying to cover the injuries. Her hands are raked by scrapes, scratches, and nicks, clearly defense wounds. More knots and welts torment what once were flawless, smooth arms. At the edge of her T-shirt sleeves, there's more deep bruising. Blood has settled under her skin, just above her bicep, likely from him grabbing there to fling her down.

This shame should not be hers to carry. This is Mario Merchant Davis's cross to bear. She's still crying, still hurting. I walk closer still, whispering in the ear of the officer who carried her into the kitchen. "Please, find me a blanket for her."

As he steps away, I inch closer. On the back of her neck and the top of her shoulders, more discolored welts. And her hair! Jesus…he did it again. Haley's beautiful, fierce red hair…butchered! God! I drop to my knees. "Haley…" My throat tightens, and my eyes well up as I whisper her name.

Another stolen daughter slowly lifts her face. I first see misshapen knots all across her hairline. The swelling around her left orbital socket is extensive, so much so that swollen purple slits have replaced her eyelids. Her brown eyes aren't much visible anymore. As tears stream down her bloated cheeks, she moves her head to the left slightly. She looks at me with the only eye she can open. The vessels inside it have burst. The once-ivory parts are blood red, a tell-tale sign of strangulation.

I gently take her hands in mine. In return, she squeezes firmly. "Haley, I'm here. Your Uncle Mark sent me."

At the mention of her family, her tears pour down like rain. She releases my hands and gingerly slides herself off the chair and onto her knees. My arms drop like weights and hang at my sides. She leans into me and wraps both arms around my torso. She's spent, but still finds the wherewithal to string together a few words. "I…I knew you would c…come…for, me. I knew wo…would find me."

My heart pours out onto the floor. In her blackest hour, when Satan himself had risen to lay claim on her life, she held out hope for me. "Shhh." I cradle her head with my right hand and feel more contusions that have formed on the top of her skull, buried beneath what's left of her mutilated hair. I wrap her in the blanket, and lift her from the chair. "Your family is waiting. We're leaving soon." I gently lift her from the floor, and carry her out to the Mustang. We pass by Mario, I make sure to keep her body and face turned away. My eyes cut through him like razors. I could kill him. Maybe in another place, in another life, I'll have my opportunity. Tonight though is about Haley, and her return from the darkness.

Safely tucked into my passenger seat, Haley tells me just enough to allow for the initial arrest. She manages to give me the tales of her torment, and how Sadie was told to deliver her to this house.

"Haley, I have CSI coming to photograph your injuries, and medical coming to make sure that, physically, you'll be okay. Once that's over I'm going to take you home. I have to handle a few things, but I'll be right back."

Haley leans her head back and exhales, she sinks into the leather as I shut the door. I'd love to stop the presses and serve another warrant on this place tonight, but Haley's been through enough, and her family has already waited an eternity for her return. I give instruction that Mario is to be taken to city jail and booked for domestic violence. Those charges should give me at least twelve hours. I just hope that's enough time for me to get her home, rest, and start again semi-fresh in the morning.

Mario's escorted from the courtyard to the transport just as he should be, in shackles and bound by cuffs. After seeing him off, I make my way back to Haley. The police photographer has just finished documenting her wounds.

After putting Haley back in the car, I move around to the driver side to join her. I pull my phone from my pocket, plop down, drop my head, and sigh.

"Chris?" asks Haley, the sound of her voice altered by her swollen lips, "my family doesn't know what I was doing for him." She seems scared, or maybe ashamed. I know what she's thinking. How can I go home? Will they ever accept me?

"I'll tell you what I know. Your family never stopped fighting for you. They would have had me burn this city down to find you, and I would have done it." With phone in hand I scroll through a list of numbers before punching the dial button. "Haley, there's someone that wants to hear your voice." I hand her the phone. She lifts it slowly, and gingerly presses it against her swollen ear.

It's quiet enough in the car that I can hear the voice coming from the phone. Mark answers frenzied, "Chris! Hello?! Chris!"

Haley breaks down in tears. Her sobs echo from the heart of my city all the way to Orange County, to an uncle who never let go. "Uncle Mark...it's me. It's Haley."

"Haley...we love you, baby." Mark's voice cracks as the weight of uncertainty is lifted from his shoulders. The words cease. Sometimes tears and silence can say so much more.

She is still a wreck as she hands me the phone, and so she curls back into a fetal position, crying into her knees.

"Hey, Mark," Silence. I can hear him, I can feel him. I know what he wants to say, and he knows he doesn't need to. "We're about to leave here. Call Mike and Betty. Tell them their baby is coming home."

After cranking the ignition, I settle in for the long journey home. Beside me sits a broken angel, one who may feel she's returning to people who don't know her.

I can't help but think of what Haley feared most. Did she believe for one moment her family wouldn't be waiting with arms stretched open to welcome her back? Life has taught me a thing or two about homecomings. Our minds are amazing creations, but not even they can fully comprehend the power of the human heart, or the undeniable strength of family.

I glance over and find her sleeping, her head resting on the door as she breathes heavily. Rest well, dear sister. Too many demons walk this earth, but for those of us called to face them we aren't left without hope, for if they exist, then so, too, must angels.

After the long drive she's starting to rouse. "Chris," she whispers, "Mario had like sixty thousand in that house."

"Shh, Haley, just try to rest. There's nothing more valuable than what I went there for in the first place. Now I've got you. We can talk about everything, but not tonight. I'll be by tomorrow evening. I've still got a lot to do."

She nods and gently lays her head back against the door. We turn another corner and pull into a quiet neighborhood at the far-east end of the city. Haley sniffles and wipes her eyes as best she can. I pull up to an older home. Parked in the driveway are a couple of weathered pickup trucks. The canopy of large tree in the front yard stretches out over both the side walk and the roof. I can't even get the car in park before two people come sprinting from around the corner. Mike is an older man who is the size of a bear; his hair is just as brown. Running step-for-step beside him is a woman–Betty, I assume—the spitting image of Haley, with the exception of a few years. She carries an unfolded blanket, its edges dance in the wind. Making a beeline to the passenger side of the car, she screams out in tears, "Haley!"

Opening my car door, I step out. The great grizzly charges me. Tears in his eyes, I can't tell if he wants to thank me or kill me. As he closes in, I get ready for the worst, quickly trying to announce that I play for the good guys. "Hi, I'm detect...Uhgh," I can't get out the words, I can't breathe. The giant scoops me up in his arms bear-hug style. My feet dangle, toes barely scraping the pavement. What else should I have expected?

He's massive, powerful, the epitome of a father, and he's in tears. He's proof that real men do cry, but only the best of us can admit it. Mike clears his throat, sets me down and wipes his face. "Thank you...thank you for bringing my baby home. As long as I live, I'll always owe you."

Betty pulls open the passenger side door and wraps Haley in both the blanket and a heart-breaking, motherly embrace. Mike rushes over and lifts his little princess off her feet. The blanket sways in the air. Haley turns her head to find my eyes once more. I'm left in awe. With Betty beside him, Mike carries Haley home. She's safe now, in the arms of her true daddy. As they move onto the house, I stand alone once again, a figure in the darkness. Perhaps I'm not alone, after all. I feel the glow, the satisfaction of my city.

I lean against frame of The Beast and wipe the tears from my cheeks. Perhaps my heart does have some life left in it. I look to the heavens in search of the Angels, "Thank you...thank you."

28
The Event

There are dozens of good reasons to return to Mario's place, since I'm sure more evidence is just waiting to be gathered there. Unfortunately, I'm up against the clock. Again. I figured I had twelve hours to complete my work here, serve the warrant at Mario's home and hopefully re-arrest him for a whole list of charges, not the least of which is first degree kidnapping. Of course, that was over nine hours ago. If I don't finish this quickly, he could make bail and vanish.

I complete the warrant for the homes–both Sadie's and Mario's–and in short order, get the judge's signature and the power to proceed.

Trey and Al meet me outside the house we pulled Haley from only hours ago. "Damn, you don't look so good, bro," says Al as he walks up, glancing into The Beast.

"Yeah. Yesterday was hell. Thanks for coming so quickly."

"So what we got, kid?" Trey crosses his arms while giving a little head-nod.

I explain the circumstances from the previous night, stressing the point that we need to find evidence to support the verbal statement that Haley gave me yesterday.

"So what are we talking about, exactly?" Al asks, now peering down the street at the house.

"Blood evidence, trace stuff, hair, soiled clothing and anything in that vein. Right after that, though, we're heading to Sadie's. I think that's where it all started."

"All right then," Trey speaks up. "Let's vest up and pay this asshole another visit."

As we move through the front yard and enter the courtyard, things feel a bit different. No shadows, no sneaking, no hiding, and no guessing. I know that what lies in this house is the key to Mario's demise. Al and Trey stand behind me, one at each side. The sound of our knocking brings Sadie Ortega to the door.

"Ummm, hi," she manages, her voice choking from shame. Nerves have her biting her bottom lip.

"We're back. Where's Mario?"

"I...I don't know," she says timidly, moving a strand of long dark hair out of her face. "After he bailed out, he came here for a second, grabbed some stuff and just left." I rest my hand on the frame of the door and lean in, tilting my head as I look into her eyes. Is she being honest, or is she still under a trance? I catch a hint of frustration in her voice.

"He left," I ask, "and didn't make mention of where he was going?"

"He just, he just does whatever he wants. He doesn't tell us shit, and we know better than to ask." As Sadie speaks, Laurie wobbles in from the kitchen and stands behind her.

"All right, we'll talk about all of this later, alone." I acknowledge Laurie's presence with a nod. "We have another warrant." Sadie doesn't bother speaking. Her shoulders drop like anchors as she lowers her head and steps aside.

"Is there anyone else here?" I ask, leading the two women to the living room couch.

"No, just us."

"Trey, Al, would you mind clearing this place?"

They un-holster their side arms and step into the depths of the house. I stand just opposite Sadie and Laurie waiting for my partners to return.

"Is, is she going to be okay?" Sadie asks, looking up from the couch, crestfallen.

Trey and Al round the corner, taking away my opportunity to answer. I'm not sure I would have anyway, given the fact she'd probably only report back to Mario.

I huddle with my partners in a semi-circle, careful not to let the ladies out of our sight, or hear our words.

"We have a little blood in one of the bathrooms," reports Al in a near whisper, "and what looks like a couple strands of hair on the floor. Red hair."

Trey picks up where Al leaves off. Frustrated, he blows air out of his cheeks and shakes his head. "So, in the southeast bedroom there's, there's a blanket laid out on the floor. It uh, it looked like a mat someone might lay out for a dog."

"Huh?" I say, raising my eyebrows. "What do you mean?"

"Chris, I think he made her lay on the floor like she was a fucking animal. There's blood on the blanket."

"What?"

"Yeah, kid. But that ain't the worst of it." Trey rubs the stress off the back of his neck. "Beside the mat," his voice drops to a whisper, "there's hair, a shit load of it, inside of a plastic grocery bag."

"Damn!" Al says, who doesn't keep his voice lowered.

"Al, c'mon, keep it low." I place my hands on both of their shoulders. "I need to speak with Sadie. Contact our crime scene analysts. Tell them we'll need them to swab some blood, collect trace evidence, and shoot some digitals."

"Sure, kid," answers Trey, tucking his gun back into his holster.

Now it's time to see what Sadie knows. She has questions about Haley, and I have questions about Mario. I take a quick stroll through the house looking for the best place to hold this conversation. I settle on the master bedroom's walk-in closet. I step back through the maze of halls to retrieve Sadie. "Ms. Ortega, it's time we had that conversation."

At the sound of my voice, she turns her head, nearly in tears. I push closed the door behind us, mindful to leave it cracked slightly. Sadie moves to the far end and turns to face me, the tears already streaming from her eyes. "Is she going to be okay?" Sadie cries out. "Please, please tell me." It pains me to hurt her, but right now, her agony's a commodity.

"So, you've got questions." I cross my arms and take one step closer. "Good. I've got questions, too. What happened, Sadie?"

"I can't talk to you. He'll...he'll..." Her face is covered in tears. She drops her head and she begins shaking it repeatedly.

"He'll what?"

Sadie still doesn't answer me. At the moment, all she can offer is more tears and an occasional gasp.

"Sadie, tell me WHAT HAPPENED."

"WHEN I WALKED IN, HE WAS STANDING OVER HER!" she screams with clenched fists. "BLOOD WAS EVERYWHERE. HE...HE WAS SMASHING HER FACE IN WITH HIS FISTS!" Sadie's face is red and her breathing is ragged. She's experiencing it all over again. "I, I screamed. I begged him to please, please stop. He didn't, though. He didn't care. I couldn't help her." She pauses, unclenches her fists and covers her face. "I started crying. He...he told me, 'Shut up, bitch...or you're next.' Haley was just lying there, like she was dead. He kept punching her face. When he finally stopped, he told me, 'Clean this shit up, and drive this bitch over to my house.' "

"Sadie..." I drop my head and massage my temples.

"So, I did it...I dr...drove her down."

"You brought her here? Of all places."

"I tried to help her, I tried." Sadie collapses, and her knees dig into the carpet.

"This? This is your idea of help?"

"I stopped at Walgreens and went inside," she replies in a whisper. "I left the car running. She could have driven away."

"Sadie. How?" I crouch down, and look onto her drenched face. "Haley couldn't walk. Her eyes were destroyed. She couldn't even see out of them."

"When I got back in the car, she was still there, still bleeding." Sadie looks at me, and brushes away tears with her hands. "She could barely talk, her mouth was so messed up. But she kept saying, 'I wanna go home. Please...take me...home. I want my mommy and daddy.'"

As Sadie tells her story, emotionally I'm caught somewhere between anger and pity. Who would place another human in such a position?

Sadie's tears are overwhelming, and sobs muffle her words. "Chris, I was crying so badly. I couldn't. I, I, t...to...told her that I couldn't or he'd kill me.'"

"Sadie, I need you to listen. You will give Mario a message for me. Tell him, if I don't hear from him before the sun sets, the next door I'm going to kick in will be his mother's. If I don't find him there, I'll go to his grandmother's house. I won't stop there. His cousins will be next, then his nephews and nieces. I won't stop. Our issue will become a family issue, his family. Do you understand?" Sadie looks up and nods, still shedding tears.

I run my hand across the top of my head, and again I ask myself, who are the victims here, and who are the monsters? "Shhh. Shh. It's okay." I extend my hand. "You know, Sadie, this doesn't have to be your life. Come on, let me help you up."

If there's one thing I know, it's that truth can weigh heavily on us. I see it in her as she stammers through the hallway on her way back to the couch. She plops down sinking into the cushions and fabric. I move back to Trey, who watches her with pity in his eyes.

"Where's Al?"

"He's outside with the evidence techs. They've already recovered and photographed everything." Trey looks awestruck, still staring at Sadie. "Jesus, Chris, she looks like a train wreck. Is that the same woman who walked back with you?"

"I pray to God it isn't, Trey. But one can never be sure."

"What the hell did you do to her?"

"Not much. I suppose if I did anything at all it was to help her see what was right in front of her. And maybe she got a good look for the very first time."

"Well, do me a favor, would you?"

"Sure"

"Don't ever do that to me. My life's been a horror story. The last thing I need is to relive it in HD."

"Deal."

"Let's get the outta here, kid," Trey grins. "We got one more spot to hit."

Sadie's house is spotless. I'm hunched over, scouring the living room floor. Not a drop of blood on the tile. Even though there's still plenty of daylight, I pull out my high-intensity flashlight and aim it at the floor. I need more illumination on the grout. The soft sound of feet stepping to and from comes from the ceiling as Al and Trey search upstairs. Still, we've got nothing. Not a sign, clue, or even a hint that this was even the original scene of the crime. It's time to take a deep breath and try to see this scene as a whole.

I walk to the front door and turn around to face the living room. Two plush, dark-colored couches fill most of the space. One is a love seat; the other full-sized. They're situated in the classic L pattern. Completing the square is a rectangular coffee table. A few small pillows meant to compliment the furniture are scattered on each couch. The white walls inside the house don't look as if they've been touched. Not one picture hangs from them.

I close my eyes and recount the details. Haley is lying on the couch, but which one? I look at them both, surmising the love seat's too small. In bursts Mario. He grabs Haley, who screams and then drops her phone. Mario flings her to the ground. But in front of which couch? It couldn't be at the elbow where the two couches meet, there's not enough room for him to stand above her.

I press the reset button in my mind I start over. Haley is lying on the couch. In bursts Mario. She screams. He flings her down in front of the long couch near the open end. He strikes her, again and again. Blood spills from her face. But where does it go? If she was bleeding as badly as Sadie said, it would have been on his fists, arms, chest, and face. A bloodbath. How hard did he drive his fists into her face, and what type of momentum did he build? And lastly, how fast was he punching her. Could there have been enough force to...

I run to the wall behind the long couch. There! On the flat white wall my eyes catch a hint of red, a tiny, near invisible speck of blood. I move closer. The spatter trails away, and the tail end of each droplet points me in the right direction. As I look more closely, there's blood everywhere. The faint trail of blood specks leads me down the hallway ending near a dull pink swipe. More accurately, smeared blood. Just on the other side of the swipe, a bathroom door. I lean in closer, and find more blood droplets on the door, but they are all incredibly small.

At last, the case against this animal starts to solidify. "Al, Trey, we got it!"

To have allies one can trust is an invaluable resource. Al and Trey will remain at this house to oversee evidence collection. In the meantime, I've got other business to tend to, and it starts at the Harrison residence.

As I pull away, a dull flashing red light catches my eye from the passenger seat. The message light on my cell phone is on fire. Four missed calls. Before I can check any of them the ringer goes off once more, on the screen, an unfamiliar number.

"Hello?"

"Hi, I'm looking for a Detective Baughman."

"You found him. May I ask who's looking?"

"Of course, of course, but first let me tell you how much I appreciate all the hard work you're doing, keeping the city safe and all."

"Hmm…" I'm reminded there are snakes in the water, and I need to mind my tongue. His words sound like the same cardboard greetings I've received from so many defense attorneys.

"Well, I'm calling on behalf of my client…" Let me guess. "…Mario Davis. I can assure you, he intends on cooperating fully, and he wants to do everything he can to help you get to the bottom of this."

What is that saying? Something to the effect of throwing up a little in my mouth? "Is that so?"

"Yes, it is. He's already informed me about the domestic violence allegations."

"Allegations of domestic violence."

"Yes, yes."

"That's funny. Running to God-knows-where and hiding after making bail on a DV charge hardly seem like the actions of a cooperative person. You know, if he told you I was coming after him because of DV, well let's just say he was being less than honest."

"Well, I don't want to know everything my client is involved in, you understand."

I continue weaving my way through the city's streets, quickly growing tired of the individual at the other end of the phone. "I'm sure you don't. But if he isn't up front with you, do you honestly think you can defend him?"

"I hope you aren't implying that I won't perform for my client." He replies in a rather maligned tone. Interesting, it seems I've struck a nerve.

"Me? Nah. You sound like a smart guy, and I've no doubt you'll treat and defend him as if he were an innocent man. But you might consider having a rather candid conversation with your client. What do you want?"

"I'm calling to ask if you'd stop hunting him."

Hunting, now that's an interesting word choice. Of course, though, it's entirely fitting. "Stop hunting him. And why would I do that?"

"Because, Detective, he wants to turn himself in. Of course, we would ask you give him some time to get a few things in order, family issues and such. Can we agree on a week?"

"No, we cannot. I'll have the arrest warrant for Mario in three days. I expect you'll be turning him in?"

"Yes, that's unless I can get you to agree to let me go before a judge to get the warrants quashed?"

He must be joking. Getting the warrants quashed would mean Mario could continue roaming the streets. Most importantly, he could avoid another booking into County Correctional, the place I seem to be making his home away from home. "That's not going to happen. I'll see your client in three days behind County. Nice talking to you."

I pull into Haley Harrison's neighborhood accompanied by a stomach full of knots. After a few knocks the door opens, I'm greeted by Betty, Haley's radiant mother. Her hazel eyes appear bottomless, and the tears in them lie still. "Chris!" she cries while folding me into a firm hug. "Please, come in. I'm sorry about the mess." I enter and scan the room. On the walls, plenty of family pictures show a proud mother, a strong father, and young lady with a head full of red hair standing beside her sister and younger brother. "I was just in the middle of spring cleaning when everything happened. Please, don't mind the boxes. Haley's been in and out of sleep since you brought her home. She's here, on the couch." I step further into the living room and look to my left. She's huddled on the couch, covered in a blanket, finally safe and resting comfortably.

"Has she been resting well?" I whisper.

"How can I rest with you talking so loud," says a muffled and still raspy voice. "And Chris, whoever taught you how to whisper did a terrible job." She laughs softly, and winces in pain.

"Hey, I told you I'd be back." I move closer, taking a seat at the edge of the couch nearest her feet. I look at her face. The swelling is getting worse, or better. At this point I can't tell.

Haley cracks her swollen eyelids, and looks at me, and in that moment I'm reminded why I'm here. Why I love. Why I hate, and lastly, why this war will define my very life. "I'm glad you're here."

"You may not be for long," I say, placing my hand on the blanket and rubbing her ankle gently. "Haley, we need to talk about what happened."

"I know," she closes her eyes, "but I'm still happy you're here."

"So, you're ready?"

"Mm-hmm. I want to tell you everything."

"I'll be in another room," says Betty. "I don't think I can bear to hear all of this." She looks at Haley, "I love you, baby."

"Haley, let me explain why I'm recording this."

"It doesn't matter. I trust you."

"All right. When I start this tape, just tell me the story. How you met, everything up until this point. Okay?"

She nods. I hit record. We begin.

29

The Void

"I met Mario on August 13th, almost seven-and-a-half years ago, through his cousin. I was at a night club. We just started talking. He was a pimp then, and I knew it. He started telling me of ways I could make money. I was on drugs then. I've been clean ever since," she says, stifling a smile. "So I guess that's at least one good thing that came from all of this. Well, anyway, everything he said sounded good, so he convinced me to start working for him.

"We'd been fighting for the past two months, off and on, basically ever since you came along. Since then, I'd been thinking about leaving. I didn't want to be there. I guess I made it kinda obvious, he noticed my demeanor changing and everything. On Friday, May 2nd, God, was that just yesterday? Anyway, I woke up around two o'clock in the afternoon, and saw him going through my phone. He found some numbers in there he didn't know, didn't like, and some text messages. We started arguing again. He picked me up off the couch and flung me across the floor." Haley pauses, tears seep from the corners of her blackened eyes.

"He sat on my arms, and beat my face in with his fists. He kept hitting the left side of my face. He hit the right side a few times, too. I remember him getting off of me and calling some of the numbers in the phone and yelling at people. He dragged me upstairs. He put me in a closet, and started in on me again. My face, my ribs…he hit me so hard in the head my whole body started shaking. I remember him standing over me. My body went numb, but I could see him, still pounding away on my head. It was like I was outside of my body, watching him destroy me.

"I finally must have blacked out. I remember opening my eyes, and I couldn't feel anything, but I was like convulsing, and he was still going. I was spitting up blood. I tried begging him to stop. I even put my hands in the air to show him how bad my fingers were shaking. I hoped he'd stop hitting me, I begged him, 'Please stop.' I said, 'You hit me somewhere wrong.' He...h...he said, 'BITCH, I DON'T GIVE A FUCK!'

"Then he called my sister. He said something to her, and she heard me screaming in the background. She hung up and called the cops. My brother-in-law called back. Mario actually told him he was busy...beating my face in."

Haley shakes her head, sniffling, and gently wipes the tears from her cheeks. " 'Yeah, I'm beating her face in,' he said. I fought to get out of the closet and made it back downstairs, and somehow ended up in the downstairs bathroom. That's when he kicked me in my kidneys. I couldn't breathe. He'd punched me in my face so many times the blood coming out of my nose had clogged it up. He covered my mouth with his hands, and I began passing out. He kept saying, 'Go to sleep...go to sleep.' I must have passed out on the bathroom floor."

Haley's tears won't stop coming. I reach to my right and grab a few Kleenex from a box sitting on an end table. With nicked up hands and swollen fingers she reaches out for them. "Take your time, Haley."

She softly blots the tears from the sides of her eyes and continues. "When I woke back up he was still going at it, still screaming, but now he was standing on my face. He was looking down at me! Laughing! His foot was on my jaw line. He was going to stomp on my face. He...he told me, 'Bitch I will break your jaw!' He said the only reason he didn't was because he needed me to go out and work. At some point, he let me go. Well, he stopped beating and kicking me, I think because one of the other girls showed up.

"They took me through the garage and put me in the car. I was begging him to let me go the whole time he was hurting me. I kept begging him, 'Please let me go home. I want to go home! Please, I just want my mom.'

"He was like, 'Bitch! I'll take you home. I'll take you home in a few weeks after you've healed up.' After that he put me in the car. I was messed up, *so* messed up. I was crying, and I begged her, " 'Please take me home. Take me anywhere, but please don't take me to his house!' She was crying, too, from looking at me. I know she was as scared as I was.

"She took me to him. She said she had to because he told her if she didn't, she was next. I mean, look at what he'd already done to me. I just remember all the blood, and the crying, both of us. She wanted to help me, but she couldn't.

"So I...I told her, 'Don't feel guilty. It's not your fault.' When we got to his house, I remember the garage door lifting up, and he was just standing there...waiting.

"He pulled me out of the car; I was too weak to fight him, too tired to stop him. He told me, 'You're in *my* house now, and no one can hear you scream.' He took me into the back bedroom and started in on me again. Slapping me, punching me. By now, my face was already swollen, I could barely see. He threatened to cut my face up, too.

"Later that afternoon, he took me to another house, because he thought the cops were going to come to his. Once it got dark, he brought me back to his place; he asked me...he asked if I wanted to be there, to stay there with him. What was I supposed to say? I told him, 'Yeah.' I was afraid if I said no, he'd hurt me worse. I didn't know what to say."

As her story comes to a close, I turn my face away and look to the light-colored carpet beneath my feet. I can feel her eyes on me, well at least what Mario had left of them. "Um, I'm going to ask you a couple of questions."

"Okay."

"So after he went through your phone, and you woke up, was he yelling at you?"

"He, no he didn't yell at me. He was calm. He just asked, 'Whose number is this? Who is this?' Before I could answer him, he hit me in the face and threw me across the floor. That's how I got this." Haley pulls back the sheet revealing her knee. It's still swollen. Some blood has begun to form a large scab over the spot where her knee should be.

"Rug burn?"

"There was no rug. This came from a wooden floor. Then he just flipped me over and just…just, that's when he sat on my arms and cut loose on me. I can remember he hit me like four times on the left side of my face. Pow! Pow! Pow! Pow! I was so scared.

"And then when he got off me, I just wanted to run, but I knew I couldn't. Who would help me with my face looking like that? There was blood on the floor 'cause my nose was bleeding. My lips were cut up and bleeding pretty badly."

"Did someone eventually show up?"

Haley answers pensively, likely not wanting to out her friend, "Yeah…um, Sadie Ortega."

"All right, and what did she have to say to him?"

"She screamed…like, like…" Haley momentarily falls silent, likely overwhelmed by these memories. "She started screaming and crying. It was like she thought he was killing me. 'Why did you do this to her? Oh my God! Look at her! What did you do? What did you do?'"

"What was his attitude?"

"He snapped at her, like he was crazy. He said, 'Shut the fuck up! Shut the fuck up! Give me the pain pills, and put her in the fucking car.'"

"Then?"

"Sadie gave me some pain medication and they walked me to her car. They put me in the car in the garage. From there she drove me, and he took the other car."

"At this point, he knew you wanted to go home. Correct?"

"I told him. At least I tried to when he was sitting on my arms smashing my face in. When he finally was done hitting me, I remember begging, 'Just let me go. I just want to go home. I just want to go home.' He laughed, 'Bitch I'll take you home in a week.'"

"And when you got to his house?"

"He just, he…"

"…he said, 'No one can hear you scream'?"

Haley shifts positions and sits up on the couch. "Yeah, he said that as soon as he got me into the garage. The garage door closed behind me, Sadie went into the house. He just had this smirk on his face, 'Bitch, I got you at my house. I can do anything to you, and now no one can hear you scream."

"Do you remember what you were thinking? I mean, at any point did you feel like you might not make it out of this?"

"Yeah, I thought he was going to hurt me bad. I was afraid for my life. I don't know if he would have killed me, or just hurt me to the point where I wished I was dead."

"What do you mean?"

Tears rain down once more. "He told me he would cut me. He said he would cut me so bad that any time I looked at myself in the mirror, even when I was fifty, I'd always remember him. That was right around the time he took me to the back of the house. He made me cut off a bunch of my hair. He said that I didn't cut off enough. I tried to tell him I couldn't reach because my ribs were so messed up from him kicking me. He put all my hair into a ponytail and chopped it off. It was down to my waist. Now it doesn't reach my ears. He kept hitting me threatening my family, saying stuff like, 'Bitch, it's me and my niggas that's gonna do your family!' I remember him telling me, 'Wait 'til I get you out of town!'"

"He threatened to take you out of town?"

"Yeah, yeah. He was saying once he got me out of town, no one would ever see me again, or be able to help me, 'cause I'd be all alone. Of course in the same breath he told me if he was wrong about all of this he would give me $15,000, and we'd leave town and have a baby together."

"What? He said that while he was beating you?"

Her silence says it all.

"Haley, is there anything more?"

"He, uh, he would act like, you know, he would be caring. Give me pain pills, and put ice on my face. It's like he'd help me get just a little more comfortable, to the point where I'd fall asleep. Then I'd open my eyes and he'd be standing over me, spitting in my face and screaming at me, 'Dirty bitch!' When I'd fall asleep, he'd come in a little later and just start beating me again. I was afraid to fall asleep. I was afraid to wake up."

"And things would go on like this for the next day and a half?"

"Yes. It started at two o'clock in the afternoon on Friday, and didn't stop until you came in through the door. Right before you got there, he laid down with me because he was afraid I was going to sneak out." Haley snickers, "Like I could run anywhere. If he wasn't with me, he would make one of the other girls watch me. He even put a baby monitor in the room so he could hear what I was doing. He finally put me in his room with him. Before he fell asleep, he cussed at me, slapped me and spit on my face again."

"All right. I know this is tough on you, but you're doing great, Haley. I've got just one more question. Did he threaten to kill you at any point?"

"Oh *yeah!* He said, 'Bitch, I could take you out to the desert and bury you.'"

"All right." I pat her ankle gently. "Operator, this is the end of this interview. The same people are present. Thank you." I stop the recorder and look into Haley's eyes. "You know, you can never go back to this man. If you ever did, he'd kill you."

Haley eyes search my own as she replies, "He would have killed me that night if it wasn't for you. It was hell, and every second he had me, I felt like I was falling deeper and deeper into it. Thank you."

I understand that hopelessness; this is a place no man or woman should ever have to travel alone. I stand and make my way to the door. "I'll call you soon, Haley. We're going to have to talk about where we go from here, okay?"

She looks at me before lying back down on the couch. Through all of this her smile is still bright enough to warm my cold heart. "Okay."

With Eliza and Haley beside us; we have him dead to rights. I pull away knowing that Hell hath no fury.

30
The Rift

In any lifetime there are factors, ebbs and flows of singular events that influence the trajectory of our lives. Behind each case are lives — people, families whose journeys have in some ways all been altered. The most elite detectives work with the idea that it's not enough to understand the elements we can control, rather we must master them. Forensics, interviews, search warrants, evidence collection, and case building all become second nature, occurring as naturally as breathing. But what is much more difficult to control are the decisions made by those we are charged with protecting, and in this instance I've lucked into having two of them. Eliza and Haley.

It's been a week since the attack and Haley's kidnapping, and soon, Mario will be taken back into custody for, amongst other charges, the crimes of Kidnap, Coercion, Battery Substantial Bodily Harm, and Pandering with Force. Once this begins, the days will fall from the calendar like dying leaves from autumn's trees. With this in mind, I pull my phone and dial Haley's number. After a few chimes Haley answers the phone. "Hello?"

"Hey, how are you feeling today?"

She answers with an exhausted sigh, "I'm tired, tired of thinking, tired of hurting. I know I'm probably not making any sense."

"I understand. Look, I was hoping I could come by this morning and talk to you. Mario is going to turn himself in pretty soon."

"Sure, I could use the company. How long 'til you get here?"

"I'm already out on the road, so I'd guess around ten minutes."

"All right, let me throw on some clothes. I'll see you when you get here."

Our call ends and her voice is gone, but something remains, a feeling, an aura, of turmoil, agitation, and extreme confusion. I could hear it interwoven through each word she spoke. Of course, if Haley is feeling this way, it won't be long before these emotions begin to manifest themselves in other ways.

Things aren't as simple as I'd like to believe. In fact, they're anything but. Deviant, manipulative, and abusive are words that best describe Mario's treatment of Haley. I can tell that Haley, for better but mainly worse, was that she believed she was in a committed relationship with him. So much so that she nearly forfeited all that she was; mind, body, and all but the last sliver of her soul. For me, saving her body was only half the battle. Truth is, if she's still in love with him, I'll have yet another mountain to climb.

Hunting these bastards isn't a science, although I often wish it were. At least in the laboratory there are absolutes, elements, equations, and measurements that produce consistent results. Scientists are bright men, so much so that they were intelligent enough to exclude the most volatile of elements of the periodic table. HE—The Human Element. Emotions hold people hostage. Love is a dangerous and complicated thing. On one hand, it's the weapon that nearly destroyed her. Of course, it was also the lifeline with which her family used to bring her back.

I park and make my trek up to Haley's home. My eyes move to the end of the walk where Haley sits outside on the porch in one of two chairs separated by a small garden table. On top of the table are two glasses of ice water. She smiles and pats the chair beside hers.

"Hey, princess," I say with a smile while lowering myself onto the empty chair and leaning back. "Ice water? Well now, aren't we the little hostess."

She smiles back at me, "The least I could do was have a cold drink ready for you." Her gaze moves to the trees branches. "Sometimes I just like to sit beneath the tree, under its shade. I've been doing it for as long as I can remember."

I take another look at Haley. Sadly, I've got to shift the conversation. "So, I got a call from Mario's attorney yesterday."

Haley sighs with obvious frustration. "Great." She drops her head and stares at the porch floor. "Everyone in this town is so damn dirty."

I don't reply, I just fiddle with my glass and wipe the moisture away with my off hand. Not everyone in my town is dirty, but the truth is that far too many are.

Haley looks up briefly, "I bet you didn't know that Mario and his attorney have been friends since high school."

I'm more concerned with her demeanor than with that last bit of news. "No I didn't know that. Go figure, a pimp and a lawyer...friends."

"Exactly. So what was he saying?" Haley's voice is full of pain.

"Just the usual, you know, 'blah, blah, blah, my client wants to cooperate. This is all a misunderstanding.' Haley, they all say the same crap. Half of the time I can't tell if they're trying to convince me or themselves that the people they represent aren't monsters."

Her eyes are still fixed on the pavement. She slowly shakes her head back and forth, "A misunderstanding..."

"Hey, don't get caught up in his words. It doesn't matter what his lawyer is saying. We have the truth, as well as the evidence to back it up. Of course that brings us to a very important topic of discussion." She lifts her head. Her eyes, dark and swollen, feel magnetic, yanking my heart right out of my chest. "Like I said, Mario is going to turn himself in soon. I need to know where you stand."

"I...I don't..."

"What I mean to say is between you and me, and this must stay between you and me, do you think you'll be able to testify against this man?" I hate that I even have to ask this question because I know the human element is a rather complicated one.

Haley takes a sip from her glass, slumps her shoulder and sighs, "I don't know if...I'm not sure, Chris. I know he's messed up, and I know he was wrong for everything he did to me, not just this time, but from the very beginning. But, I...I still kinda care about him. It sounds crazy, even to me. I know you probably don't understand."

She's wrong, I understand far more than I'd like to. Her heart is my Achilles' heel, and I fear it may leave this maggot room to fester. "No, I get it, Haley. But you have to know that you can't save him. He's lost, and if he had his way, you'd still be there with him, locked up in that house. You know there's this saying that no one man, or woman for that matter, can serve two masters. You'll have to decide what you want."

Haley wipes away tears from her eyes, "I know, it's just, it's just so hard. I've seen him do things to the other girls, but I never, I never thought he could do those things to me."

Frustrated, I fall back in my chair and look away. My qualms aren't with her, but life. Love shouldn't be a sentence; it shouldn't keep monsters safe, and set abusers free. It's bad enough I've got to fight hate, but now I've got to face off against love as well. This just keeps getting better. "I know, Haley, it's always hard. But here's something to think about; another woman came forward, another woman he hurt. You wouldn't have to do this alone."

Almost instantly she lifts her head. "Who?"

"Well, at this point I can't say because, just like you, I've got to protect her." An intermission of silence seizes the moment. Haley sniffles and cries silently. "If you know in your heart you can't, all you have to do is tell me. I'm not here to force you into anything. But I can't allow this other woman to take a risk for you that you aren't willing to take for yourself."

Still in tears, she looks into my eyes and shakes her head. "I know, I'm just afraid. I'm sorry. I hope you aren't mad at me."

"No, but are you sure about this, Haley?"

With a nod, Haley breaks down in tears. Her face sinks into the palms of her hands. It is finished. I can't press her, as much as I'd like to, it's not within me. "It's okay, Haley," I whisper. "I'll figure this out. But I'm going to need you to do something for me."

"Whatever you need," she sniffles, wiping away the last of her tears.

"I need you to swear you won't tell anyone about our conversation today. Nobody can know that you don't want to testify. I can still do a few things, but if word got out, I'd be dead in the water."

I understand. She doesn't want to play the role of executioner. I suppose that black hood is mine alone to wear.

With another nod she answers softly, "I swear. I won't stand in the way of you doing what you have to."

I'm given her word, and I accept it on its face. After all, the only things we can afford to invest in are each other, in this, the new underground railroad. Who needs to travel back five hundred years to find an America where lives are owned, collected, traded, and eliminated without a so much as thought? I still see it every day.

I finish the last of my water and stand. "All right, Haley, there's a couple things; I want you to get down to the hospital and get checked out. We just need to make sure there's no internal damage. But before you do that, I'm going to give you the number of a woman I need you to meet. Her name is Regina. She'll help with things that are out of my area of expertise."

Haley looks at me hesitantly. "Haley, she's good, she's safe, and she understands. Will you call her for me? Just a call if you get a bad feeling. I won't push it any further."

She sighs and answers. In the tone of her voice I catch a tinge of embarrassment, "All right, I'll call her today."

Haley uses her bruised arms to balance herself as she rises from the chair. After a quick hug she steps inside the house closing the door behind her. Although Haley is still with me, it's not exactly in the manner I hoped. The Human Element strikes again.

Next stop, Eliza Serra. She deserves to know what I know. I park and take my time stepping up the walkway. Now close to the door, my sense of smell kicks into high gear. It seems like the cooking never stops at their home.

After two knocks Adelia opens it. The smile on her face is warm, "Christobal, please…" she extends her right arm and guides me to the front office area. Before I can take my seat I'm engulfed in a motherly embrace. "Now, you sit. I go get Eliza."

I hear the light patter of feet bounding down steps and twist my neck just in time to see Eliza hop off the last step. "I was starting to think you'd forgotten about me," she states in her usual light manner.

"You know better than that. I've just been busy dealing with a few new developments." Eliza plops down in the seat beside me. I lower my head as I tap my thumb on my thigh with nervous anticipation. "I need to fill you in on everything that's happened."

"Developments?"

The serious look on my face all but kills the smile on hers. "All right, um, Eliza, something, something bad has happened.

31
The Pain

This culture is designed to protect the men who rule it; they destroy women, causing such damage. Physical, psychological, and spiritual, and the turn of recent events have left me frustrated.

"Chris, you can tell me."

"All right. Mario…he, uh, he did it again."

Eliza wrings her hands and hunches closer. "Did it again? I don't understand."

"Eliza, he hurt another woman badly, a woman whom you know."

Eliza's warm aura grows cold. She slowly lifts her legs onto her chair and wraps her arms around her knees as she speaks through a whisper, "No, no, not again Chris."

What's there to say? I don't even bother trying to make sense of it.

"Who was it this time?"

The air leaks out of my lungs as I sigh; a natural reflex that only stalls the inevitable. I have to tell her. I just don't want to. "It was Haley. Haley Harrison."

"Oh God," she whimpers. That's all it takes for rivers of regret to fall from those brown eyes. As I look at her, she looks towards the ceiling, "I don't understand. Why does this keep happening?"

Still perched in her seat, Eliza wipes away tears with her hand. "How bad? Is she gonna be okay?"

I lean forward in my seat. "She's getting better every day, well, at least her physical wounds are. I worry about her emotionally, though."

"Chris, can I see her? Please? I just want to tell her that I love her, and that I'm sorry."

"Sorry? You didn't do anything."

"Chris, sometimes we were so mean to one another. I'm telling you, it was like he controlled everything. He even manipulated the way she and I felt about each other."

"I understand, but I can't let you guys see each other just yet. Give me a little time. I'll try to arrange something. I promise."

Eliza composes herself, slowly lowers her feet the floor and runs her fingers through her dark hair. "Okay. And to think I'd planned on surprising you with how my mom and I went and enrolled me in college this week. It doesn't even feel like it matters right now."

"It matters. Every decision you make matters. I'm so proud of you. At least now, one of us can say we've been to college."

"So, what happens next? Is there going to be a second case against him with Haley as the victim?"

"Well, since you brought it up. That's something else we'll need to discuss. Remember I told you she was torn, emotionally. She doesn't want to testify against him in court, and that brings us to you. I need to know how you're feeling about all of this."

"I guess I'm not sure how I feel. On some level, I never really thought we'd get here. I'm not even sure I believed you guys would be able to catch him. He seemed so smart."

"If it weren't for you, we may have never found out about him, and its likely Haley might have been killed."

"I don't know, I don't feel like I did anything."

"You took a stand, for yourself, your family, and whether you knew it or not, every woman he was hurting."

"Chris, if I testify against him, is it gonna to be hard?"

I want to be selfish. It would serve both my pride and spirit to euthanize Mr. Davis. With her on the stand, I could do it, no question. But there's a saying, "Pride goes before destruction, and a haughty spirit goes before a fall." This isn't the time for me to bolster my pride or my concern myself with legacy. Rather, it is a time for honesty between a brother and his sister. "It isn't going to be pleasant. To be perfectly honest, this may be the most difficult thing you'll have done in your life since leaving him."

She's still silent, pushing away a bit of her bangs that hang in front of her eyes.

"If you weren't so far along with your new life, I wouldn't be so worried. You're doing so well now. You've enrolled in school, and you're even smiling again. Mario has a very capable attorney. I'm familiar with his work, and I know what they'll try to do to you on that witness stand."

Eliza sits and stares into my face, absorbing my every word. I need to couch this carefully. She's made tremendous progress, and has already reset the trajectory of her life's course. She is now surrounded by people who believe her. But even more importantly, she now has people who believe *in* her, plain and simple. "I don't wanna disappoint you," she says softly, still looking into my eyes. "What do you think?"

In this situation, I worry about two things. The first is that her new-found sense of self hasn't yet had an opportunity to mature, to strengthen and develop a skin that's tough enough. Secondly, what is the likelihood that Eliza will be able to recover from being re-victimized? That is exactly what would happen should she take the stand. I can see it. I have seen it, and far too often.

Once they've managed to tell their own life story, the defense attorneys move in. They pace round and round the victims, all the while grinning. "This has all been a huge misunderstanding," the lawyers claim. "My client is a fine, upstanding citizen, a man with an unblemished criminal record. He's simply a business owner who attended college and has led an exemplary life."

In closing arguments, these women are again belittled and attacked with words. They are picked on the same way hyenas tear at a carcass. "Ladies and gentlemen of the jury, please don't forget that this woman, this so-called 'victim' is a prostitute! She is a criminal who destroys families every time she makes the conscious decision to go out and sell her body for money."

I lean back, sigh and drop my hands into my lap. "I think right now, we have to do what's best for you. Either way, we are going to make him pay. There's only one question that matters, and the only person that can answer it is you. What does Eliza need in order to move forward?"

"I don't know, Chris. I don't know if I could take being dragged back through all of that. I'd be so embarrassed. His lawyer would try to make it look like we're the bad ones. Having that happen in front of my family, my mom?" She pushes her hair back once again, clearing the way for more tears. "I'm scared, Chris, I'm scared."

"I understand."

"If we, I mean, if I don't get on that stand, could you still get him to plead guilty?"

"To hurting you?"

"Hurting all of us! All of us, Chris."

I drag my fingers across my scalp. I feel like Mario's slipping through my hands. "Is that what you need for me to make happen? Will that be enough?"

A heavy heart keeps her from speaking, Eliza replies with a head nod. A few strands of dark hair sway in the air.

"All right, all right, Eliza."

She takes my hand, and for the next ten minutes we sit in silence. Brother and sister. Survivor and hunter.

If the value of my life is judged by how well I have lived up to and fulfilled my purpose, at this moment, all I can see is how short I have fallen.

Nearly eleven months into this investigation, I step through the gated parking lot of the Triangle with another thought in mind. Come tomorrow morning, this will all come to a head. The hunted will surrender himself with his attorney standing beside him.

At the entrance of the Triangle, I swipe my proxy card. At the sharp sound of a pop, I step back in.

How much pain is too much? At least Eliza and Haley are smart enough to know that. As for me, pain is instrumental. It is fuel. Right now, though, I feel hollow. The crater inside of me is only getting bigger, and without the testimony of the girls, I may not be able to cast Mario down into it. Surely, with him as a sacrifice, wouldn't that satisfy, even if just for one moment, the beast inside me?

"*Que pasa?* You look a little flustered, bro. Everything good?"

"No, everything is not good. We need to chat, all of us." I look past Al and spot Trey, who leans back in his desk chair with the phone receiver pressed against his ear. "Trey, when you're done, meet us in the conference room." He nods and slowly lifts his index finger.

I step in after Al and quickly glance around the room. The white dry erase boards are still covered with the tactical plans for our last strike. I drop my backpack on the table and plop down beside Al with a sigh.

"Is it that bad?"

"I'll let you be the judge after Trey gets in here."

"If it ain't one thing…"

"…it's another," I answer.

"Another meeting of the minds?" Trey asks as he steps into the room, swinging the door shut behind him. "Let me guess, once again, the wheels are falling off the truck. Am I right, or am I right?"

"You're right, Trey," I manage. "We have an issue. Well, actually two."

"I know you're about to give us some bad news, Chris, but do me a favor, and make it sound good." Trey kicks his feet up and leans back in his chair. "If you're gonna make us eat a shit pie, the least you can do is put a little whipped cream on top."

"All right boys, tomorrow we're taking Mario into custody."

"Hell," Al pipes in, "that's not so bad."

Trey grins. "Patience, my friend, patience."

"The not-so-good news is that the girls want us to make him an offer."

"What?" Al winces as he leans forward. "What is that? What the hell are you talking about?"

"What did I tell you, Al?" Trey sits forward. Propping his elbows on the table, he tosses out a bitter laugh. "Chris, what are we doing here? What's the point? This assignment is going to drive me insane. I don't know about you two, but I find this shit nerve-wracking."

Al's still in shock, "I don't get it. We have this case sewn up. We can't lose it. Don't the girls understand that?"

Al would be right if the only people who had to testify were him, Trey, and I. The problem is, we won't be the ones who are dragged through the mud on the witness stand. "Al, Trey, I know neither of you want to hear this, but I'm not so sure winning was ever an option for us."

"Un-*fucking*-believable," Trey whispers under his breath.

"Look, I'm frustrated, too, but you aren't new to this. Now, I'm sorry we don't have the girls. I know it's not ideal, but we still have an advantage. His defense doesn't know that the girls are tired and scared. We can use that. We'll get him to take a deal. I know what I have to do; I guess the only thing I need to know is whether or not I'm going it alone."

Although still demoralized, Al is the first to speak. "We started this together."

"So, let's end it the same way," Trey replies. "But I want the record to reflect that this is not healthy. It's bad, boys, bad on the nerves."

I stand, grab my backpack, and sling it over my shoulder. "And so the record will reflect, Trey. We start early tomorrow, around ten a.m. I'll want you two watching my back, but out of sight, see if you can't find a place to park behind County."

"All right," Al says. "Where you headed now?"

"The District Attorney's office. I need to make sure Mario gets the shittiest deal possible. I doubt I'll be back tonight. This could take a while. I'll see you boys in the morning."

32
The Collectors

Last night was hellish, but after hours of discussion, the district attorney and I did come to agreeable terms. The charges are now in place, and an offer is ready to be made. As I wait behind the Clark County Detention Center, Trey and Al watch me like hawks from inside their cars. Both of them are parked at separate ends of the street. I'm confident they've got me covered, even as I stand with a backup officer beside me. The small of my back presses against the front quarter panel of The Beast. This is the day Mario Davis surrenders to me.

Question: What gift do you hand the man who use to have everything? Money? Cars? Jewelry and slaves? I'll start with the steel bracelets tucked in the back pocket of my jeans, one for each of his thin wrists.

Next, an all-expenses-paid weekend retreat inside of County, compliments of my city. Finally, the amended criminal complaint. I look down and massage the papers in my hand with my thumbs and forefingers. The stack ruffles as a breeze whips past. Mario will plead guilty to three counts of Pandering, and one count of Pandering with Force. He must admit to the pandering of not only Haley and Eliza, but to the fact that he did commit crimes against each and every one of their sisters–Sadie Ortega, Laurie Blackmon, Katie Coughlin, Marissa Shipley, Georgia Andrews, Haley Carter, Faven Drazkovich, Alisson Becker, and Carmen Wilson.

He'll be tabbed a felon several times over, lose his right to bear arms, vote, and then be saddled with a strict five-year probation. Should he refuse, then hell awaits. The dark ink imbedded into the white sheets of paper reads "for crimes committed against Eliza Serra,

Count 1–Pandering with force; Count 2–Living from the earnings of a prostitute; Count 3–Living with a Prostitute; Count 4–Pandering: Furnishing Transportation; Count 5–Coercion.

"For crimes committed against Haley Harrison, Count 6–Pandering with force, Living from the earnings of a prostitute; Count 7–Living with a prostitute; Count 8–Second Degree Kidnapping; Count 9–Conspiracy to commit second degree kidnapping; Count 10–Coercion; Count 11–Battery with substantial bodily harm.

"For crimes committed against Sadie Ortega, Count 12–Pandering; Count 13–Living from the earnings of a prostitute; Count 14–Living with a prostitute.

"For crimes committed against Katie Coughran; Count 15–Pandering; Count 16–Living from the earnings of a prostitute; Count 17– Living with a prostitute.

"For crimes committed against Laurie Blackmon, Count 18–Pandering; Count 19–Living with a prostitute; Count 20–Living from the earnings of a prostitute.

This twenty-count indictment could garner up to seventeen years in prison. It isn't ideal, hell, it's not even fair. Five years probation for what he's done doesn't begin to wipe clean his sins. But this does keep the victims safe, and allows me up to five years to catch him should he fall back into his old habits. For now, however, I'll just wait. I twist the stack of papers into a tight roll and slide them into the rear pocket opposite my cuffs.

The silence of the lonely stretch of road I'm standing on is cut by the sound of an oncoming engine. I lift my head and peer down the street. A garden-variety luxury sedan banks right at the intersection and rolls in my direction. Al and Trey both flicker the headlights of their cars warning me that someone is approaching.

I stare down the sedan and fix my eyes on the interior. I can make out two figures. The driver is a full-faced, middle-aged white male with brown hair. How nice. This lawyer also serves as a chauffeur for his trafficker client. I shake my head at the thought. It's amazing who a little cash can buy these days.

To his right sits the coward who attacked Haley and stole Eliza away from Adelia. His shaven head catches a beam from the sun, slumped shoulders and skinny neck. I'd know his profile from anywhere, and it makes me sick.

I stand up straight and step to the rear of The Beast, my hands hanging at my sides as I clinch my fists. My knuckles crack and pop from the tension. At about fifteen feet out, the car slows to a halt. The first to appear is Mario's hired help. "Hello, Detective," he calls out. "As promised, Mario is turning himself in, and he's ready to cooperate."

I move a step closer. "Well, if he wants to cooperate, he can start by getting out of the car."

The lawyer bends down and peeks into the car window, nodding his head. Mario instantly exits the passenger side and steps onto the sidewalk. I look him over. Blue jeans, T-shirt, and gym shoes. I'm sure he didn't work for a single cent of the money it took to pay for the clothing he's wearing. Leach.

Mario looks over at his attorney for re-assurance. "Call my office once you've gotten booked in. We'll talk then." Mario nods and hangs his head, stepping in my direction.

I match his speed, taking a few steps in his direction. So, here we are again. For a moment we're face-to-face, eyes locked. In his, I see nothing more than the darkness I've come to despise. "Turn around! Put your hands on your head! Interlock your fingers!" With my left hand, I reach back for the cuffs. Click...click. Shiny and new, they're perfect addition for his wardrobe.

Mario doesn't speak. At this point what's left to be said? The malevolence I feel at this very moment may stop me from entering any kind of paradise. When my time comes, will I be welcomed to walk through the Halls of Valhalla? Is there a place in Shangri-La for someone as maligned as me? Will Heaven wait for me to find my way through my malcontent? May God have mercy on me. I fear that I'm already right where I'm meant to be...in Hell.

"Move!" I blurt out behind him, just an inch or two from his ear. Mario steps forward, making his way towards the intake area of

County. While he marches on ahead, I glance back at his lawyer. I think on the many who defend these men. How can they stand to look in a mirror? Then an even more frightful thought pops into mind: What in God's name looks back at them?

The thick sliding doors retract. Welcome back to County.

After parking their cars, Trey and Al join our delegation and lag just a few feet back. I can hear them snickering, making snide comments. They're enjoying every minute of this, and they should. I'm sure he can hear them as well, but all he does is drag his feet along the cement floor. I wish I could parade him through the streets of my city marked as a trafficker, a destroyer of women, and a devourer of purity. This last walk is as close to that satisfaction as I will get.

"Sit down over there, Mario," I instruct him, pointing to the row of chairs furthest from me. "Wait for them to call your name. You've been here enough. I'm sure you know the routine by now. Enjoy the visit."

Trey walks beside and tosses his left arm around my shoulder. As we watch Mario step to the far corner of the booking area, Trey whispers under his breath, "Asshole!"

Al is the last to step up. The final member of our trio stands at my left side with crossed arms, staring at Mario in disgust.

"Come on boys. Let's get him booked in."

After the arrest it only took a few weeks before Mario's attorney bit at the offer. At last comes sentencing day. Neither Eliza nor Haley are here to watch him cower. Instead they've sent us. This day, we three will stand in their place as detectives and the collectors of an un-payable debt.

District Court. To my left, Al sits. He's cleaned up quite nicely. After a few quick tugs at the sleeves of his dark blue jacket, he sits back and waits. The white dress shirt and red tie that he matched with his suit rivals anything you'd see in a race for Congress. Trey's navy blue suit is freshly pressed. It's complete with thin pinstripes.

Honestly, he looks more prepared for a *GQ* shoot that a sentencing. As for me, I'm not as dashing. It's always the same: tie, shirt, slacks, belt, socks, shoes, skin and soul…all black.

There is a creak from rich oak doors as they swing open into the court. I look back and spot one of our antagonists. Today, with his dark suit, tie, and attaché, he resembles the notion of Attorney more than Chauffer. His driver's cap must be buried beneath all the papers in that briefcase.

Not far behind is his client, the rodent, Mario Davis. He steps through the doors and scurries to the front of the courtroom. He can't bring himself to look anywhere near our direction. For our part, we will not look away. Instead, our eyes burn holes of contempt throughout his body.

"ALL RISE!" The bailiff's voice pings off the hard walls, floors and every bench. "COURT IS IN SESSION!"

From a door in the far corner of this regal place, the magistrate enters and takes a seat at the bench. The judge flips through the sheets of paper on his desk before calling both Mario and his attorney to attention. "It's my understanding that your client has had an opportunity to review the charges being brought against him?"

"He has, Your Honor."

"Very well." The judge's eyes move from the attorney and zero in on Mario. "So, Mr. Davis, do you understand the charges brought before you?"

"I…I do, Your Honor," he answers, his voice in a well-rehearsed stammer. He reeks of humble sincerity, and even his posture suggests he's repentant. I know better, though.

"And are you prepared to enter a plea of guilty to the crimes of Pandering and Pandering with Force?"

"Well, Your Honor, if I could just explain?" Mario begs, adjusting his body language, and standing a bit straighter. "See it's not the way it looks. I…"

Perhaps the good judge can see through his act, too, and quickly cuts him off. "The time for explanation is over. You either did this, or you did not. Now, how do you plead in this matter?"

Mario melts in his shoes from the heat of the judge's words. The coward inside him rises once more. He hangs his head and answers in near whispers. "I, I plead guilty."

Trey and Al crack slight smiles and pat me on the back. Even as they celebrate, I feel empty. This isn't right. This doesn't feel like justice to me, and I'm left reeling with the thought that my greatest test only resulted in my biggest failure. The remains of this man's life should be spent behind the glum steel bars of some penitentiary, a quiet, dark and dingy place where he can slowly wilt away.

I can't smile, but I don't rain on the parades of my partners, either. With the plea in, we excuse ourselves from the courtroom. The three of us step through the halls of the Regional Justice Center back into the fire, right back into the heart of our city.

Beneath a late afternoon sky, we stand in a secured parking lot, each of us leaning against our cars. Trey, ever insightful, offers a kind word. "Hey, you should be ecstatic. We did everything we could, kid. The girls didn't have to testify. He pled guilty, and now you have five years to catch him dirty. That ain't bad."

"Chris," says Al, chiming in, "Trey's right. What else could we have done? This is what the girls wanted. We did right by 'em, you gotta know that."

"You're right. Both of you," I say, loosening my tie and unbuttoning the top of my shirt. "Still, it doesn't make me feel any better. He'll still be out there."

"And guess what, Chris?" Al cracks an infectious smile. "So will we."

I place my hand on his right shoulder, "I never feel like I tell the two of you this enough, but thank you."

"Hey, kid, that's what friends do," says Trey. "So, I'm guessing now's as good a time to tell you as any. I passed the Sergeant's exam. It's just a matter of time now until you two have to call me Sir."

"Damn." I smile warmly. "Al, you ready for that? You're going to have to show Trey some respect now." I look over at Al who just shakes his head and smiles. "I have one other order of business to take care of. I'll call you guys in a few hours, we'll grab some coffee."

As my partners pull away, I dig the phone from my front pocket. I have two very important calls to make. At the top of the list is Haley. "Hey, Chris!" I can hear the smile on her face.

"Haley, it's done. He pled guilty this morning. I was wondering if maybe I could pick you up and grab a bite. I could use the company."

"Don't be silly. Of course, I'd love to. But you should know my face is still healing. You don't mind going out to eat with a bruised up woman, do you?"

"Come on now."

"Then good," she replies. "How much time do I have?"

"I'll see you in one hour. And Haley, I can't think of anyone I'd rather enjoy a meal with. I'll be there soon."

I hang up knowing that I wasn't entirely honest with Haley. In fact, I can think of one other person, and her phone is the next to ring.

The ever-bubbly Eliza answers with a giggle. "CHRIS!!!"

"Hey, Eliza. You sound wonderful."

"I feel wonderful, thank you very much!"

"So, I have a little news for you. Mario pled guilty today. He admitted to everything."

Her voice cracks. "Thank you. Thank you so much."

"You really wanna thank me?"

"Of course I do. You want me to bake you a cake?"

"Oh no, I'll pass on the cake. How about we go grab a late lunch? My treat. Say in thirty minutes? Can you be ready?"

"I'll get dressed right now. I can't wait to see you."

"Good, because I'm on my way."

From where I'm located downtown, I'm at Eliza's in twenty minutes. I pull up beside the curb and honk the horn twice. Eliza bursts through the front door and sprints to the car. Even from ten yards, her smile says it all. She is a free woman. Looking past her, I see Adelia standing in the threshold, a vindicated mother.

Eliza hops in the front seat, smiles and wraps her arms around me. Hope lives. Not in me, but in her, and the promise of what she might do with her life, one renewed, reborn from the flames of despair.

"All right, all right. I missed you too, knucklehead." I wrap my right arm around her and squeeze. "Now get your seat belt on. I'm taking you somewhere special."

The setting sun has left the sky splattered with tender orange hues, soft white clouds, and a cool violet wash. Eliza cracks the window, and the wind whips her hair, which also has new life. It's now grown well past her shoulders. She speaks of school, of family, and even the nice young man she's seeing.

We race from one corner of our beautiful city to the other. The ride doesn't feel long, and if it were, what would it matter. For now, we are just two individuals, made family by this war, and forever connected by our pasts.

We stop at a red light only a few blocks away from Haley's house. Just long enough for me to send a text.

Me: I'm right around the corner. I'll honk when I'm out front."
Haley: Okie!

I bank left from the main street and continue through the well-worn neighborhood. At last we're right in front of Haley's parents' home. Eliza's never been here, so she naturally looks over at me with raised eyebrows. "I thought we were going to eat."

"We are. The place is right around the corner. I just need to make a really quick call. You mind?"

"No, not at all." She replies nonchalantly. Eliza's eyes are fixed on the house in front of us. Occasionally, she scans left and right, taking in all the surroundings. Keep looking, sis.

With Eliza occupied by the scenery, I press the icon on my phone for Regina. Then I beep the car's horn twice. At this point, Eliza's looking back at me, maybe growing slightly suspicious.

"Ooops, sorry about that. My hand must have slipped. Twice."

Regina answers the phone just as the front door to the Harrison household opens. Haley steps out and moves toward the car with a slight limp.

At the sight of Haley, Eliza starts to shriek. Tears flow down her face as she looks back to me, "I can't believe you!" She explodes from the car, all full of screams, and sprints toward Haley with arms outstretched. Haley's mouth drops in astonishment, and she tries to wipe tears from her own face just before Eliza engulfs her. I see two souls in full blossom beneath a pastel sky.

While I savor the sight of this amazing, timeless embrace, Regina's voice comes from the other end of the phone line. "Chris? What in God's name do you have going on over there?"

"I'm not sure. I think I might be experiencing forgiveness and redemption all at the same time."

"Chris?" Regina asks sternly, "what are you talking about?"

"Mario pled guilty today, and I just surprised Haley and Eliza. They're together now, and it's really something to see, Regina."

"Oh, Chris, that's wonderful! So you know I have to ask you, how do you feel about all this, Mr. Doom and Gloom?"

"I don't know," I laugh. "I wanted so much to destroy that man. He slithered out from underneath me by taking a deal. Obviously, the girls didn't have to testify, but what kills me is that he's avoided prison. Instead he has a five-year probation hanging over his head. Maybe he'll slip up. I just hope I get to drop the hammer on him, whenever that day comes."

She replies with all the patience of a mother. "Chris, I know you hate it when I do this to you, but you haven't left me with a choice. Did you ever stop to think that maybe, just maybe, you weren't supposed to destroy this man?"

"I don't understand. He needs to pay for what he…"

Regina interrupts so softly, so compassionately. "Christopher, 'Vengeance is mine, sayeth the Lord. I will repay.' You really need to consider the fact that maybe this was never about destruction. Perhaps, this was always a mission of rescue, of redemption, for you and them. Now, try to take part in their happiness."

The sound of Regina's voice is interrupted by an alert to some incoming text message.

Chris, it's me, Sadie Ortega. Please call me back. I need your help. I want out!

I shake my head at the probability. As Haley and Eliza walk toward the car, hand-in-hand, I quickly respond to the text.

Me: Are you safe?

Sadie: Yes

Me: All right, I'll call you later this evening.

I sit in the driver side of the Beast, still amazed by Regina's insight. Unreal. A rescue mission, indeed.

As I thank Regina for her wisdom and hang up, I am reminded of a saying, "Lean not unto thine own understanding."

Eliza pulls the car door open, and I see the smiling faces of my sisters.

Acknowledgments

To my mother and father, Cynthia Baughman and Daryl Horne, thank you for your steadfast encouragement and support of me as both a writer and hunter of men. I wouldn't be the person I am without your heart and wisdom. To Tiersa, thank you for being the woman that you are, a solid place for me to lean when I am tired, and an unfaltering pillar of strength for our daughters. To my brothers and sisters, Anber, D.J., Daniel, David, and Sarah…you all make me a better person.

To Al B and Trey G, the saga continues. I can't think of anyone I'd rather have so intimately involved in this phase of my life than you two. You are both Legendary.

To Cathy H, so honored to have had the opportunity to learn from and grow with you as a person and an investigator. To S. Dirks…aka Garcia, I love you girl!

To Karen H, a leader is not something you become when you pass a test. There is an innate quality engrained in the greatest of them. In my estimation, you have met the mark. To Don H, what more needs to be said than thank you for everything.

To Judge Tim Williams and Angie, over the years you've made me feel more like a son than an official. I love you both. To Judges Cadish, Villani, Tobiasson, L. Bell, Earley, Miley, Allf, all of you have either presided over some of the most important trafficking trials our valley has seen, or assisted, through search warrants in the decimation of many of thee most dangerous people in Las Vegas. I am forever indebted.

To Deputy DA District Attorney Elizabeth Mercer, I am not ashamed to admit when someone is smarter than I am; in fact I'm thankful that you are. You are and have long been just the prosecutor I prayed for when this all began. To my friends, Deputy DA District Attorneys M. Thompson, N. DeMonte, M. and B. Schifalacqua, A.

Albritton, S. Jimenez, D. Pieper, G. O'Brien, B. Turner, A. Ferreira, and L. Robinson, this is our city...let's take her back! To District Attorney Wolfson, you have an amazing staff, take pride in and lead them well.

To Professors K. Bergquist, S. Bradley, A. Kennedy, and P. Davis, who knew at 37 years old I'd still need the counsel of teachers? Maybe God did. Enforcement without education is a futile endeavor. Thank you.

Mike Bartel...Free International! Thank you for shining a light on my abilities as a public speaker. To Jan Langbien, Bill Walsh, Brooke Wyatt, Stacey Cramer, Esther Rodriguez-Brown, Debbie Johnson of Without Permission, Jane Wells of 3 Generations, and J.K. Wasson thank you for allowing me to become a part of your families. To Andy Cashman, onward and upward, I'm ready when you are. To Gene Greenberg and Martin Bergman, I am glad to have you in my corner; let's take this to the next level. To C. Perkins and T. Montoya, you have been instrumental in helping me educate our city...thank you both for your friendship and support.

To Brian Rouff and the team at Imagine Communications, you all are like a second family. I love you.

To every survivor, every family affected, every prosecutor, detective, officer, social worker, and care provider fighting fatigue and logging ridiculous hours, remember that we are the last hope for so many. I know, that as more people learn of our war, our numbers will grow, and we will become that much more powerful.

To Verna Dreisbach, I promise, I will continue to work as hard for you as you have for me. We have already made the difference we hoped to. To my editor, Lynn Price, thank you for your belief in my work, as well as your instruction and patience. Between the constraints on time between my duties as an author and Detective, it's a wonder I have any time to sleep. But hell, even when I can, I am roused by nightmares of your red pen hunting me.

To J. Ross Baughman, here we are, nearly three years later, I am still your padawan, and I am thankful to hold that distinction. Thank you, Ross, for all that you have given, shall we to do it once more?